**Pra**
*SOG Code*

"I thought I was crazy until I saw what Dick Thompson did when he became my SOG Team leader in 1969. I learned a lot from Dynamite during our time together at CCN and grew up a lot—especially after getting the crap shot out of me a couple times. I got focused on what was right and what leader responsibilities were in combat. He was a great role model for me."

—**Eldon Bargewell**,
Major General (Ret.), MACV-SOG 68–69, 70–71

"Dick Thompson served as a One Zero, Recon Team leader at Command and Control North (CCN) during the height of the Vietnam War. His journal takes the reader on numerous covert missions across the border into Laos, where he and his RT engaged North Vietnamese Army forces from the company to division levels, during the conduct of their missions.

Each mission is described in detail, from the insertion to extraction and the employment of close air support. What is unique in the account of each mission is that following each mission is an After-Action Review (AAR), lessons learned and the follow-on action items in preparing for the next mission. This is the hallmark of a good combat leader, as I often saw that 'lessons learned' were often mistakes repeated as they only were captured in the after-action reports and then filed away and never followed up by unit or leaders.

The lessons learned described in this book still apply to our Special Forces units. The enemy and conditions have changed, but not tactics and techniques. Today's Special Forces leaders and Operational Detachments need to learn from Dick's experiences."

—**Ken Bowra**,
Major General (Ret), MACV-SOG, 70–71, US Army Special
Forces, One Zero, RT Idaho and RT Sidewinder Command and
Control North (CCN), TF1AE

"Having served with Dick Thompson in recon companies at SOG bases FOB 1 and CCN, I never realized the epic nature of his missions. Years from now, scholars will turn first to his book for the historic and jarring SOG-related action. Readers will learn what happens when he opens fire on fully automatic on an enemy's head three feet away from him."

—**John Stryker Meyer**,
MACV-SOG, RT Idaho, 68–70

"I have read Dick Thompson's book and it takes me back to my SOG days at FOB-2, CCC. The book is so real it took me back to jungles of Southern Laos. It especially meant a lot to me because I had many similar experiences. Dick has done a great job of painting a picture of how it was. For those who weren't there it gives you an insight that is unique. For those who lived it, it will take you back to the sights, sounds, smells and fear you once felt."

—**Richard Todd**,
COL (Ret.), MACV-SOG, HF CO, 68–69

"This is an eye-opening account of Dick Thompson's experiences as a MACV-SOG Team Leader assigned to CCN, a top-secret covert operations organization tasked with observing, interdicting, and destroying NVA units 'across the fence' in Laos, Cambodia and North Vietnam during the Vietnam War.

Dick's demanding, intensive training prior to each mission resulted in a multiplier effect on his small team against a determined enemy that always greatly outnumbered them.

This book is highly researched, fast paced, exciting and at times extremely brutal. Written by a highly respected, courageous American hero, this is a book you won't be able to put down."

—**Bruce Lombard**,
MACV-SOG, RT Indiana and RT Intruder, 68–69

"Having assisted with two Vietnam-related Medal of Honor upgrades, I have no doubt in my mind that Dick Thompson deserves America's highest military honor for the valorous acts he committed whilst a volunteer in the top secret world of MACV-SOG. As you read about these—what most people would call insane missions—you'll see for yourself that Thompson is a daring, thoughtful, brutal and fearless warrior, who took on and destroyed well over 10,000 enemies toe-to-toe.

People not in-the-know might consider it all bullshit. Listen to his podcasts, his quiet, considered responses to questions, his gentle humor and humility, and you will know, as his friends do, that Dick is the real deal.

Future movies will be made about these unsung heroes of the Vietnam War, the real John Rambos—men like Dick Thompson, Lynne Black and Eldon Bargewell, who went out time and again to face an overwhelming, highly trained and equipped enemy determined to hunt and kill them. This book is a must-read account of a man in extreme combat, who calculates his next missions with a clear and focused mind, and steps off the helicopter skid, aiming to come and kill you. You would not ever wish to be his enemy."

**—Rob Graham**,
CEO Savage Game Design, Creator SOG: Prairie Fire

"When I watch a stupid action movie and some guy jumps off a helicopter skid into 150 feet high trees, I always think, that's BS! That'll never work. Apparently, I need to spend more time with Dick Thompson to know what works."

**—Jocko Willink**,
Retired Navy SEAL Commander

"Dick Thompson artfully describes how he was born on the path to becoming a warrior, from growing up in rural South Carolina where he played 'army' in the foothills of the Blue Ridge Mountains, to giving up his chemistry scholarship at the University of South Carolina to pursue his destiny. As a SOG 1-0 he methodically dissected each mission as he continued to hone his skills and develop into the ultimate SOG ninja. Always outnumbered and often one mistake away from death, Thompson shows that he had more lives than a cat as he cheated death time and again. Each mission will have you hanging on every word and leave you clamoring for more.

It's raw, it's gritty and not for the faint of heart, but if you really want to know what it was like to work in the black world of special operations, *SOG Codename Dynamite* is a must read.

—**Barry Pencek**,
COL (Ret.), US Marine Cobra pilot (Scarface 42) supporting MACV-SOG Operations, 70–71, author of *Operation Tailwind: Memoirs of a Secret Battle in a Secret War.*

"*SOG Codename Dynamite* is a blood and guts account of the great heroism and battlefield camaraderie of MACV-SOG, the Vietnam War's unconventional warfare combat element in the Southeast Asian conflict. It was, by design, the most secret, elite US Military unit to serve in Vietnam—so secret, its existence was not only concealed but denied by the US government. Dick Thompson superbly describes his military training, and the minute by minute first person account of extraordinary men living and dying on the edge behind enemy lines. His and his team's battlefield heroism is revealed in each and every one of their cross-border missions—in explosive, heart stopping detail."

—**David Carr**,
LTC (Ret.), MACV-SOG, Recon Company Commander, 68–69

"Dick Thompson will take you inside the heart and mind of one of the most elite MACV-SOG warriors. This book is a journal of his time as a SOG RT team leader conducting combat operations across the border in the Top Secret war in Southeast Asia. 'Not for the faint of heart' is a mild quote. A must-read book to understand what it's like to constantly look death in the eye."

—**Carl E. Hudson**,
75th Rangers, Vietnam, 66–69

"Dick Thompson should have seven Medals of Honor and Ford should give him a new car every week."

—**Andy Stumpf**,
Navy SEAL Team 6

"*SOG Codename Dynamite* is written like no other book on MACV-SOG, a 'Must Read.' Once I got into this book I could not put it down for hours. It is about the brutal combat between highly trained, motivated, professional NVA soldiers and SOG's Special Forces and indigenous Recon teams operating Across the Fence in the NVA's backyard, Laos, Cambodia, North Vietnam and the DMZ. He describes the horror of being chased by hundreds of angry NVA, burnt, mutilated, screaming bodies in brutal, sometimes hand-to-hand combat told as Dick Thompson, *SOG Codename Dynamite*, saw it. I inserted and extracted the SOG legends of CCS, and Dynamite is a legend among legends."

—**Don "Ghost Rider" Haase**,
195th Assault Helicopter Company
MACV-SOG Gunship Support, 68–69

"There's a saying that goes something like, 'The world needs good men who are skilled at violence.' Dick Thompson is one of those men. His account of his time in Vietnam serving in MACV-SOG is deeply personal and pays tribute to his fellow warriors who never made it home. They are the men who put honor, country, and self-sacrifice above all else. Men who were asked to do the hard stuff. It's a humbling read. It's also a fascinating look at what shapes a warrior mindset. How to prepare physically and mentally, to use stress, adapt, overcome, and succeed. Lessons anyone can apply to their own lives and individual circumstances."

—**Holly H. McClellan**,
Spouse of Army SF combat veteran and daughter of
Air Force Vietnam B-52 pilot.

# SOG CODENAME DYNAMITE

A MACV-SOG 1-0's Personal Journal

Book 1

*SOG Codename Dynamite A MACV-SOG 1-0's Personal Journal, Book 1* by Henry L. Thompson, Ph.D.

Cover design by Rich Niles

Interior formatting and design by Jacqueline Cook

ISBN: 9798399424354

10 9 8 7 6 5 4 3 2 1

BISAC Subject Headings:
BIO008000 BIOGRAPHY & AUTOBIOGRAPHY / Military
BIO026000 BIOGRAPHY & AUTOBIOGRAPHY / Personal Memoirs
HIS027180 HISTORY / Military / Special Forces
HIS027070 HISTORY / Wars & Conflicts / Vietnam

Published by Wormhole Publishing
PO Box 868
Watkinsville, GA 30677

# Dedication

*This book is dedicated to my friend,*
**1LT Robert (Bob) E. Sheridan.**
*Rest in Peace, my friend.*

MACV-SOG, CCC, 1968–69
Killed in Action March 26, 1969
Posthumously awarded the Silver Star and Purple Heart

# Contents

Preface.................................................................................xiii

## PART 1

Chapter 1: Born on the Path ........................................1

Chapter 2: Becoming a Warrior....................................14

Chapter 3: Do Not Volunteer for SOG! ........................31

## PART 2

Chapter 4: Phu Bai: FOB-1............................................49

    RT Alabama ...........................................................53

    Mission Preparation ..............................................55

    RT Alabama: Wiretap SOG #1 ............................63

Chapter 5: Into the Darkness .......................................82

    RT Alabama: S & D SOG #2................................83

    RT Alabama: Eldest Son SOG #3.........................101

    RT Alabama: Road Interdiction SOG #4 .............108

## PART 3

Chapter 6: Command and Control North (FOB-4) ......129

    RT Michigan: Walk-In SOG #5 ...........................140

    RT Michigan: PW Snatch SOG #6 .......................164

    RT Michigan: Marble Mountain .........................192

RT Michigan: S & D SOG #7 ..............................................207

RT Michigan: Pipeline SOG #8 ..........................................212

RT Michigan: BDA SOG #9..................................................214

Acknowledgments ................................................................220

Glossary ................................................................................224

About the Author..................................................................240

Veteran Support ..................................................................243

# Preface

*You have never lived until you've almost died. For those who have fought for it, life has a special flavor the protected will never know.*
**—Guy de Maupassant**

*You are volunteering to go anywhere and do anything, no questions asked. You agree not to disclose to anyone in any way where you went and what you did for at least 20 years. Sign these documents. Welcome to SOG!*
**—LTC Jones**

The two books in this series are about how I got to the Military Advisory Command Vietnam-Studies and Observation Group (MACV-SOG) and experienced life and war during my time there. Don't be misled by the name. We were not an academic group studying the war in Vietnam. We were not "advising" anyone. MACV-SOG was a top-secret group of the most elite Special Operations warriors in the world. Let me be very clear: This book is about the top-secret war in Southeast Asia that took place from 1964–72. This book is not for the faint of heart or people who do not want to know the poignant reality of what really happens on the top-secret black ops battlefield. Every time I led my team on a mission, it was a kill or be killed event. Every time hundreds, sometimes thousands, of people would die. It was not about rules of engagement, was this person an enemy, does this person have a weapon, is this person about to kill me or the many other questions and rules today's special operators may have to deal with. SOG rules were very different and simple. EVERYONE was the enemy. The enemy had to be terminated—or you would be! And, if the enemy caught you, the United States government would deny any involvement with you or what you were doing. You had no protection under the Geneva Convention. You were a spy. You were on your own. Make no mistake. SOG was not fighting the Viet Cong (VC) or some rag-tag, made-up group of old men, women and kids who called themselves soldiers. We fought the hard-core, North Vietnamese Army, by most estimates the third or fourth best Army in the world at the time.

SOG missions, by definition, were missions conducted outside of South Vietnam in other Southeast Asian countries to include North Vietnam. We conducted military operations inside Vietnam for practice, training, and mission preparation. By today's terminology all of these combat operations would be called combat deployments. And there were a lot of them!

Our cross-border (sometimes called "over the fence") operations proved an effective economy-of-force, compelling the North Vietnamese Army to divert over 50,000 of their best soldiers to rear area security duties, far from the battlefields of South Vietnam (cited from the Presidential Unit Citation for Extraordinary Heroism) to try and counter SOG team missions.

It has been documented that SOG teams had the highest kill ratio of any unit during the Vietnam era. SOG teams also had the highest casualty rate, over 200%, of any unit of the Vietnam era. This means each SOG team member was either killed or wounded multiple times. For example, SSG Robert Howard (later Colonel Howard) was wounded on at least 11 occasions, was awarded eight Purple Hearts, the Distinguished Service Cross (the second highest medal for valor in combat) AND the Medal of Honor (the highest award for valor above and beyond the call of duty). He also received numerous other medals for heroism. Bob is one example of what a SOG 1-0 (pronounced "one-zero," a team leader) was like. Twenty-two men received the Distinguished Service Cross and 13 received the Medal of Honor on SOG operations. It is safe to say that SOG team members were the most BA men walking the face of the planet from 1964–1972.

I waited too long to write this book. Too many surviving SOG operators have passed, most parents have passed. I am not going to include a lot of historical detail around units, battles, SOG, etc., unless it pertains to the missions I discuss. There are many great SOG books that contain that kind of detail. My focus is on describing what I, as a SOG 1-0, experienced and felt during my time there—and afterward. I feel a need to get this message out while I can of what it was like to be a young soldier (21–22 years old) leading the world's most elite military combat teams on what have been described by many as "insane" missions. These are missions you would never be allowed to conduct today.

As I said, this is not an academic SOG history book. Plenty of those are out there and more coming. This is a journal of some of my experiences that I think represent much of what all SOG 1-0s experienced. My focus is on the missions I went on because those are the ones I know best. It is about what I experienced as a SOG warrior. It is not a pretty story. It is raw, about war and war is about death, killing, horror, fear and heroic actions by the people with whom I crossed paths. There are things in this book that many people do not want to know or believe happened. If you are one of those people, this book will upset you if you attempt to read it.

The actions described here are about the elite of the elite desperately fighting for their lives and the lives of their teammates as vastly, numerically superior enemy forces closed in on them, and in many cases, killed them and left their mutilated bodies behind for the animals and jungle to consume. Any North Vietnamese soldier who killed a SOG team member received a "Killed an American" award and was guaranteed to be set for life by their government. The North Vietnamese Army had dossiers on SOG operators and posted bounties on SOG team members—dead or alive—that extended beyond the borders of South Vietnam! The deaths of some SOG team members, for example Jerry "Mad Dog" Shriver, were announced and celebrated on North Vietnam radio stations.

There has never been a war where such small teams of young warriors were set against such overwhelming numbers of enemy forces on every mission. This fact has been documented in many other places by historians. There are names of some heroes that I can't remember at this point and have not been able to find those who do. In these cases, I gave these warriors names so their stories would not be forgotten. In other cases, I changed names as a courtesy to warriors who do not want to relive their stories.

SOG missions were not fought alone—you were always part of a team. Internal battles, however, were and still are being fought alone by what has been burned into each SOG Operator's brain. Once seen, you cannot unsee. Once you do, you cannot undo. There are experiences on the battlefield that you can never un-see, un-hear, un-smell, un-feel or un-taste. Once you pull the trigger or detonate an explosive, the lives you have just terminated cannot be un-killed. The enemy soldier's spouse, kids, grandkids, great grandkids, future relatives and potential roles they all play in the history of the world are immediately and permanently erased. You can never forget the look on the person's face when you pull the trigger or penetrate him with your knife. These are part of you for the rest of your life. You can never remove the experience from your brain. It is part of you until you die.

You cannot do what SOG Operators did without experiencing Post Traumatic Stress (PTS), Post Traumatic Stress Symptoms (PTSS), or Post-Traumatic Stress Disorder (PTSD) and Traumatic Brain Injury (TBI). It just wasn't talked about much in those days. All SOG operators had PTSD and TBIs to some level and those who are still alive continue to experience it today. In some cases, it is lying just beneath the surface ready to emerge again with the right "trigger." The six-mission/six-month commitment was designed to let warriors out before they had severe problems. But it only took one mission to change your life forever—if you lived.

Today the Veterans Administration (VA) estimates that an average of 22 veterans die by suicide per day—a figure that's skewed because more than half of US veterans are not registered with the VA. More recent and robust national research puts the estimate at 50 or more per day. Over the years, some of these have been SOG operators.

I learned from everyone I worked with, came in contact with or heard on the radio—including the enemy. This is not a political book or story. I admit that I have some strong opinions about the war in Southeast Asia and how the US conducted it, but you will not find them in this book. **This book is to honor the memory of all those who served in or supported MACV-SOG.** I consider all of them to be American heroes of the first order and men I am honored, humbled and proud to have served with. Many men of SOG were recognized for their heroism, such as Bob Howard mentioned above, who at the end of the day would say, "Just another day in SOG." There are many heroes who were not recognized with medals or publicity for various reasons. They know what they did. Their teammates know what they did. And most importantly, the enemy knows what they did.

My friend, retired Navy SEAL Jocko Willink, talks a lot about "getting and staying on the path." I believe some people, like Jocko, Eldon Bargewell, Dick Meadows, Ken Bowra and many others mentioned in this book were "born" on the path.

I consider myself extremely fortunate to have worked with, fought battles with, and been friends with legends like Dick Meadows, Bob Howard, Eldon Bargewell, John Stryker Meyer and many others who are mentioned in this book. I have carried the memory of 34 personal SOG friends and teammates who made the ultimate sacrifice with me for over 55 years and have swum, biked and run tens of thousands of miles in their memory over the years. I say their names as I begin my exercise every day. It has been said that a warrior dies twice. Once when their heart stops beating and finally when people stop saying their name. These heroes will not die the second death as long as I am alive because their names will be spoken every day until I meet with them again on the other side.

You may find that some of my accounts of the circumstances around the death of someone you know do not match up with what you have read on the Internet or been told by someone who heard about these incidents. I find many inaccuracies with stories and reports on the Internet, in articles and books. In many cases I was there. I know what really happened. I heard the heroes' last words, last breaths and saw their life leave their eyes. I carried their bodies out of the jungle.

I am using my experiences as a platform to describe what SOG operators went through and lived through. It is about the lives and actions of SOG operators. **If you choose to continue to read, fasten your seat belt and brace for impact!**

# SOG CODENAME DYNAMITE

**A MACV-SOG 1-0's Personal Journal**

**Book 1**

Henry L. (Dick) Thompson, Ph.D.

Wormhole
PUBLISHING
P.O. Box 868, Watkinsville, GA 30677

# PART 1

# Chapter 1

## Born on the Path

*On the plains of hesitation lie the blackened bones of countless millions who at the dawn of victory lay down to rest, and in resting died.*
—Adlai Stevenson

I was in a prone position in knee-high ribbon grass. I had a death grip on the shoulder of a North Vietnamese Army (NVA) soldier. Our eyes made contact as I grabbed the barrel of his AK-47 and pushed it away from me. At the same time, I realized I was in trouble. I had no strength. The pain in my back was debilitating! I was having difficulty breathing. We were grappling and he was terrified and determined to kill me. He yelled for his teammates who were crawling in the grass about 40 meters away to help him, then pulled the trigger on his AK-47 trying to shoot me. The bullets just missed me. I was getting weaker and having more difficulty breathing, but I was determined to take him prisoner!

He rolled on top of me and started fighting harder. I managed to get my CAR-15 pointed toward him and shot him in the shoulder. I thought that would take some of the fight out of him, but I was so weak he was still overpowering me. He kept yelling for his teammates and firing off rounds trying to hit me as we continued to wrestle. I was about to pass out from the excruciating pain. He was holding the barrel of my CAR-15 and I could not get it pointed at him. He could see that he was beginning to overpower me. I could tell I was about to become the victim. But I would not give up!

Suddenly, he turned loose of the barrel of my CAR-15 and punched me really hard in the nose. My nose was bleeding, and my vision was blurry. Our eyes locked again. This time I could see the look in his eyes that people get when they know they are going to die. He had realized that turning loose of my CAR-15 allowed me to point it toward his face and that this would be what killed him. He knew he had less than a second to live.

I had moved the muzzle of my CAR-15 so it was pointed toward his head about six inches away from his cheek. At this point there was nothing he could do. He knew he was dead. He closed his eyes. He had not been cooperating with me. I only had one option left: I had to terminate him. I squeezed off a five-round burst on full-auto directly into his face. His head literally exploded, covering my face and head with blood, brain matter, bone fragments, and yellow fatty tissue followed immediately by a stream of hot blood from his carotid artery. As his mostly headless body went limp, the sounds of the firefight and reality came back loudly. I could hear his teammates yelling to him that they were almost to us. I sprayed the grass with 20–25 rounds of automatic fire, threw a frag grenade in their direction and began rolling away toward the bomb crater as some of his teammates returned fire. As I rolled, I remembered being a little kid playing army in the woods alone, a lifetime ago.

I was born January 3, 1947, and grew up in South Carolina in a small town called Walhalla, not far from Clemson University. I came from a military family. My father, SGT Henry L. Thompson, Jr., was a veteran of both WWII and the Korean War. He and my mother's five brothers, PFC Clyde J. Hudson, PFC Ray Hudson, S1C Harold Hudson, SGT Alton Hudson, and PVT Doyle Hudson were all deployed in WWII at the same time. My mother, Christine Hudson Thompson, was a member of a six-time Blue Star Family. On November 19, 1944, one of the Blue Stars turned Gold. My uncle, PFC Clyde J. Hudson, was killed in action (KIA). She became a member of the club no one wants to belong to—a Gold Star family.

I heard talk about the war and the military from the time I was old enough to remember. My family was together a lot, so there was a lot of discussion about the war and things that had taken place on the battlefield and the home front. As I got older, I was able to ask my father and uncles more specific questions. I wanted to know how the Army was structured, what a platoon did, etc.

My father was in the infantry most of the time but spent some time in the Rangers. Sometimes I would hear him talking to my uncles about the kinds of operations he participated in. He was in the Army about four years and got out when WWII ended.

When the Korean War started, my father was called back to active duty and deployed to Korea. That's when I really started to hear about war because I was old enough to better understand what people were talking about. My father wrote letters home and told my mother about how deep the mud was, how cold it was and what the war was like. War and the military fascinated me, and I was hearing about the Korean War firsthand.

The house we moved into when my father returned from Korea was on a small farm with lots of space for me to roam, learn and grow. We had running water in the house but not an indoor toilet. You had to brave the elements to go to the outdoor toilet. I didn't realize it at the time but going to the toilet was "on the path." A dirt road that went past our house separated the house from the barn—and toilet. You had to cross the road and approach the barn to get to the toilet.

When I was six years old my father bought a large turkey. Large in the sense that when the turkey and I stood face-to-face we were the same height and eye-to-eye. Luckily for me, the turkey was very aggressive and territorial. He claimed all the area on the barn (and toilet) side of the road as his and guarded it fiercely. When he would see me crossing the road, he would run after me and flog me, often knocking me to the ground and preventing my use of the toilet. When

PFC Clyde J. Hudson   PFC Ray Hudson   S1C Harold A. Hudson

SGT Alton Hudson   PVT Doyle Hudson  SGT Henry L. Thompson, ˒

*My Uncles and Father in World War II*

I complained to my father he said, "You have to stand up to him. Show him you are not afraid of him. Make him back down." I said, "I do stand up to him, but he's bigger, stronger and faster than me. When he knocks me down, he pecks me." He said, "True, but you are smarter than he is. Figure out a way to show him you are not afraid of him and that it's your side of the road, not his."

And so, my special operations field training began. I learned how to infiltrate the other side of the road, to use cover, concealment and distraction to get to the toilet before he could respond. Then how to arm myself with rocks and a sling shot so I could hold him off during my ex-filtration. I also watched what my parents did when he went after them. They would just jump at him, yell at him and chase him away. I decided to try this. Armed with my sling shot, I yelled at him to get away, fired a rock into his chest and ran toward him yelling. He ran from me until I turned my back to him. It took a few iterations of this tactic, but I eventually convinced him I would only run toward him, not away. My final victory came when he was invited to Thanksgiving dinner.

When I was about seven, I decided to form an army. More specifically, Thompson's Rangers. My Cousin Eddie, who became Carl when he joined the Army later in life, helped me organize it and recruit other members. (Carl spent three years in Vietnam and was a member of G Company, 75th Rangers.) Cousins Joe, Larry (a.k.a. LD) and Danny were the first recruits. Later, Cousin Patsy (a.k.a. Pat) became our only WAC (Women's Army Corps) member. We grew from there, bringing in other cousins and friends from outside the family. We found it necessary to have a logbook to keep records of all our members and their performance. One member, not a cousin, was court-martialed and booted out. He was our first and only dishonorable discharge. And just for the record, according to the logbook I was General Thompson in charge of the 69th Ranger Regiment, Company A, 2nd Platoon. I still have the logbook.

I had been thinking about being in the Army when I grew up from the age of four. I was "on the path." According to my logbook, I locked on to the decision to become an actual Ranger the day my cousins and

*Ranger Logbook (Courtesy of "General" Thompson)*

I saw the movie *Darby's Rangers* in 1958. We were hooked. My actions and interests became more and more focused on Special Ops from that time forward. I became more interested in not just shooting guns, but marksmanship. Not just firecrackers but building explosives. Not just playing army in the woods but becoming invisible and learning to live off the land.

I grew up in the woods. When I was five years old, I would go to the woods whenever I had the chance. Most of the time I would go alone, unless Carl was available to play, track animals, listen to the sounds of the woods and work on how to be invisible when you move or stop moving. I wanted to have the skill to track an ant through a cornfield, but I don't think I ever reached that level.

By the time I was six, I had an army pup tent and I would take it up on a wooded hill about 200 meters from our house, put it up and sleep up there by myself some nights. On weekends, Carl and I would take eggs and bacon up there, build a fire and cook them for breakfast. When I got a little older and had a BB gun, I would take out birds and roast them over the fire. Carl and I did a lot of things we thought Rangers did. I was also discovering that I seemed to have Spidey senses. I could hear a silent dog whistle, see a gnat climbing a pine tree at 500 meters and tell you its sex, see in the dark and smell snakes.

We discovered that our Uncle Alton had brought a German Dress Knife back from the war. He said he took it off a dead German officer. We were not allowed to touch it but knew where he kept it. Sometimes when he would leave the house, we would get it out and play with it.

The perfect storm that disrupted my future plans came together when I was 13. Math and science had always been my favorite subjects in school. Santa gave me a chemistry set for Christmas and things were never the same after that. I developed a passion for chemistry, which put me on a dual track: the Army and chemistry. I watched monster movies on Shock Theatre at midnight on Saturday and tried to replicate some of the experiments I saw on these shows.

In addition to the Ranger stuff, I set up my own laboratory in the barn. I spent all my allowance and money from part-time jobs on chemicals and lab equipment. Back in those days, you could go

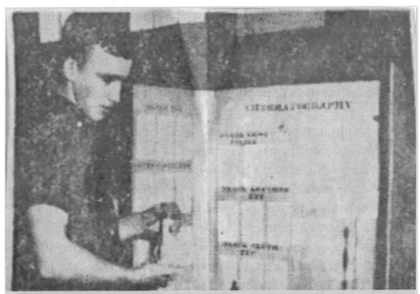

**OCONEE COUNTY'S** Science Fair attracted several hundred persons to Walhalla yesterday. One winner was Dick Thompson of Walhalla, with an exhibit on chromatography—separation of dyes and mixtures.

*One of many Science Fairs*

to a drug store (pharmacy) and buy all kinds of chemicals. It's almost unbelievable to people today that I could buy then what are considered dangerous chemicals today; particularly if my mother signed for me and said, "Yes, it's okay for him to have concentrated nitric acid." I stocked my lab with all types of chemicals and equipment for my experiments. At one point I thought I was getting close to a successful brain exchange between birds and frogs. I could get the brains in the skulls, but just couldn't get my patients to start breathing again afterwards. I also worked on heart exchanges and had the same problem getting the hearts to start beating again. It didn't seem to matter how much electricity, even 120 volts, I ran through them.

I also became interested in building solid fuel rockets, starting small and graduating to rather large ones. One of the larger ones exploded on the launch pad and took out some of my neighbor's windows so I had to go back to the smaller ones just to be safe. Fortunately, my mother never knew how many pounds of rocket fuel components I had in my bedroom.

I had a great relationship with my high school chemistry/physics teacher, Mr. Sid Ballenger, who took me beyond high school level in these subjects. He loved my science fair projects even though I tended to take a different approach than what he recommended. Occasionally he let me borrow pieces of lab equipment that I could not afford for my own lab in the barn.

Mr. Ballenger had a state-of-the-art driver's ed machine that allowed a student to practice driving skills. One test was how fast you could take your foot off the gas pedal and apply the brakes when the emergency stop light came on. I had the fastest reaction time in our high school—with one exception: Mr. Ballenger also had a daughter, Joyce. She was my age, an athlete, the star of the Majorettes in the High School Marching Band and lettered in sports. But I was more impressed with her reaction time. She was the queen of reaction time. I just could not beat her.

During my senior year I borrowed the school's very expensive Bausch and Lomb™ high-powered microscope. About a week later, after I had shown him a picture I had taken with the microscope, he dropped by my lab after school to see what I was doing. He almost had a cardiac arrest when he realized that I had disassembled the precision microscope and built a more powerful system with the components integrated with a photographic system I had created. My system was more than twice as powerful as the school's microscope and it took pictures! When he was able to speak, he said I needed to have the microscope back at school the next day as re-assembled as I could get it. I put it back together as good as new, but it ended his willingness to loan me expensive equipment from the school.

In high school I played football and ran track. I was strong and fast, and could hit really hard, but I wasn't college material because of my size. I actually played defensive end my senior year on a defense line that weighed over 200 pounds, and I was 140. One did not, however, want to try to run around my end. Newton's second law says force equals mass times acceleration. My mass was relatively small, but I was very fast, and I would still be accelerating when my force impacted a running back or quarterback. They learned it was painful to come around my end. A quarterback would drop back and see me in his face because I could get there quickly. My cousin and good friend, Derrill Thompson, played the other defensive end. Our plan was to meet at the quarterback and make a sandwich out of him.

In June 1962, my buddy, Hal Ballenger, asked me if I wanted to go SCUBA diving. I watched *Sea Hunt* starring Lloyd Bridges every week and had read Jacques Cousteau's book. I had also done a lot of snorkeling and free-diving and really wanted to SCUBA dive. Hal's father, Howard Ballenger—an attorney and former bomber pilot and POW in WWII—owned a couple of tanks and regulators. Our football coach, Charlie Johnson, dabbled in SCUBA and had a small SCUBA air compressor that he let us use to fill Mr. Ballenger's tanks.

When we got to the lake, Hal hooked the regulators to the tanks, used the straps on the tank to tie it to me, and told me to put the mouthpiece in my mouth and just breathe in and out. He asked me if I had any questions. I said, "No," and down we went. Somehow, I managed not to drown or have an air embolism.

A couple of weeks later my dad's brother, Uncle Robert, arrived on a 30-day leave from the Navy. He had some dive gear to include fins at least three feet long and stiff as a board. He said he was in the Navy's Underwater Demolition Team and was going to teach me how to SCUBA dive. I was all in. This began my serious SCUBA journey. We were in the water almost every day. I continued to dive throughout high school and into college and became a certified dive master and instructor on 3 November 1966 along with another high school buddy, Mike Hamor, who later joined the Navy Seabees and visited me in Vietnam at Da Nang in 1969. I didn't realize it at the time, but I was continuing to build my mental and physical skill sets for the path ahead. I was also beginning a life of SCUBA around the world, to include the South China Sea.

I graduated high school in 1965 and started college at the University of South Carolina on a chemistry scholarship. I continued to SCUBA dive and began to study martial arts. At the University it appeared to me that our country was dividing into two groups: the long-haired, drug-using, anti-war, hippy people and the patriots who wanted to crush the North Vietnamese. I knew I was in the second group and began thinking seriously about volunteering for the war.

After a year and a half, I could see that Vietnam was going hot and heavy. It was on the news every night. This was also about the time the US discovered that the North Vietnamese had a "real" army that was much better than anyone thought at the time. The North Vietnamese Army probably ranked in the top four armies in the world. Plus, we were fighting in their backyard. They knew how to train and how to operate there. And they didn't stop; they would just keep coming at you! Their biggest disadvantage was they didn't have the technology that we did. They also didn't have air superiority. There were a lot of things they just didn't have that held them back or it would have been much worse for the US than it was.

I decided to take a break from school and do my patriotic duty to help crush our enemy in Vietnam. I felt an obligation to do my part and thought it was something everyone should be doing. My father supported me going into the military, but my mother was not happy! She wanted me to finish school. I told her, "I'm just taking a three-year break. When I come back, I'll finish my doctorate, and everything will be fine." She said, "No, you won't." I assured her I would come back and finish school.

I was actually on my way to the Marine recruiter (I had obviously gotten off the path), because the Marines were on TV every night, but stopped by the Army recruiter who was next door just to see what they had to offer. They seemed to be excited and willing to give me anything I wanted. "You want chemistry? The Army has a Chemical Corps." I went with the Army because of the promise of a chemical corps assignment, and I knew that being in the Army would also give me the chance to become a Ranger if I chose to. I was on the path!

*Cousin Carl as a machine gunner in Vietnam.*

I was always impressed with this picture he sent home.

**Lessons Learned**

- When you are on the right path you can feel it. When you step off the path it doesn't feel right. Get back on the path and stay on the path.
- In reality, there are multiple paths for everyone, but one is the best for you.
- Things you experience and see on the path fit together. Keep moving.
- Before I joined the Army, Cousin Carl—who was already in the Army—said, "When they give you a job to do, even if you don't like it and no one is around, always give it your best effort. It will pay off in the long run." I never forgot this—and he was right.
- The Army did not like nick names. I was called Henry (and a few other less flattering names) when I joined. Only my close friends knew me as Dick.
- Events come together to form patterns. Patterns lead to systemic structures. Systemic structures have rules. Learn the rules and you can control your path.
- Cousin Carl would spend three back-to-back tours in Vietnam.

# Chapter 2

## Becoming a Warrior

### I am the Infantry!

*I am the Infantry—Queen of Battle!*
*For two centuries I have kept our nation safe,*
*Purchasing freedom with my blood.*
*To tyrants, I am the day of reckoning;*
*To the suppressed, the hope for the future.*
*Where fighting is thick, there am I. . .*
*I am the Infantry! FOLLOW ME!*

—Poem Adapted by LTC Stephen H. White

It was January 1967. I was on a long bus ride from Seneca, South Carolina to Columbia, South Carolina, the home of Fort Jackson. Once our bus load of recruits got through the main gate and onto Fort Jackson proper, it was several miles to the Recruit Induction Center. A railroad track ran along one side of the road, and a single line of coal about 20 feet high ran along the other side of the road for several miles.

14

The bus driver announced with a Southern drawl, "You boys, see all that coal piled on the side of the road? When I drove my bus load of boys in yesterday, all that coal was on the other side of the road. And by this time tomorrow, you boys will have it moved back over there! (Followed by a big laugh.) You boys are in for the shock of your lives! It won't do you no good to cry for your mama. She can't help you in here! Most of you are probably going to die before you ever get to Vi-et-naam!" I didn't believe it at the time, but some recruits did die before they finished training. One was my bunk mate during Advanced Infantry Training.

## Induction Center – Fort Jackson, South Carolina

When I first entered the Army, my thoughts were that I'm here for three years, then I'll get out, go back to school, get a Ph.D. and be a research chemist. This pathway began to change at 0330 hours the first morning at the Induction Center. We were asleep in bunk beds in the barracks. The lights came on and someone started shouting and screaming to get out of the @$#&* bed and to fall in formation in front of the bunks. Apparently, we weren't moving fast enough. I heard bunk beds crashing to the floor with people still in them! I quickly jumped to the floor, stood at attention in front of my bed and started looking around for the giant ready to crush anyone who talked back!

I saw a guy my size wearing a big Smokey the Bear hat and a black and gold Ranger tab on his left shoulder! And I thought, "Wow! This drill sergeant is an animal, and no one is going to talk back to him! When he says jump, everyone asks 'How high, Drill Sergeant?'" That was when I thought, "Okay, I've got to start rethinking my path. This guy is a Ranger. He is very impressive." That brought back all my pre-adolescent desire to be a Ranger. When he marched us to the mess hall with the Jody call, "I want to be an Airborne Ranger! I want to live a life of danger," I was hooked. Why would I want to be anything else for the next three years?

It was a week of taking one test after another, marching, KP (kitchen police—peeling potatoes, washing dishes and cleaning the grease trap) and police call, which sounded cool, but turned out to be picking up trash, especially cigarette butts. On the first day when the drill sergeant asked me why I was not picking up the cigarette butts, I replied, "I don't smoke. I'm not picking them up!" You could have heard a pin drop. After I had pushed Fort Jackson a little closer to China by doing over 100 push-ups, I agreed to make an exception this time and pick them up. I was not happy about it but I was doing enough push-ups for other things, so it seemed logical to play the game. Plus, I knew we were leaving Fort Jackson in a couple of days.

Hundreds of us were loaded on literal cattle cars (tractor trailer trucks) and transported to Fort Gordon, Georgia, for Basic Training. It was a long, cold, miserable ride. Cattle cars have plenty of holes in them to allow the cows to get fresh air, but it was January and below freezing.

When my group of about 200 arrived that evening, a knuckle-dragging drill sergeant boarded our cattle car and in a loud voice said, "From this point forward, I am your mama and your daddy. You don't do anything, even breathe, unless I tell you to. No one knows where you are, no one cares where you are, or if you are tired, hungry, cold or want to go home! Do not dare say any of that @$#* ##@** to me. DO YOU UNDERSTAND ME?" We all responded with a very loud, "YES, DRILL SERGEANT!" to which he replied, "When I say go, get off my bus with all your equipment and line up on the cables in the sawdust pit!" He got out of the way, shouted "Go!" and we almost killed each other trying to get off the bus.

We discovered that this was not our lucky day. Once we were lined up, the Drill Sergeant said, "When I call your name, you say, 'Here, Drill Sergeant,' and bring your mullet body and equipment and line up behind me. DO YOU UNDERSTAND ME, TRAINEES?" We responded, "Yes, Drill Sergeant!" That is, everyone except one guy in the front row who responded with "Yes, Sir!" "Drop, trainee, you little piece of %$#. I am a Staff Sergeant in the United States Army! I work for a living. Don't ever call me Sir. You keep doing push-ups until I get tired."

"Listen up! Adams!" No response. When I call your name, you sound off with 'Here' and line up behind me with your equipment. Am

I clear?" Everyone sounded off with "Yes, Drill Sergeant." He looked down at the guy doing push-ups and said, "Did you call me Sir again?" Before the guy could answer, the drill sergeant said, "Alright, dirtbag! Crawl on your belly like a reptile to the far end of the line and back as fast as you can. Move out!

"Listen up, scumbags! We're going to try this again! Adams!" No response. He put us all in the push-up position called "front leaning rest" and told us to start doing push-ups. He went to the next name on the list, "Addis!" No response. This went on for a few minutes until another drill sergeant arrived and said something to him. He yelled, "All of you dirtbags, pick up your gear and follow Drill Sergeant Ruiz at a double time. Go! Get out of my area!" Drill Sergeant Ruiz was a good guy. Unfortunately, he was killed in Vietnam the following year, 1968.

Turned out we had been dropped off in the wrong battalion area. Our Company was five blocks down the street. We got to jog in double time all the way there carrying our duffel bags and equipment. It was not a pretty sight. People were scattered out all along the way. All of our drill sergeants were there impatiently waiting on us like a pack of hungry pit bulls. At least we knew what to do and not to do when we got in that formation—not that it made any difference! Welcome to the Army. We would soon learn about "hurry up and wait!"

## Basic Training – Fort Gordon, Georgia

The Vietnam buildup was so massive there were not enough buildings available to put us in, so the lucky platoons, like mine, lived in general purpose large tents—18' X 52', 12' high in the center with 5'8" sidewalls—with a small oil heater in each end. They would always clog up during the night and begin putting out more soot than heat. When you got up in the cold tent, below freezing most mornings (this was before climate change), your nostrils would be clogged with soot, and it would be all over your gear. The bathroom was a PortaJohn located outside the tent in Siberia.

It snowed several times while we were there, and the tents tried to fall in on us because of the weight of the snow. Fun times! Training and

*Company E, 3rd Tng Bn, 1st Tng Brigade Fort Gordon, Georgia*
*20 JAN – 24 MAR 1967*
*Front row, fourth from the left with Sergeant stripes*

actually the food were great. I didn't mind potatoes at all three meals and SOS—sh*t on a shingle—for breakfast.

After watching our platoon perform for a few days, SSG Beasley selected a trainee to be the trainee platoon sergeant and gave him an arm band with sergeant stripes to wear that also put him in charge of the platoon. I was selected as the assistant platoon sergeant. One night I was on trainee Charge of Quarters (CQ) duty and had to work in the orderly room with the drill sergeant who had CQ duty that night. I saw an Army Field Manual, FM 22-5, Drill and Ceremonies laying on the desk. I picked it up, started looking at it, and realized it described everything about right face, left face, when to call the commands—it was all written out right there. If I had had this book for the last couple of weeks. . . . So, I read the book that night. The next day, I could see the mistakes that the drill sergeants were making. I made the mistake once of pointing out a mistake and got to work my triceps and pecs while I pushed Fort Gordon a little bit closer to China. Within a few days, SSG Beasley made me the platoon guide. Mentally, physically, and now drill and ceremonies wise, I was separating myself from the pack. I was highly motivated and eating this stuff up!

I almost lost my platoon guide stripes during Army hand-to-hand combat training when SSG Beasley was teaching us how to do the Army's version of a front kick. Suddenly, I heard myself say, "That kick won't work. It's too slow and your head is too exposed." You could have heard a pin drop! Total silence.

Beasley said, "Come over here, Thompson. If you think you are fast enough to stop my kick, go for it or you will be lying on the ground crying like a little girl!" Before he finished saying girl, he launched his kick at my groin. I executed a blocking kick with the hard edge of my combat boot that hit his front shin bone about halfway up and caused him to spin to the ground. Based on the blood I could see beginning to seep through his fatigue pants leg, it cut a nice gash on his shin. He had Drill Sergeant Ruiz take over the training while he counseled me off to the side of the formation. Beasley was not happy the rest of the day. He had a limp for about three days.

When we started going to the firing range I was fired up, no pun intended. It was great! A few trainees refused to shoot at the silhouette targets, which were designed to prepare us to fire at a human form in combat. I soon qualified expert with the M-14 rifle and won the company marksmanship trophy. At the time, there were approximately 15 different weapons systems soldiers could quality as expert with if they met certain standards. Hand grenades were one of those systems and I got my expert badge with them. The last week of training I maxed the marksmanship course and came in second in physical fitness.

At the time, a lieutenant had a life expectancy of about a day and a half in Vietnam. Lieutenants were getting killed so fast the Army couldn't produce them fast enough. Drill Sergeant Beasley insisted that I apply for Officer Candidate School (OCS). He made sure that my application had been approved before I left Basic Training. Beasley also made sure I was promoted to the rank of Private E-2 at the end of Basic Training. Given the death rate of lieutenants, I'm not sure if that meant he liked me or not! I thought I was hot. My parents and younger brother, Butch, came to see me graduate as Outstanding Trainee of our Training Company. After graduation I got ready for my first commercial airline flight to travel to Fort Lewis, Washington, for Advanced Infantry Training.

## Leadership Preparation Course – Fort Lewis, Washington

When I arrived at Fort Lewis, I discovered that I had been selected to attend a two-week leadership preparation course (LPC) to prepare me to be a trainee platoon leader during Advanced Infantry Training (AIT). The LPC was great. Everyone in the course had been chosen because they had demonstrated above average leadership abilities during Basic Training. They were all sharp and great to work with. I met two guys who would become good friends of mine, Bob Sheridan and Pete McMurray.

The cadre almost treated us like soldiers rather than trainees and I learned a lot. The time flew by and then it was time to join our AIT company and assume a leadership position. In addition to learning a lot about leadership I learned that it rains almost every day at Ft. Lewis in Seattle, Washington!

## Advanced Infantry Training – Fort Lewis, Washington

The leadership team arrived a couple of days before the trainees. We got to know our drill sergeants, the company area and what our roles would be during AIT. We were ready to go when our "trainees" arrived. AIT seemed to be more like I expected the Army to be. We trained hard, worked with a variety of weapons, learned basic patrolling and combat maneuvers.

After becoming relatively proficient in day land navigation working in buddy teams, it was time to learn how to do it in the dark. The second night was long and wet. We got back to the barracks in the wee hours and got a little sleep before more day land nav training. That night we reported back to our night land nav instructors. The first thing my instructor said to me was, "Where's your compass buddy, Thompson?" My quick reply was, "He died, Sergeant." That perceived "sarcastic" reply did not go over well. He immediately dropped me for push-ups while he talked about my ancestors. Finally, our company drill sergeant saw what was happening and came to my rescue. He told the instructor that my compass buddy was found dead in his bunk (below me) that morning from meningitis. John was a good guy and I enjoyed working with him. I guess the old bus driver was partly right—some of us did die before finishing training.

It was a great, wet eight weeks of Advanced Infantry Training that allowed me to qualify as expert with the M-14 A1 fully automatic rifle, M-60 machine gun, 3.5-inch rocket launcher and M1911 .45 caliber pistol. I was promoted to private first class (E-3) at the end of AIT and flew home for a short leave before going to Ft. Benning, Georgia, for Infantry Officer Candidate School (OCS) with Bob and Pete.

## OCS – Fort Benning, Georgia

I reported to OCS 92nd Company a little after 2000 hours dressed in my khaki uniform with my Infantry cord on my shoulder, National Defense Medal and PFC stripes on my uniform. I looked good. The senior cadet in charge of quarters that night didn't think so. He went ballistic! How dare I come into his orderly room dressed like that. I was a low-life cadet who had no rank or awards. I was sent outside to rip off my stripes and anything else attached to my uniform before I could sign in. I knew I was going to get six months of harassment, but I wasn't expecting it to start so soon.

More bad news was coming. When I got upstairs and met my two roommates, they told me we had reported five weeks early because of a scheduling mix-up. (Everyone who has ever been in the military can tell you about "hurry up and wait!") The seniors had moved out of the barracks so we would have a place to stay, but they would be back every day to give us things to do for them and harass us. It was going to be a fun five weeks!

Later in the week, Bob and I met Keith Pennington from Griffin, Georgia. The three of us became close friends and remained together until we arrived in Vietnam (Bob later became engaged to Keith's sister).

*Second Lieutenant's Gold Bar Commissioned as a
Second Lieutenant 22 JAN 1968*

CPT Pollack was our Company Commander. He had recently completed a combat tour in Vietnam, which gave him a lot of street cred. Unfortunately, he was killed on his second tour in Vietnam toward the end of 1968.

I did well in OCS and requested to go to Airborne school followed by an assignment with Special Forces (which included the SF qualification course) after graduation. It was approved almost immediately. I was commissioned a Second Lieutenant in the Infantry on January 22, 1968. My father asked me why I wanted to be in Special Forces. My reply was, "If I'm going to Vietnam, I want to be the best of the best."

### Airborne School – Fort Benning, Georgia

Bob, Keith and I rented an apartment for the three weeks we were running and making parachute jumps. Airborne school was outstanding. It prepared me to do one thing: throw myself out of a perfectly good airplane traveling over 120 MPH at an altitude of 1250 feet and survive! I was really impressed with the training process. From Airborne school, Bob, Keith, Pete and I traveled to Fort Bragg for a Special Forces assignment—provided we passed the qualification course. Bob, Keith and I moved into a trailer in a trailer park just off post. It was a tight fit, but it was mostly a place to store our gear and sleep out of the rain, sometimes.

*Airborne Tab*
*Graduated Airborne School, FEB 68, Ft. Benning, GA*

**Assigned to 3rd Special Forces Group – Fort Bragg, North Carolina**

We began our assignment in the 3rd Special Forces Group while we waited on the Special Forces Officer Qualification Course (SFOC 68-4) to begin. It was a challenging mixture of academics, tactics, strategy, physical fitness, field operations and training in the basic Special Forces skills. Q Course students were assigned to "A-Teams" for the duration of the training. That's where Bob, Pete, Keith and I met and became friends with Chuck Adams, Ray Stacks, MAJ Denton, Dr. John Bosco, Rich Todd, Pat Cunningham, Joe Gayer and Hal Hepler.

Three months later, our entire team graduated from the Q Course, received our "Flash" and credentials that signified we were Green Berets.

**Special Forces Qualified – Fort Bragg, North Carolina.**

*100 men will test today, but only 3 win the Green Beret!*

Special Forces Qualified at last and assigned to the 3rd Special Forces Group! Special Forces was not just about going in to conduct a raid or ambush. SF in Vietnam was more about going in to win the hearts and minds of the people. In the qualification course we trained on insurgencies, how governments are overthrown, different things like that as well as raids, ambushes, underground railroads, explosives, lock picking and the major specialties in which the Non-Commissioned Officers (NCOs) were trained: demolitions, light weapons, heavy

*Special Forces Flash and Unit Patch Graduated*
*Special Forces Officers Course, Ft. Bragg, NC, MAY 1968*

weapons, communications, and combat trauma care, except in less detail. For example, the medical specialty for the NCOs was 12 months of intense medical training including basic surgery.

As an officer leading an A-Team, two members of my team were Special Forces medic qualified. When I was in the Special Forces Officer Q Course we did a lot of work on large scale insurgencies, escape and evasion processes, winning the hearts and minds of the people, and training the indigenous population in guerrilla operations. Officers were trained in all the primary skill sets of Special Forces, whereas NCOs coming out of the Q Course, went to an in-depth training program for a specific specialty, for example, light weapons, heavy weapons, medical, communications, etc. Officers had to be trained in the basics of all the skill sets to be able to appropriately use the team's abilities.

### Mission Prep for Africa – Fort Bragg, North Carolina

Bob and I were assigned to a B-Team in the 3rd Special Forces Group at Fort Bragg, North Carolina. The 3rd Group's target area was Africa. Our B-Team was preparing for a mission in Africa. Not what Bob and I wanted to do. We submitted a Form1049 (paperwork to volunteer for an assignment) for immediate assignment to the 5th Special Forces Group in Vietnam. We had joined the Army to go to Vietnam, not Africa.

Our preparation for the Africa mission continued and involved getting a lot of vaccinations. We also began training with the types of weapons we were likely to encounter there including the AK-47 rifle. I enjoyed the weapons training.

## Quick Kill

When training to fire a weapon, you typically turn sideways and shoot. But when the enemy is shooting at you, your brain takes over and says, "Face the enemy." Your body instinctively turns toward the enemy. For short distance encounters, you need to train to shoot without aiming. Pointing is much faster and can be as accurate as aiming since your eyes find it difficult to focus on the sights under high stress. Our group went through an intensive course called Quick Kill where we trained to shoot from the hip or under the armpit. We started with BB guns and shot at miniature silhouettes on a 2x4, shooting from the hip until we could knock them all down. Then we started throwing three-inch disks up in the air and shot until we could hit that moving disk. The disks got smaller and smaller until we were shooting quarter-sized disks in the air.

Next, we moved to a course where targets popped up and we used M-16s and live ammunition until we could hit all the targets without aiming. This included target discrimination where some targets that popped up were good guys. We had to make split-second decisions whether the target was friend or foe. It was amazing how quickly we became proficient after only practicing a few days. This technique would soon prove to be a lifesaver for me. It was one of the most valuable skill sets I learned for surviving in the jungles of Southeast Asia. Life or death is often determined by a fraction of a second.

Special Forces was an airborne unit. We found ourselves making a lot of parachute jumps from different types of aircraft, with and without rucksacks, day and night. Our parachuting skills increased rapidly. So did our tolerance to resist air sickness on the planes. We flew low and it was always a rough ride.

Demolition training was one of my favorites. We moved from the intermediate level taught in the Q Course to advanced techniques. For example, how to drop a bridge, wire cars to detonate, building lots of different booby-traps (IEDs). We used all kinds of fuses, detonators, explosives, trip wires, mines, etc.

## Ranger School – Fort Benning, Georgia

Bob and I had also volunteered for Ranger School, nine weeks of brutal mental and physical training. We got a lot of extra harassment because we were from a rival elite unit, Special Forces. For example, to report into Ranger School we had to knock on the training company admin door and request permission to enter. Bob and I watched others in line ahead of us go through the reporting process. It appeared that students couldn't knock on the door hard enough without having to go through the process several times with lots of push-ups in between.

When it was our turn, Bob and I backed up and ran into the door together so hard we knocked it off its hinges. The door landed with a loud bang in front of the table where two Ranger Instructors were seated. We reported to them, (Ranger Thompson reporting for training, Sirs! Ranger Sheridan reporting for training, Sirs!") The legendary MSG Brunel looked at us, looked down at the roster, and told the other Ranger Instructor, "We've got two snake-eaters here. We have to keep our eyes on them and make sure they don't crap in the company street. You never know what these &%$#* are going to do!" It went downhill from there. Ranger School became a tug-of-war between Special Forces and Rangers. When they dropped us for push-ups, we were required to do an extra push-up for the "Big Ranger in the sky" before we could get up. Bob and I always added "And two more for the big SF Trooper who watches over the Big Ranger!" That never went over well, and they would put us back down again. We developed a reputation that went with us from the Ft. Benning training phase to the Mountain training phase to the Florida training phase.

We tried to have as much fun in Ranger School as we could because it was tough; being able to put a little humor in it along the way helped.

Our class started at Ft. Benning with 248 Ranger students and picked up some recycles along the way. We graduated 135. Of these, 75 earned the coveted black and gold Ranger tab, less than 30% of the original class. Bob and I were among them. In reality, I was the outstanding graduate of our class, but politics came into play and Major Berzotts edged me out the night before graduation when a Spot Report (10 points) was miraculously discovered that put him two points ahead of me.

*Ranger Tab*
*Graduated Ranger School, Fort, Benning, GA, OCT 1968*

Once we graduated from Ranger School, most of the class, including Bob and me, traveled to the nearest steak house and bought big T-bone steaks. We only ate about a quarter of the steak before we had to run to the parking lot and throw up. The small amount of food during the Ranger course had caused our stomachs to shrink and reject big greasy steaks! It was all part of the Ranger experience. The hardcore Rangers, like Bob and me, tried to re-eat the larger pieces we threw-up, but they wouldn't stay down the second time either.

Bob and I had been together since Basic Training. We had attended the same training, at the same time and always in the same squad because the Army made assignments alphabetically. When we arrived back at Fort Bragg, we discovered that our orders had been changed. We were no longer going to Africa with our team. Our new destination was Vietnam with a 5th Special Forces Group assignment! We had a couple of weeks to make arrangements to leave Fort Bragg, then take a leave before traveling to the other side of the world "to exotic places to meet interesting people and terminate them."

*5th Special Forces Flash*
*Assigned to 5th Special Forces Group, Vietnam, OCT 1968*

## Lessons Learned

### Special Forces

- Special Forces are hardcore warriors. Not everyone can eat glass.
- Special Forces operators were the "intellectual, quiet professionals."
- We did a lot of physical training in our preparation for deployment to Africa. This helped to prepare us to meet the physical and mental demands of Ranger School.
- "Quick Kill" training continued to forge my mindset of speed (fraction of a second) and accuracy (multiple bullets on target vs one in a very specific location).
- Sniper skills are different than those needed for close quarters combat.

### Ranger School

- Special Forces and Ranger are states of mind. These mindsets allow you to do the impossible. Everyone does not have the ability to develop/use these states of mind.
- Your body will quit if your brain lets it.
- You can always do more than you think you can.
- You can perform a long time with little food, sleep or rest— but your decision-making effectiveness degrades rapidly.
- I became very skilled at land navigation, especially at night.

- Very impressed with what I learned from SFC Shelly, one of the Ranger Instructors at the Mountain Ranger Camp. He was the definition of hard core.
- Becoming an expert in one area creates unconscious bias in that area that results in blind spots in other areas. Blind spots lead to poor decision-making.
- Stress creates blind spots through focusing of attention.
- Pain really is weakness leaving the body.
- Pain occurs in levels with the most intense pain hiding the less intense pain. If I poke my finger in your eye, the pain from your broken ankle will temporarily disappear.
- Exhalations allow you to manage more pain.
- Special Operations training (Special Forces, Ranger, SEAL, etc.) is designed to be mentally and physically difficult. Training any other way creates a false sense of ability that will get more people killed during the intense combat situations these warriors face.

*SSG Gilmore Shelly*
*My friend and one of the most hardcore and dedicated Ranger*
*Instructors in the US Army Ranger Department.*

# Chapter 3

*Do Not Volunteer for SOG!*

### Old Blue

*Old Blue runnin' through the yellow corn Blue come a runnin' when I blew my horn. Hey, Blue, You're a good dog, you. Old Blue died, and he died so hard it shook the ground in my backyard.*
*Hey, Blue, You're a good dog, you. Dug his grave with a silver spade. Lowered him down with a golden chain. Hey, Blue, You're a good dog, you. Link by link I lowered the chain, And with each link, I called his name. Hey, Blue, You're a good dog, you.*

At this point SOG members would start adding the names of those who were killed, such as, "Reno, Thorne, McNam, too." They would sing the same song over for each Recon Team member who was recently killed in action or missing in action—a long list—and toast to each.

**Travel to RVN**

After a 30-day pre-deployment leave, my parents took me to the Atlanta airport to begin my long journey to Vietnam. My mother wanted to

31

come in and stay with me until my plane departed, but I told her I didn't want a long goodbye. I would be back in 12 months. It wasn't a big deal. She was not happy but agreed. After some hugs and tears I was off on an adventure of a lifetime!

I navigated the airport wearing a Green Beret. It was amazing how well-known John Wayne in *The Green Berets* movie and Barry Sadler with his song "The Ballad of the Green Berets" had made that beret. People tended to give me a wide berth as I moved through the airport. I heard a few derogatory remarks shouted from a distance but took some deep breaths and kept going. Soon I was on the plane to Los Angeles.

I linked up with Bob in LA for the long flight to Vietnam. We stopped once for fuel, then headed for Cam Ranh Bay, South Vietnam. It was a very long flight! It was 1968, and the Tet Offensive was full-on; it had begun on 31 January 1968 and would last until 23 September 1968. That year would see the highest weekly death rates of the war (250–300 Americans a week). Shortly before arriving at Cam Ranh Bay the pilot came on the intercom to brief us on what was going to happen when we approached the airport. He encouraged us not to panic even though our descent was going to be a steep nosedive and flare out just before touching down. We needed to keep our seat belts fastened because it was going to be a fast taxi with several turns to the off-load ramp (steps to the ground).

The pilot announced that we needed to be prepared to off-load quickly and safely through the front exit doors. He wanted us to be aware that personnel leaving Vietnam would be loading the plane through the rear of the aircraft as we were deplaning out the front. The engines would continue to run. The plane would spend the minimum time possible on the ground. It would be a dangerous time while so many personnel were congregated in one small spot. The enemy liked to attack the planes on the way in, on the ground, and during take-off. He was sure we would be fine. "And, by the way," he added, "enjoy your stay in the exotic country of South Vi-ettt-Naam!"

The descent was quite an experience. It felt like we were going to crash. Everything was in fast motion. The flight crew and ground crew were like a well-oiled machine. They did this several times a week, every week. When I stepped out into what I thought was going to be fresh air, I was immediately hit with the smell of JP-4 jet fuel and other strange smells, some that burned my eyes. Red dust was in the air all around the airfield and it looked like pure chaos on the ground. Aircraft of all types were taxiing, taking off, landing and flying over us. Vehicles were scampering all along the taxi ways. It was very loud and windy. The civilians looked very different. (The good news was I felt tall.)

There was no doubt that I was not in Kansas (South Carolina) any longer. This was a different place with a different set of rules! A major transition from the country and culture I had known all my life to something bizarre and extremely dangerous. My world and life had changed forever in less than 24 hours. Even the time was 12 hours different. Day was night and night was day. We entered the plane in one world, then stepped off the plane into what seemed like another dimension, a strange and perilous planet.

We went quickly through customs/arrival procedures, then were transported to the reception center for in-processing. A Special Forces sergeant gathered up those of us who were going to a Special Forces assignment and took us on a short ride to Nha Trang. There we were assigned temporary quarters, given instructions for the next day, and fed. Bob and I made contact with CPT John Smith, a friend of ours from Ft. Bragg. He got to Vietnam a few weeks ahead of us and was already working in a Mike Force. Another good friend of ours, 1LT Ray Stacks, from Ft. Bragg had left four weeks ahead of us, but we had no idea where he had been assigned.

John updated us on things that were going on in-country, especially with the Tet Offensive, Special Forces and the types of SF assignments we might want to ask for the next day. He said, "Tomorrow, toward the end of the day, one of the last things they are going to do is ask you if you want to volunteer for SOG. DO. NOT. DO IT! Regardless of how cool they make it sound, DO NOT VOLUNTEER FOR SOG! Just tell them NO! If you volunteer, you WILL die! Almost all of them die! The ones who don't die get the crap shot out of them several times and return to the States as nut cases! DON'T DO IT!"

"Just say No! They'll say 'thank you,' and you'll move on to your Special Forces assignment. We'll meet back tomorrow evening, and you can tell me about your assignments. I might know some people where you are going."

We spent the evening talking about old times and various aspects of the culture. His parting words were, "Remember what I said. DO NOT VOLUNTEER FOR SOG!"

The next day, toward the end of the day, Bob and I sat in an office waiting to meet with Colonel Jones for our assignment, and Bob said, "What are you going to do if he asks about SOG?" I said, "If he does, I'll make my decision and you make yours. This might be the last decision we ever make. This is not a joint decision. I'll make mine. You make yours. Just think carefully about what John said." Consciously or unconsciously, my decision had been made. I strongly suspected that Bob's had too. But, if he chose to die, it had to be his decision.

I had heard rumors of SOG. At Fort Bragg, once in a while someone would mention SOG, and if you asked what it was, you heard things like, "Oh, man . . . it's top secret. No one can tell you what it is, except that it is the most BA unit in the world. They really do some cool missions. They are the elite of the elite. Only a few survive and they are bat @#*$ crazy. Most who go there are KIA or MIA. But nobody can tell you what they really do—or where they do it."

Bob, Keith, Ray and I were in a bar one evening in Fayetteville, North Carolina, and one of the guys with us nodded toward a guy and said, "The rumor is that he was in SOG. Don't make eye contact. Those guys are totally crazy. They will kill you at the drop of a hat and think nothing about it. And your body will never be found!"

We had to meet with Colonel Jones individually to get our final Special Forces assignment. I went in first. He went over the highlights of my background and qualifications and said, "I see that you volunteered for the Army, OCS, Airborne, Special Forces, Rangers and Vietnam. And now you have the opportunity to volunteer for the most important job that you will ever have. Based on what I see in your file, you are perfect for the job." He continued, "This is a job that is so elite that only the people who do it know what it is. If you take this job no one will ever know that you did it, where you did it or what you did. It will not be in your records. You cannot tell anyone. And you will have to sign papers agreeing not to tell anyone. It is very rare that I offer this opportunity to anyone, but I'm offering it to you. (I did not believe this statement.) What do you think?"

I said, "It would help if I knew what the job was." He said, "I understand. All I can say is that you will be volunteering to go ANYWHERE and do ANYTHING. No questions asked." I asked, "Are you asking me if I want to join SOG?" He asked, "Is that what you want to do?" I looked him in the eyes and said, "Yes." "Are you sure, Lieutenant?" he replied. I repeated, "Yes."

"If you are serious, you will have to sign some documents. The first says that you are volunteering to go anywhere and do anything for six months or six missions, whichever comes first. You need to understand that I am saying anything. Do you agree?"

"Yes," I replied.

"Then sign this document agreeing to go anywhere and do anything for six months or six missions. You also have to sign a non-disclosure form that says you can't tell anyone in any manner about what you did or where you went for a minimum period of 20 years. If you violate these agreements in any way, you will be prosecuted to the fullest extent of the law. You are voluntarily agreeing to and signing these documents."

I signed the documents.

"Thank you, Lieutenant Thompson. I sincerely wish you the best of luck. And remember, this conversation never took place." (Someone actually said this for real!) He handed me a note with instructions on where to be at 1300 the next day for transportation to Da Nang. He sent me out the back door and brought Bob in the front door.

I went to the bar to meet John. When he saw me walking up to the bar, he said, "You did it! I can see it on your face! You are a &%$* DEAD MAN WALKING! $#&* @@#$ *&^%! I told you not to do that. Crap! I thought you were smarter than that. Bartender, give this stupid SOB a double Jack and coke!"

When John saw Bob walking up to the bar, he said, "You did it too.

I can see it on your face. YOU ARE BOTH DEAD MEN WALKING! $#&* @@#$ *&^% I told you two not to do that. Crap, Bob! I thought you were smarter than Thompson. Bartender, give this stupid SOB a double Jack and coke!" John repeated his remarks about what we had done several times that evening.

The chances for survival, if you ended up on a SOG team were very low. You knew that at a minimum the best thing that could happen to you on a SOG mission was to get the crap shot out of you. That meant you had a good mission. The other option was you got killed. SOG operators had the highest casualty rate in Vietnam. They just didn't survive. That was scary, but at the same time exciting!

John had a surprise for us. He had arranged for us to be guests of honor at a Chinese wedding that evening. The wedding was interesting, but what happened after the wedding was even more so. The groom's friends escorted him to each table of guests where he had to chug what looked like vodka with the table. There were a lot of tables. His groomsmen were literally carrying him before he finished visiting all the tables.

Then the food was served beginning with the head table where we were seated. We each were given a big bowl of soup. As I dug around in the soup, I could feel something in it. I could see that the guests at the tables were eating big pieces of chicken. When I lifted my Chinese spoon out of the soup, I had a big chicken head with everything except the feathers. John said, "Eat it. You don't want to insult them. Everyone is watching." Bob had a pair of chicken feet—complete with toenails. Our Chinese hosts considered what we had in our soup to be the best parts of the chicken! Needless to say, we had to get something to eat after the wedding. We were learning something new every day.

## Traveling to CCN

The next day we had to fly from Nha Trang to Da Nang, because if you were going to SOG you had to start at Da Nang. From there you literally disappeared! You went through a black hole and no one outside of a few people in SOG knew where you were until you and your coffin (empty or not) arrived back in the States.

When we got to the airfield, the escort took us to a restricted (classified) area. The C-130s and C-123s that came into that part of the airfield were black and were called Black Birds. That added to the sense that we were going down a black hole. We had not seen or heard of black C-130s before. When we boarded the aircraft, we realized it didn't have seats! The seatbelts were on the floor! The plane was gutted of everything else. Toward the front there was a big red line painted across the floor that said: Do NOT Go Beyond This Line. Classified Area. Something was happening in the front of these planes that we were not allowed to see or know about. Even with our top-secret security clearances! I asked Bob what kind of security clearance he thought you had to have to go beyond the red line. He had no idea.

We sat on the floor and fastened our seat belts. The crew chief came by and said, "We don't have seats in this plane. Sorry about that. When we take off we will immediately go into a steep climb. When we get ready to land, we'll go into a steep nose-dive, pull out at the last minute and hit the runway a few seconds later. Fasten in tight and be ready to experience some serious g-forces. Enjoy the flight!" The takeoff and landing were definitely an experience. We were beginning to notice a pattern in takeoffs and landings.

It would have been a "fun" experience if I didn't have that little voice in the back of my mind saying, "There must be something pretty dangerous outside to require this kind of flying." We didn't ask. Just something else to get used to.

An escort met us when we got off the Black Bird. He said, "There'll be a bus here to pick you up in about ten minutes to take you to FOB-4." A few minutes later, a black school bus arrived. But not just any school bus. This was a SOG school bus. We knew that it was a SOG school bus not just because it was black, but because we could see that all the windows were shot out, the seats were ripped apart from being hit with bullets and there were at least 200 bullet holes in the bus— that we could see! As Bob and I looked at the bus I said, "What have we gotten into?" The young sergeant driving the bus called for us to get in. He said, "We'll leave in a few minutes. We're picking up a team here too." Bob said, "What happened to the bus?" The driver responded,

"Well, we have to go through a pass on the way to Da Nang and we get ambushed there a lot. If it happens today, the main things for you two to remember are, get on the floor of the bus and do whatever the team leader tells you to do. The team will take care of everything. Just do what they tell you to do if you want to live." At that point, Bob said, "Man, this isn't looking good. We might not even get to FOB-4!"

Suddenly, a group of seven of the most BA, meanest, deadliest looking men, animals, warriors—I don't know which—literally appeared out of thin air and approached the bus. The one in the back was walking backwards and looking to the rear as if he thought someone might be following them. Even 50 years later, I can still feel the adrenaline rush generated by the force field of awe surrounding those warriors as they approached the bus. Bob and I had been through a lot of training including Special Forces qualification, an SF assignment, Ranger training and training for a combat mission in Africa, but this team did not look like anything we had seen before.

Two of the seven appeared to be Americans because they were taller than the others. They were all camouflaged, heavily armed with strange weapons and loaded with all kinds of gear, a lot of which we had not seen before. Hand grenades and smoke grenades hung all over them. In addition to their primary weapons each had a knife and most had pistols. Two had what appeared to be M-79 grenade launchers with the barrels and stocks sawed off so they looked like big, fat pistols. They wore pouches of ammunition hung around their waists and some type of ruck—no flak jacket; no helmet; just rags tied around their heads; no patches or markings on their uniforms; no dog tags; and a demeanor that seemed to communicate, "I will rip your face off and eat it if you make eye contact with me!" These guys evoked the kind of fear that would make the hair stand up on the back of your neck and arms if you saw them. It was surreal.

Bob and I were in awe of this team! They boarded the bus and immediately took up defensive positions. It seemed they hoped that the NVA would ambush us along the way. One of the Americans, we assumed the team leader, said, "If anything happens on the way to FOB-4, you guys get on the floor of the bus and stay there until we

38

tell you to get up. Is that clear?" Bob replied in his most macho voice, "Yeah. We got it."

These were serious warriors of the first order, and it was reassuring to have them to protect us. And we knew that in a few days we would be on teams like this one. That was exciting to think about. I really liked that short-barreled, collapsible version of the M-16 they were carrying! We arrived at FOB-4 (CCN) late afternoon—without getting ambushed. The team seemed to be disappointed that we didn't! They moved quickly off the bus and instantly disappeared. It was as if they had walked into another dimension. We were welcomed by another escort and because it was getting late in the day, we were assigned to guest quarters and briefed on which defensive bunker to go to if we heard the "incoming" siren go off during the night.

He said, "If the siren goes off, whatever you do, don't sit up in bed. If you do, your head will be higher than the sandbags around the building. A few weeks ago, we had a guy killed his first night here because he sat up and a bullet hit him in the head. Roll off onto the floor, crawl to the door, peek outside from the floor to make sure there's not an NVA standing there waiting to kill you. We've had lots of guys killed that way too."

I asked, "Can we get weapons? We're unarmed." He responded, "Sorry about that! You'll be issued weapons tomorrow if you stay here. Just be careful tonight." He told us we would be briefed in the Command briefing room by the Camp Commander, Colonel Warren, at 0830 the next morning and not to be late. He then took us to the mess hall and told us to eat and relax. He reminded us again not to be late!

The food was much better than I expected—and there was plenty of it. Looking around the mess hall it was relatively easy to pick out the Operators from the REMFs (Rear Echelon Mother F$@&s). The Operators dressed, looked and acted differently. There was a coldness about their eyes. Probably resulting from what they had seen and would see again. These people were truly the elite warriors of the world. The elite of the elite. The most dangerous men on the planet. I thought I had been around some bad people in my time but never anyone like these guys. They literally made the hair stand up on the back of your neck. No one would ever know the horror these men had experienced. It was as if they had an invisible bubble around them like a warning to "keep your distance." You could physically feel it if you got too close. I wondered if people would ever experience me that way. A strange thought.

Our escort said a John Wayne movie would be showing that night. "A movie?" I asked. He responded, "The camp's Vietnamese carpenters constructed some bleachers in a small open area, nailed up a few sheets of plywood, painted them white and set up a movie projector. The Supply Sergeant gets movies from somewhere and they show a movie out there most evenings if it's not raining."

As it started to get dark Bob and I made our way to the small movie theater. The bleachers were facing Marble Mountain, a prominent mountain that jutted straight up out of the sand 450 feet just outside of the compound's defensive wire. It had two peaks; each peak had a combat outpost on it because if the bad guys got up there, they could shoot down into the FOB-4 compound.

We were sitting in the bleachers, in the dark watching the John

*Marble Mountain*
*Outside the FOB-4 (CCN) Compound, Da Nang, RVN*

Wayne movie, when suddenly the mountain lit up like a 4th of July fireworks display. Red and green tracers went back and forth all over the mountain along with a series of loud explosions and flares. Bob and I jumped out of the bleachers and landed prostrate on the sand. Everyone else just sat there watching the movie.

I asked a guy in the bleachers what was happening. He said, "Sorry about that, Lieutenant! It happens almost every night. ("Sorry about that" was becoming ubiquitous.) The NVA try to take out the two combat outposts on the mountain. They put on a pretty impressive light show up there. Eventually the teams will kill the NVA and it'll get quiet, except for the NVA snipers who will continue to shoot at the team throughout the night. It will be fine. Enjoy the movie. They don't shoot down here. They just shoot at each other. Remember that the red tracers are the good guys, and the green ones are the bad guys. If you stay at FOB-4 (CCN), you will get plenty of time on the mountain. Teams are sent up there between missions to get some rest and target practice against targets that shoot back."

## SOG Briefing & Assignment

The next morning after breakfast, we went to the Command Briefing room and discovered there were seven other new SOG recruits. Bob and I knew LT Jones from Ft. Bragg. Like us, he could not resist an "experience/opportunity" like SOG. SGM Johnson took us into the briefing room and gave us the briefing before the briefing. All the walls were covered with curtains. He said, "Gentlemen, this is a Top Secret Limited briefing room. Once this briefing begins, you cannot change your mind about being in SOG. If you have any doubts, step out of the room now! Am I clear?" We all responded, "Yes, Sergeant Major!"

"You will not take any notes about what you see or hear in this room. You are not to discuss anything said in this room outside of this room. Am I clear?" We all responded, "Yes, Sergeant Major!"

"When the Colonel finishes his briefing, you will stand at attention as he is leaving. Then, you belong to me! And make sure you do not ask the Colonel any stupid questions! Am I clear?" We responded, "Yes, Sergeant Major!"

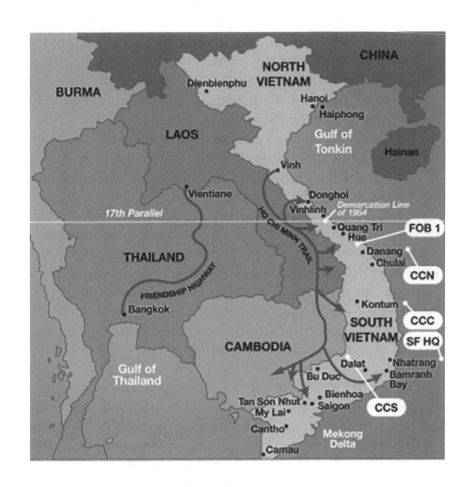

*Southeast Asia*
*Key SOG Locations*

When the FOB-4 (CCN) commander walked in, we all stood up at attention. He said, "At ease. Take your seats. I'm Lieutenant Colonel Warren. Let me tell you what SOG is about and what you have volunteered to do—that you can never tell anyone about.

"You have volunteered to serve in the Military Advisory Command Vietnam, Studies and Observations Group (MACV-SOG). This is your official assignment. And if you believe you are here to do Studies and Observations on what happens in Vietnam, then you are dumber than an effing board and need to leave now! If you stay, you can never leave, not alive anyway. You have just become a member of the most elite fighting force in the world. You have volunteered to go ANYWHERE and do ANYTHING! And you can never tell anyone about it! If that is not what you are here for, leave now! Once I start the briefing, you are all in. Am I clear?" We responded, "Yes, Sir!"

LTC Warren explained that MACV-SOG was a top-secret multi-service US Special Operations Force unit, established 24 January 1964 to conduct unconventional warfare operations in Southeast Asia associated with the Vietnam War. Operations took place in South Vietnam, North Vietnam, Laos, Cambodia and other Southeast Asia areas as required. MACV-SOG had participated in the most significant campaigns of the Vietnam War.

"In short, we are North Vietnam's worst nightmare!" He uncovered some maps on the wall and started talking about the kinds of missions we would be conducting. I had heard rumors that SOG possibly operated outside of Vietnam, so I wasn't surprised Vietnam was just a training range for preparing for our missions. SOG missions were mostly conducted outside of Vietnam. We would be going into other Southeast Asian countries. There were others, but they were too classified for this briefing.

He said that SOG was structured with three primary commands: Command and Control North (CCN) at Da Nang, Command and Control Central (CCC) at Kontum and Command and Control South (CCS) located at Dalat (see Map at left). Each of these commands had a Recon Company with Reconnaissance Teams (RTs) originally called Spike Teams, which at full strength had three Americans and nine indigenous members.

Hatchet Force (HF) companies were also located at these commands. An HF platoon had approximately 42 members. SOG had Forward Operational Bases (FOBs) located in specific areas to support the missions, numbered FOB-1 to FOB-6.

Launch sites were set up along the Vietnam border to support the insertion of teams into Areas of Operation (AOs). There was also a launch site located in Thailand at Nakhon Phanom (NKP) approximately 75 miles from the North Vietnam border. The northern teams were named after states, central teams named after snakes and southern teams named after tools. (FOB-1 was closed in January 1969 resulting in some teams being shuffled around among the Command and Controls.) The RTs and Hatchet Forces were composed of Vietnamese, Montagnard, Chinese Hmong, Laotian or Cambodian mercenaries. LTC Warren said that in general we would be conducting cross-border operations to disrupt the Viet Cong, Khmer Rouge, Pathet Lao and North Vietnamese in their own territories. These missions included:

- Recover imprisoned and missing Americans
- Training agents for insertion into North Vietnam
- "Black" psychological operations
- Raids and ambushes
- Prisoner snatches
- Assassinations
- "Doctored" ammunition
- Document retrieval
- Wire taps
- Pipeline destruction
- B-52 bomb damage assessment
- Search and destroy
- Other missions as assigned

The kinds of missions didn't surprise me much. Well, maybe a few did, but for the most part, I felt like I had arrived at the James Bond level. The world elite level. The bat @#*$ crazy level—but very cool.

I also realized that now I had gone into a black hole for sure. I looked around expecting to see Alice or the White Rabbit at any time. Then I realized that LTC Warren was Alice!

After LTC Warren finished his briefing and left, the SGM took over. He gave us his overview, covered some administrative things (like how the mail system worked) and more about security, classified information and mission compartmentalization—we would only know what our own team was doing. If the NVA captured us, no matter how much they tortured us they would not be able to get information about other missions.

We also got to pick our official Code Names. I wanted "Ranger," but Bob spoke up before me and asked for Ranger. Then I saw "Dynamite," and I thought it was fitting for me seeing as how I had always liked to blow things up and I was relatively small. "Dynamite" would work for me. I had blown my neighbor's windows out when I was a teenager with a rocket that exploded on its launch pad. I didn't intend for that to happen, but I was always blowing things up. I figured I would probably be blowing things up in Southeast Asia. (And I did get to blow up a lot of things, for example, bridges, helicopters, bad guys, ammunitions dumps, etc.) I always carried a lot of C-4 and other explosives with me. It would be my code name to identify myself if I were wounded or something bad happened to me. (There would be occasions where my code name would be used as my call sign.) Normally, mission call signs were three alphanumeric characters assigned to each mission, e.g., Alpha Tango 7.

We were also asked to give answers to three security questions that, interestingly enough, are the same ones we use 50 years later with credit cards and computers. For example, the name of your first dog, the make of your first car.

Then, the bad news. The Sergeant Major (SGM) read out our assignments. I would be going to FOB-1 (at Phu Bai) up North. Bob would be going down to FOB-2 (at CCC around Kontum). It would be the first time in almost two years that Bob and I did not get the same assignment. We were not happy about it, but we had a war to fight.

When the meeting was over, we left to fly to our respective assignments. Bob and I said goodbye, made the appropriate comments about keeping your head down and see you in 12 months. The last thing I said to Bob was, "Bob, make sure you are here!" I did not have a good feeling about our separation. Was this the last time we would ever see or speak to each other?

**Lessons Learned**

*MACV-SOG Patch*
*Officially in the Black Hole*

- I boarded a plane in a world I had known all my life and got off the plane in a strange, dangerous, wild west world on steroids with a very different set of rules. It was like entering another dimension.

- All my senses were confused. Nothing made sense. My circadian rhythm was 12 hours off.

- Death was in the air. You could smell it. You could feel it.

- Bob and I made a decision a lot of people questioned—we volunteered for MACV-SOG.

- We had approached the event horizon of a black hole and were being pulled inside where nothing escapes.

- We were at the elite of the elite level. The best of the best—or craziest of the crazy.

- In the new world I was given a new name, "Dynamite," and sent North on a quest to hunt down and terminate the enemy.

# PART 2

# Chapter 4

*Phu Bai (FOB-1)*

*We don't receive wisdom; we must discover it for ourselves after a journey that no one can take for us.*

—Marcel Proust

### Teammates/Friends KIA/MIA OCT-NOV 1968

SP5 Gary L. Matson, KIA OCT 30
SSG Arthur E. Bader, Jr., KIA NOV 30
SGT Gary R. la Bohn, KIA NOV 30
SSG Michael H. Mein, KIA NOV 30
SFC Klaus D. Scholz, KIA NOV 30
1LT Raymond C. Stacks, KIA NOV 30
MAJ Samuel K. Toomey, III, KIA NOV 30

After we finished the briefing at CCN, I walked with the other new SOG volunteers going to FOB-1 at Phu Bai to the helipad at the far end of the compound. The helipad was constructed from PSP (perforated steel planks). There we boarded a CH-34 "Kingbee" helicopter without doors. It was about a 30-minute noisy, windy and bumpy ride. When we got to Phu Bai, an escort took us to the FOB-1 compound and to the mess hall for a short briefing before lunch.

SGM McIntosh gave us a briefing on the FOB-1 compound, security, safety, rules and the general area of operations. Then he said everyone would be going to 1-0 school, a week-long course to teach us how to lead a SOG team on top secret missions across Southeast Asia. Actually, he said everyone was going except me. When I asked why I wasn't going, the SGM said, "Lieutenant, you are Special Forces and Ranger qualified. There are a few things they might teach you that you have not done already, but not much. You can learn those things from your team which you will be assigned to tomorrow afternoon. We are putting you to work."

"Get settled in your quarters this afternoon. Learn your way around the compound and which defensive bunker to go to if we are attacked. Go to the supply room and draw your initial equipment, weapon and ammunition. While you are in the supply room, tell SSG Jones you are the officer that will help him with his task in the morning."

When I got to my quarters, I met my new roommate, Captain Alonzo Smith, the FOB-1 supply officer. We hit it off right away and he showed me around the compound. I met him again at 1730 for dinner. He suggested that since this might be my last free night, I might want to go to the movie. I thought, I've heard that before! I asked, "Are you going?" He replied, "No. I don't have time."

As it turned out, we had a little theater at FOB-1 that had a tin roof on it so you wouldn't get wet when it rained, and it rained a lot. There were also small benches to sit on. A piece of plywood painted white was the screen. I went to the movie that evening and thought it was pretty cool. We were in a combat zone. It was 97 degrees and 96% humidity. It was night and I was sitting in a pretend movie theater next to an old, live French minefield watching a movie—with no popcorn.

The movie had been on for about 15 minutes. I was sitting in the middle of a group of 12 guys, mostly indigenous team members, when I heard a loud, POW! The Montagnard (we called them Yards) sitting next to me fell off the bench to the ground. People scattered. I went to the ground with the Yard who was hit in the shoulder. Twelve inches to the left and it would have been my chest. After we got his bleeding under control, the medics took him to the hospital. That effectively ended the movie for that night. I wasn't that much into movie night for a while. Just wasn't having a good experience with movie nights! I remembered hearing in my training at Fort Bragg, "If you can be seen, you can be hit. If you can be hit, you can be killed!" I was beginning to gain a lot of respect for not being seen—or hit!

The next morning, I went to the supply room after breakfast. When I got there, SSG Jones the supply sergeant, told me that several SOG team members were killed a few days earlier and their personal effects had to be inventoried by an officer before they could be sent to their families. He took me to a room with seven duffel bags on the floor and said, "Dump the bags out one at a time and go through the contents. Look for anything that might be classified: maps, operational pictures or anything like that. If there is any correspondence, read it to see if it says anything about any of the missions. If there are pictures, take them out." I was to sterilize their gear. It sounded simple enough.

I picked up the first olive drab canvas duffel bag and read the name stenciled in big white letters on the outside, 1LT Raymond C. Stacks. I felt like I had been kicked in the groin. SOG just got real! Ray was Bob's and my friend at Fort Bragg. He left for Vietnam about a month before we did. Ray had been in SOG for a month, and I was already inventorying his personal effects to send home to his family. Ray was a good guy, totally dedicated to Special Forces and the United States. I had no idea he had volunteered for SOG. And now he was dead. Killed in Action on a SOG mission in some Southeast Asian country. Actually, it was worse than that. He and his six teammates and four-man air crew were Missing in Action. Their remains could not be recovered. Their helicopter was hit with anti-aircraft fire at an altitude of 3,000 feet and after falling like a rock into the jungle canopy below, it exploded and burned.

When you joined SOG, you disappeared into a black hole. No one knew you were in SOG, where you were or what you were doing. No announcements in the hometown newspaper, no articles—just gone. Your mail went to and came from an address in Saigon where it was screened, going and coming, for classified information. Your friends and family assumed you were in Saigon. They had no idea that only your mail went to and from Saigon, but you were located somewhere else. Vietnam was just the "base" you staged your operations from to hit targets all around Southeast Asia. If you were killed, like Ray and his six teammates, your family would be told that you were killed or missing in action in Vietnam. Your family would not know that you were killed or missing in some other country.

It seemed like every day I learned more about my own disappearance. I was moving deeper and deeper into a dark, secret and extremely dangerous world. There was a reason we could not talk about SOG for 20 years and I was just on the fringes of learning the truth. And these books will only tell part of the story.

I quickly looked at the names on the other duffel bags to see if I knew anyone else—SP5 Gary L. Matson, SSG Arthur E. Bader, Jr., SGT Gary R. La Bohn, SSG Michael H. Mein, SFC Klaus D. Scholz, MAJ Samuel K. Toomey, III, SSG Richard A. Fitts.

Before continuing I went back to SSG Jones and asked him what these men were doing when they were killed. He said no one there knew. It was classified top secret. Not even the FOB-1 Commander knew.

Going through the personal effects in each bag became a very personal and emotional task that caused a bond to form between me and each hero, and to some degree, their families. As I laid the contents of a bag out on the table, I put together a mosaic of each American hero's personal life. His wife, kids, parents, plans for the future, dogs, family pictures of missed birthday parties, holidays, first steps, first words, pictures the kids had drawn, how much time he had left before going home and small talk with his wife and parents. All the time hiding the extreme danger of his missions.

When I was going through SSG Richard Fitts' effects I was struck by a picture of his small two-year-old son and the conversations about him and how much SSG Fitts missed him. I did not know why his son had such an impact on me. But I never forgot him. Fifty-two years later, almost to the day, I would see a Facebook post on a SOG site by Richard Fitts, Jr., asking if anyone knew his father in SOG. I responded and began to communicate with him. We agreed to meet at the Special Operations Association Reunion in October 2020. There would be no way to know at the time that the world would be struggling with the corona virus (COVID-19) in 2020 and the Reunion would have to be canceled.

Later it was reformatted into a virtual meeting/reunion. Rich and I were not able to make contact there but became friends and our friendship continues into the future. Rich also eventually produced a movie, *21 Years and a Folded Flag*, about his father and his experience in life growing up in the SOG shadow.

Eventually, the personal effects inventory was over. I had lunch and headed out to meet my new team.

## Lessons Learned

- If you can be seen, you can be hit. If you can be hit, you can be killed.
- Life is short and can end any second without warning.
- We had to stay situationally aware of the surroundings.
- The enemy was real. Bullets were real. Death was real.
- We had to learn how to live in the now, always on high alert.
- The now drains your energy.
- Death can come so quickly that some people never know they died.
- Movie night could be dangerous but watching movies could be a good diversion from the war.

# RT Alabama

My son-in-law Eric's father is a retired Navy Captain. Randy is a big man. He looks like he could have played football before the Navy. In fact, Randy did play football for the University of Alabama under the coaching of the legendary Bear Bryant. Randy understands discipline,

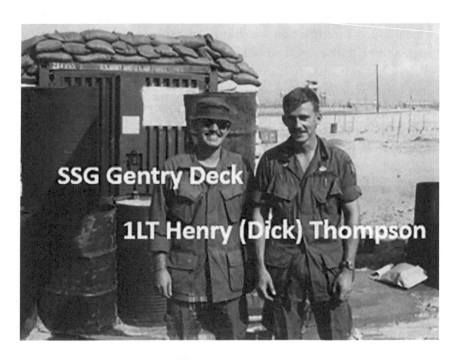

*SSG Gentry Deck and me, 1968*

no quit, giving 110%, responsibility, leadership and teamwork. I had nothing but respect for Bear Bryant and the Crimson Tide, but I was not a fan. Sorry, Randy. That's part of being in the SEC. Looking back, I find it interesting that the first SOG team I was on was RT Alabama. I don't believe it was a coincidence.

That afternoon I was officially assigned to RT Alabama as the 1-1 (pronounced "one-one") assistant team leader/radio operator. I met SSG Gentry Deck, the 1-0 or team leader, and he gave me an overview of the team, our upcoming mission, what kind of equipment to get from the supply room and our schedule for the next few days. Even though I was an officer and technically outranked SSG Deck, I was going to be second in command. No one was allowed to lead a SOG team, regardless of rank, without experience.

You had to go out as a 1-1, 1-2 or straphanger (extra member of the team) and learn how to lead a team until you were checked off (certified) by your SOG 1-0. SSG Deck had to say, "Lieutenant Thompson is cleared to be a 1-0. He can lead a team now." That would put me on the 1-0 list to take over the next team that was available. I discovered that teams could go through several 1-0s in just a matter of days. SOG had the highest casualty rate of any unit in Vietnam. Every operational team member would be killed (KIA), wounded (WIA) or missing in action (MIA).

A good friend of mine, Rich Todd, from Fort Bragg was assigned to CCC. He and I had been on the same team in the SF Q Course, attended the Infantry Officer Advanced Course (IOAC) together, and completed lots of free-fall parachute jumps together. He wanted to be the Commander of the Hatchet Force (HF) whose Company Commander was killed the day before he arrived. The CCC Commander told him it was too late; the position had been filled the night before. He would get a different assignment. That evening at dinner the Commander called Rich over to his table and asked him if he still wanted to be the Company Commander. Rich replied, "I thought that position had been filled." The CCC Commander replied, "It was, but it's vacant again. You want it or not?" Rich took the command and did an outstanding job!

Later, Rich would become the 3rd Bn Commander of the 1st Special Forces Group when it was reactivated in 1984, and then the 1st Special Forces Group Commander in 1990. After SOG he had a string of special warfare assignments: 1/10th Bad Tolz, 70–73, ODA-3 HALO team leader; 5th Group S-3, 78–80. SF Department Director SWCS, 87–88, Director of Training and Doctrine SWCS, 89–90. After 1st Group Command USSOCOM J-3 Division Chief, he retired from the military and spent 20 years as a contractor in Croatia, Iraq, Thailand, Uganda, Somalia, Niger, Benin and Togo. Some people just can't get enough.

## Mission Preparation

SSG Deck also started teaching me. "This is what I need you to do as my assistant in preparing the team. When we go over the fence and

| LEVEL | EQUIPMENT |
|---|---|
| Level 1: Survival: Carried on my person / uniform | Uniform; boots; gloves; triangular bandage; fishing cord and hook; signal mirror; pen-flare gun and 10 multi-colored flares; small VS-17 panel; one meal; URC-10 emergency radio (2.5 lbs.); field hat with sewn-in panel; notebook; ink pen; pencil; topo map; compass; insect repellent; water purification tabs; radio frequency and code book; multi-tool pocketknife (demo-knife); strobe light; compression bandage; CS powder; backup Med kit; plastic bag/scoop; 4-mag bandolier; CAR-15 w/ cleaning rod. |
| Level 2: Mission Essential: Carried on my Load Bearing Equipment (LBE) & Ruck | LBE (approximately 35 lbs.) w/(min. 5 Frag grenades; 4-smoke grenades; WP grenade; 24 magazines 5.56 ammo (plus 1 in weapon); 2-4 quarts water; Ringer's solution; CAR-15 w/clean-ing rod; .22 cal. pistol with silencer, 50 rds 22 cal. long rifle ammo; strobe light; Swiss seat rope w/snap link; KA-Bar knife; compression bandages; Med kit; pistol (.38 or .45 or 9mm) w/40 rnds to match; CS powder with black pepper; water pu-rification tabs; mini-smokes; mini-frags; pen light w/red pilter; insect repellent; camouflage sticks; sweat rag; gas mask) Ruck (approximately 50-75 lbs.) w/2-3 claymore mines w/ detonators; 5-10 M-14 toe poppers; 2-5, 2lb blocks C-4; 10-15 non-electric blasing caps; crimpers; 2-5 electric blasting caps; 1 roll of trip wire; 10 fuse ignitors; 15 feet of time fuse; Indige-nous poncho w/liner; Olympus Pen-EE camera; extra film; 3 smoke grenade fuses w/blasting caps crimped; 3-5 meals; 21 magazines 5.56mm; flashlight w/filters; 2-pair socks; 5-10 frag grenades; 2 qts. water; insect repellent; black electrical tape; 2-4 smoke grenades; VS-17 panel; chem lights; luminous tape; Eldest Son AK mag; PRC-77 Radio; long & short antenna; 2 extra radio batteries; 12 rnds of 40mm HE; 4 rnds 40mm CS; 2 white phosphorus grenades; 2-5 mini-frag grenades; 2-5 mini-smoke grenades; sometimes 200+ rnds M-60 ammo. |
| Level 3: Special Mission Equipment: Carried in ruck | SLR camera w/telephoto lens; extra film; Starlight scope; wire-tap equipment; Eldest Son ammo; KY-38 w/extra batteries & KY-28; crypto book; other mission specific equipment, e.g., AK-47 & ammo; NVA uniform, etc. |

*Typical Loadout I carried (Yes, it was VERY heavy)*

when the shooting starts—and know that the shooting will start—this is what I'm looking for. This is where we're going and we're going to do a wiretap," he told me. The team had already been in mission prep for a few days. I participated the rest of the time.

The team consisted of SSG Deck, me, SSG Davis and seven indigenous Vietnamese mercenaries. As RT Alabama continued mission preparation, we took the team to the range outside the FOB-1 compound and did simulated and live-fire immediate action drills (IAD) to get ready for what we were going to do on the mission. It was six days before we launched on our mission. This gave me very little time to get to know the team and to learn all the immediate action drills and the team's standard operating procedures (SOPs). I felt like I had joined a professional football team and did not know the playbook. The interpreter, Cowboy, spoke very good English. The others understood common words and phrases like "get down, stop, contact right" that we used all the time, but I could not carry on a real conversation with any of them except Cowboy. They also knew all the hand and arm signals. Very rarely did anyone talk during a mission before making contact with the enemy.

SSG Davis took me to the supply room and made sure I got all the equipment I needed for the mission. I was surprised at how much it weighed—and I didn't have my 35 pounds of ammunition, five-day food supply or four quarts of water yet!

## Sterile

SOG teams were inserted "sterile." That is, nothing to identify team members with the United States. No name tags, dog tags, ID cards, nothing. Of course, this was in violation of the Geneva Convention. Combat troops had to carry identification. No identification meant, if captured, you would not be afforded rights under the Geneva Convention. You were a spy and could be executed on the spot. Going in sterile was necessary as part of the United States' plausible deniability. The US would deny any knowledge of our actions or presence in the country. We were on our own.

I was totally focused at this point because I knew this was real. My life depended on learning everything I could. There was nothing else on my mind.

I arranged my equipment in three "levels": Survival, Mission Essential and Special Equipment.

The full loadout was very heavy. For example, my LBE typically weighed 35+ pounds and my ruck weighed around 75 pounds. My individual survival equipment carried on my person including my CAR-15 and pistol was another 15–20 pounds. My body weight at

*CAR-15 Sub-machinegun (left) and*
*Hi Power .22 LR with integrated silencer (right)*

*A base configuration of Ruck Loadout. Modified according to the mission.*

the time was 140 pounds (with very low body fat), and my loadout was approximately 125 pounds. I had arrived in Vietnam in excellent physical condition, but my shoulders were not used to supporting that much weight. My LBE straps and ruck straps were literally cutting into my shoulders and rubbing them raw. As soon as I put on all my gear, I knew I had to begin a strength and balance program immediately, which I did that day.

Two of the guiding principles for my teams' ruck loadouts were:

1. Things you use most often need to be easy to get to, e.g., the radio, Claymores, ammunition and toe poppers.

2. Blasting caps need to be separated from Claymores, frags and C-4 and carried in a metal or wooden safety container for protection.

The equipment the team members and I carried changed across time as I learned what was needed for specific types of missions and terrain. I also modified some of the equipment, e.g., I replaced the metallic snaps on canteen covers with wooden buttons (so I could drink water without making noise) and adjusted any other things that might make noise pre-contact. During the Final Combat Inspection (before the aircraft engines were running), each team member—including me—had to jump up and down to check for sounds. If you could be heard, you could be found. If you could be found, the team could be killed. Our lives depended on silence.

One of my rules during combat was to get as close to the ground as possible. My rucksack was shot up on most missions. If I had not been close to the ground, it would have been me that was shot up.

What I carried on my LBE and person evolved across time. I used four canteen covers with six mags each on the left side, one cover with five frags on my right side, a canteen in back, med kit, and sometimes WP and smoke on the front of my belt. One or two combat bandages in front, a black snap link on right shoulder for CAR-15 sling, a can of Ringer's solution on the back of the harness behind my neck, strobe light on my left shoulder, a frag under it, and sometimes a smoke. I also carried a coiled 12-foot nylon rope on a black snap link that could be used for constructing a Swiss seat, etc.

I wore a level of survival gear on my person, as follows: a 4-magazine (20 rounds each) bandoleer, KA-BAR knife (with a survival handle I made) on a belt; compass (on lanyard) in my front left pants pocket; map in left cargo pocket; demo knife in right pants pocket; small notebook and pen and pen light with red lens in left sleeve pocket; pen flare gun and flares in right sleeve pocket; URC-10 survival radio in left shirt pocket (over heart, with lanyard); one LRP meal in right cargo pocket with water added; M-17 protective mask on left leg; bloused boots with black electrical tape around top; sleeves down with tape around cuffs; an OD triangular bandage (Rambo rag) around neck; black electrical tape on muzzle of CAR-15; black leather issue gloves with fingers cut off at first knuckle; watch under my sleeve; and other equipment as needed. This would become the Standard Operating Procedure (SOP) for where standard equipment was carried. If we needed to retrieve something off someone—even in the dark during the heat of combat—we knew where to look.

The M-16 had a bad reputation in Vietnam for jamming a lot, especially with full magazines. By association that reputation was passed on to the CAR-15. Everyone I knew only loaded 17–18 rounds in their magazines. I loaded mine full, but only used new magazines that had been loaded within three days or less. I fired 500–800 rounds on most missions and never had a malfunction. I carried an extended cleaning rod attached to my CAR-15 just in case I had a round or casing hang in the weapon. I gave my team members the option to use full magazines or not.

On my first few missions I carried Long Range Patrol Rations (LRPs) for food. The food was okay, but it was noisy and required a lot of water (it was dehydrated).

### LRP Entrees Included

| | |
|---|---|
| Menu #1 | Beef Hash |
| Menu #2 | Chili con Carne |
| Menu #3 | Spaghetti with Meat Sauce |
| Menu #4 | Beef with Rice |

| | |
|---|---|
| Menu #5 | Chicken Stew |
| Menu #6 | Pork with Scalloped Potatoes |
| Menu #7 | Beef Stew |
| Menu #8 | Chicken with Rice |

Later, I changed to the indigenous PIR ration. It was less noisy to open and easier to eat.

Weather was a major consideration for our missions. If we got in trouble when we were across the fence (border) and had bad weather, no one would be coming to help get us out. CCN, CCC and CCS had their own Air Force meteorologist who tracked the weather and gave briefings several times a day to the command group. The teams would get a weather briefing before launch so they would know what weather to expect. Teams didn't launch on the mission unless the weather looked like it was going to be good for a few days. We did not want to get on the ground and all of a sudden not be able to use the air assets available to the team. Operators soon discovered that the best weather predictions were the ones made the day after. The meteorologists were much more accurate in hindsight.

Most of the time CCN teams were inserted into the mountains of northern Laos, the DMZ or North Vietnam. These were mostly rain forests, so we knew it was going to rain every day. When it rained, the clouds would roll right down on top of the mountains and totally conceal the ridgelines. Not only were you under double and triple canopy jungle, but when it rained, a thick cloud cover formed over the canopy. The cloud cover could make it impossible for the air assets to pinpoint our location. Even when we fired flares up through the canopy, the clouds covered them.

**Duty Officer Shootout**

I found myself on the Duty Officer roster the second day that I was at FOB-1. I was briefed that it was a Sunday evening/night and everything would be very quiet. If anything came up, all the answers were in the Duty Officer's three-ring binder. That comment should have been a red flag, but I guess I missed it. The Duty Officer was required to "inspect the compound" and log the times he visited certain locations, e.g., the ammunition bunker. This inspection had to be done several times during the night. It was time to make my first inspection.

I walked out of the orderly room onto the company street. About 40 yards in front of me was the compound gate. A three-quarter-ton-truck carrying a team returning from the firing range was waiting for the gates to be unlocked and opened so they could come in. A small South Vietnamese Army compound shared a fence on one side. I was aware that a Yard team was coming in and I could hear yelling. Then, Holy M-60, Batman! A Yard with an M-60 machine gun had opened fire toward the ARVN (Army of the Republic of Vietnam) compound, but the angle caused the bullets to be coming at me. The first one hit the corner of the orderly room about two feet from me and the others stitched across the side of the orderly room.

I hit the ground as the ARVN returned fire. I began yelling "Cease fire!" as loudly as I could. The team leader and several other people on that end of the compound were yelling as well. The Yard stopped shooting and things quieted down. As I stood up and started toward the gate, the FOB commander came out and yelled a few choice words. I learned that the Yards really did not like Vietnamese, and vice versa. We had to keep them separated in the compound. It was another exciting learning day in SOG.

**Lessons Learned**

- If you could be heard, you could be found. If you could be found, the team could be killed.
- The mission loadout (equipment, ammunition, etc.) was VERY heavy (80–100 pounds).
- The Vietnamese and Yards had a strong, deadly dislike for each other.
- I had a lot to learn (the enemy, tactics, SOPs, processes, team communication, immediate action drills, field trauma procedures, loadout, etc.) and very little time to learn before my first mission.
- I was the FNG (effing new guy) but had a lot of responsibility

on the mission.
- I discovered that our "little people" were harder than woodpecker lips.
- Looking back, I find it interesting that RT Alabama was the first SOG team I was on. I don't believe it was a coincidence.

# RT Alabama Mission 1: Wire Tap SOG #1 (6 DEC 68)
## Mission 1 Team Roster

| | |
|---|---|
| Deck | 1-0 |
| Thompson | 1-1 |
| Davis | 1-2 |
| Cowboy | Interpreter |
| Hoa | Pointman |
| Du | M-79 |
| Quang | Tail gunner |

My first mission with RT Alabama was to conduct a wiretap on a communication line running along a road being used as a supply route for North Vietnamese supplies through Laos into South Vietnam.

In addition to sending us on a wiretap mission, CCN was testing the optimal time to put a team on the ground. Should a team be inserted at first light so they could get away from the LZ quickly? The NVA would figure out that an RT had been inserted and come looking for the team. Or was the optimal insertion time to go in at last light so the team could get off the LZ, set up in a remain-overnight position (RON) and then head out at first light? If the NVA or trackers were coming after the RT they would have to do it in the dark. RT Alabama had been selected to be inserted at last light.

## Travel to Launch Site at Quang Tri

It had been a full six days and nights of training for me with the team. Now the time had come to execute the mission. I was a little more than excited about my first SOG mission and first time in combat. This was what I had been waiting for. The excitement about the next day's mission caused me to wake up a few times during the night, but overall, I had a good night's sleep. At this point I did not fully comprehend what it would be like.

Right after breakfast we did a full equipment check to make sure everyone had everything they were supposed to have for the mission, then rehearsals for IADs, RON, etc. We had an early lunch and flew to the launch site at Quang Tri. This location put our launch site and launch activities much closer to the Laos-South Vietnam border, the DMZ and North Vietnam.

Once at the launch site the team was allowed to relax while Deck and I met with the launch site commander and operations NCO about enemy activity and weather in the area. We verified mission radio frequencies, codes and call signs, then returned to the team.

About 45 minutes prior to launch, Deck and I attended the Final Mission Brief (FMB) with all the key players: launch site personnel, lift ship pilots, backup lift ship pilots, gunship pilots, Air Force A-1 Skyraiders and F-4 liaisons, Forward Air Controller and Covey rider

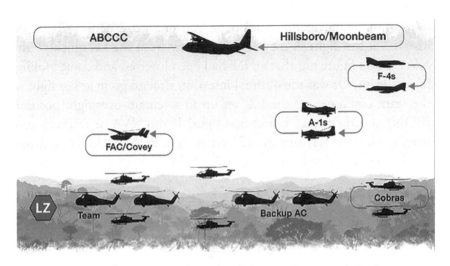

*Typical mission package (and the one for our mission)*

(an experienced SOG team 1-0) by radio, meteorologist and medics. This was the final briefing to make sure everything was in place, that every asset knew their role in different situations that might develop during the insertion and were aware of the AAA (anti-aircraft artillery) threat enroute and at the site. It was a lot of information!

A SOG mission was not just hop on a helicopter, fly 30 minutes to a site, shoot some bad guys and fly back. It was very complicated with a lot of moving parts. All of these assets were totally focused on getting the team inserted into the area of operation, supporting it while it accomplished its mission and getting the team back out as safely as possible. I was quite impressed.

We were using what I found to be our standard FOB-1 mission package for our insertions and extractions.

- **Airborne Battlefield Command and Control Center (ABCCC).** This was an EC-130E aircraft that provided a tactical airborne command post that orbited very high above the SOG team's AO. It monitored all radio communications and provided SOG teams 24/7 radio contact. The daytime call sign was Hillsboro and nighttime was Moonbeam.
- **FAC/Covey** was an Air Force Forward Air Controller that flew into the team's AO with a Covey rider on board. The FAC could talk to and control Air Force assets (A-1 Skyraiders & F-4 Phantom jets) and Covey provided control of Army, Marine and ARVN assets and communicated directly with the SOG team. The Covey rider drew on his extensive ground experience to provide recommendations and calming words to teams—especially during a Prairie Fire Emergency. Covey was the team's lifeline, without which the team would probably not survive.
- An **F-4 Phantom** was a two-seat, twin-engine, all-weather, long-range supersonic jet interceptor and fighter-bomber (often called "fast movers"). The F-4s provided Combat Air Patrol missions when operating close to the North Vietnam border to ward off NVA MiGs and maintain air superiority.

They also provided bomber support to teams in contact or to attack ground targets.

- **A-1 Skyraider** (sometimes called Spad or Sandy) was a single-seat, propeller-driven attack aircraft that was used between the late1940s and early 1980s. The A-1 could carry a very heavy load of a variety of ordnance, fly low and slow, and provide very accurate close air support.

- **AH-1 Cobra** attack helicopters could carry mini-guns (firing 4,000 rounds per minute), a 40mm grenade launcher (firing up to 250 rounds per minute) and up to 48, 2.75-inch rockets with 17-pound high explosive warheads. They provided exceptionally effective close air support.

- **Lift Ships** consisted of CH-34 Kingbees flown by the 219th Squadron, Vietnamese Air Force (VNAF) or UH-1C/D Army helicopters. Two sets of lift ships were involved in the insertions and extractions. One set of aircraft carried the team to the insertion Landing Zone (LZ) and from the extraction LZ. A second set of lift ships flew empty as "chase" aircraft prepared to pick up crew and team members of aircraft that went down during the mission.

When the final mission briefing was over, it was time to make one last trip to the latrine, gear-up, do a quick team meeting, go to our aircraft and get ready to board. By the time I got to the helicopter, I had the urge to pee again, but it was too late. I would have to hold it. Stress does that to you. But it was too late to go again. My education on the physiological and psychological effects of stress was just beginning—and I had a lot to learn. I had two near-death experiences before the Army but had never experienced this level of stress and the things your body and mind do that are beyond your wildest imagination.

We were using a small team and would all be on one UH-1D aircraft. Deck and Cowboy (the interpreter) would be in the door on the left side and Davis and I would be in the right door. The three remaining "little guys" (Hoa, Quang and Du) would be in the center of the helicopter. Du (M-79 gunner) would follow Cowboy and Deck out. Hoa (pointman) and Quang (tail gunner) would follow Davis and me out. Deck, Cowboy, Davis and I would climb out on the skids as we started to approach the LZ.

While Deck was briefing the team, I could hear the insertion aircraft engines starting to make their high-pitched whine as their rotors began to spin up. The smell of JP-4 burning in the engines was in the air. The noise level was rapidly increasing. Sand and dust were filling the air. The team was standing by the UH-1D insertion helicopter waiting on Deck's signal to "lock and load" (put a round in the chamber and make sure the safety was on so we wouldn't shoot our own helicopter down) and board the aircraft. The adrenaline and cortisol levels were beginning to climb. Deck gave the thumbs up and we boarded the helicopter. There were no seats in the aircraft cargo compartment (except for the door gunners) but there were a few straps on the floor of the aircraft and the doors were locked open.

## The Flight Out

As the UH-1Ds started to wind up, I could also hear the high-pitched whine of the Cobras revving up about 200 meters from us. The launch site became very noisy, and the smell of JP-4 (jet fuel burned in the helicopter engines) was strong. The excitement was building as the noise kept increasing. My heart rate was steadily increasing. My mouth was getting dry. This was exhilarating! We had gone over this part of the mission many times, but it's different when you are sitting in the middle of the multidimensional event with all the sights, sounds, smells, tastes, adrenaline, cortisol, butterflies in the stomach, a vibrating aircraft and starting to lift off the ground for your first SOG mission.

And here we go! My first combat mission had started. I said a quick prayer. Davis and I were sitting on the floor with our legs hanging out from the knees down. As the helicopter increased speed, the fast-moving air pushed our feet and legs toward the rear of the aircraft. I was taking it all in, like a dog with my head hanging out the car window.

About 20 minutes into the flight, I saw the river that marked the South Vietnam–Laos border fast approaching. A voice in the back of my head started saying, *It's okay to shoot these people. They are the enemy.*

*My job is to terminate them,* over and over. Suddenly, I heard the door gunners open fire with their M-60 machine guns! I thought, *Holy crap! Are we already under attack?* Then I remembered they planned to test fire their guns once we were over bad guy country. As I was getting my heart settled back down, I heard the song "Amazing Grace" playing in the back of my head. Songs were always in tune in my head. It was when they came out of my mouth that there was a problem. This song had a calming effect and would become my battle song for future combat.

As we were flying along, I was enjoying the relatively cool air blowing on me, playing out all the things I had to do during the insertion, reminding myself it was okay to shoot the bad guys and keeping my anxiety under control. We had climbed to 3,000 feet above ground level (AGL) to avoid the small arms fire that came up at us every few minutes. Some of the bullets were close enough that I could hear the "crack" as they went by. The sun was getting low. The light was starting to fade. Deck gave the team a ten-minute warning. Another surge of adrenaline. We were just about there. I saw the Cobras slowly coming up next to us and easing on by us headed for the LZ. Things were about to get exciting. Another quick prayer. I continued to run through what I was supposed to do during the insertion. My right hand gripped my CAR-15 tighter. My thumb was on the safety/rate of fire selector switch.

**Insertion**

I saw the Crew Chief lean over and say something to SSG Deck. Deck turned and gave the team a thumbs up, meaning we were going to start our descent in 30 seconds! I could feel the next surge of adrenaline and the accompanying increased heart rate. Conceptually, I understood what was about to happen, but I didn't know the reality of what it was going to be like. I discovered that this happens a lot in war. You are always discovering new realities.

Suddenly, the helicopter banked almost 90 degrees to my side, started autorotation (the rotor was turning, but not grabbing the air) and the floor fell out from under me! To say I was not quite prepared for this would be a huge understatement. I was initially just hanging out there in the air, holding on to the side of the aircraft with one hand, looking down 3,000 feet to the ground and thinking, This is not good. My stomach was up in my throat. It was like a thrill-ride at the fair, except this was for real. I was trying to hang on and stay with the aircraft as we spiraled downward toward the jungle canopy. Eventually, the pilot got the aircraft to where he wanted to pull out of the spiral and make his short-final approach to the LZ. He put the power back on, and we experienced strong g-forces as the aircraft began to vibrate violently and started slowing down fast.

When we came out of the spiral, we were on the short-final to the LZ. It was on a ridgeline where the Air Force had dropped a daisy-cutter, a 2,000-pound bomb, to blow a hole in the jungle canopy just big enough that we could land the helicopter down through the hole. As we approached the LZ on short final, I saw what appeared to be a hole in the solid jungle canopy. Must be the LZ, I thought to myself. We were slowly flying over a small pond on the ridgeline when I saw what appeared to be eight to ten hooches off to the east side of the ridge in a little valley. Must be a small village, I thought. I didn't remember that being in our mission briefing. Something was not right. Davis and I climbed out on the skid of the helicopter. Quang and Hoa were pushed up against us ready to jump out. Deck and Cowboy were climbing out on the other side, and Du was pushed up against them. We were going very slowly, and I felt like a sitting target. An NVA soldier could have thrown a rock and knocked me off the skid at any time.

We were slowly approaching the insertion hole flying with the skids dragging across the jungle canopy. The hole looked small. The aircraft vibrated as we literally dropped straight down into the bomb crater. The pilot was trying not to clip trees as we were setting down. It was just getting dark. Davis and I were on the skid. We rapidly scanned the jungle around the crater, but it was too dark and the vegetation was too thick to see into the jungle. Our descent stopped. We were still about six feet above the crater floor and were going to have to jump into the bomb crater. I thought it was a long jump carrying 95 pounds of weight! I knew I had to just suck it up and jump.

Davis and I bent our knees to jump, and just as we did, I saw an NVA soldier pop up on my right about ten feet off to the side with an AK-47 pointing at me! Instantly, instead of jumping, I pushed up and back on the edge of the helicopter floor. Just as I jumped up, the soldier opened fire with his AK-47. The bullets came right across where my legs had been a half second before and hit Davis in the legs. He screamed and yelled, "I'm hit! I'm hit! Help!" as his legs collapsed and he started to fall. The fire ball coming out of the AK-47 barrel was blinding and the sound deafening. Simultaneously, the whole jungle lit up all around us and made an unbelievably loud roar as 20–30 NVA opened fire on automatic at once. I grabbed the back of Davis' LBE harness with my left hand and used my right hand to put half a magazine (10 rounds) on full auto into the NVA soldier who was less than ten feet away. The impact of the rounds ripped him apart and blood splattered on me as he went down.

Aided by adrenaline and cortisol, I managed to jerk Davis up onto the floor of the helicopter. Blood was going everywhere. Then I saw muzzle flashes right in front of me. There was nothing but air between me and the NVA who were shooting at me from 20–30 feet away. I was totally exposed! I could be seen! I could be hit! I could be killed!

Everyone in the aircraft was returning fire. The two door gunners with their M-60 machine guns (550 rounds per minute each gun) and the team members, two of whom were using me as cover and one firing on each side of my head (at 800 rounds a minute each). Their CAR-15 muzzles were so close I was getting powder burns from the muzzle flashes. My ears began to go numb, and I knew I was losing my hearing. Hot brass was going all over me and the floor of the helicopter, and the floor on my side was covered with blood that was getting deeper. Hundreds of bullets were coming at us traveling faster than the speed of sound. I heard them crack as they passed through the cargo compartment or by the helicopter. Some were green tracers—I could actually see them coming out of the dark jungle vegetation and trees. I tried to lean back to present a smaller target. I heard the metallic clangs of bullets hitting the helicopter. *Crap! We were going down!*

Davis was in pain, rolling on the floor and screaming. Blood continued to run out on the floor. I put the other half of the magazine into the muzzle flashes coming from a tree directly in front of me and saw the NVA soldier fall out and hit the ground hard. I heard myself say, "That's two!" Now my magazine was empty.

We were in a full-fledged ambush now all the way around us. Our two Cobra gunships had opened fire with their miniguns, each firing 4,000 rounds a minute. It looked like two hoses were spraying red water all around us. Every fifth bullet was a tracer, but when they were coming that fast, all I could see was red. The bullets were ricocheting off the trees, rocks and the ground. "Friendly" bullets were going in all directions! The helicopter vibrated violently as the pilot tried to lift us out of the bomb crater. He had not planned to lift off with all of us still on board.

Some of the bullets were hitting trees and limbs were flying off, and some of the trees were falling. Rocks were being hit sending fragments flying. Everything was so loud! The second set of Cobras followed right behind the first two firing miniguns (4,000 rounds/minute) and 40mm grenades (at 250 per minute per Cobra). Explosions went off all around us. The air was full of shrapnel, smoke, the smell of gun powder and burned JP-4.

The team was shooting, the door gunners were shooting, the Cobras were shooting, and the NVA were shooting, determined to take our helicopter down. I was having trouble getting the magazine out of my pouch. It appeared to be stuck and my fingers were slick with all the blood on them. I finally got a magazine out, then had trouble getting it in the magazine well of my CAR-15. I could see hundreds and hundreds of bullets and green NVA tracers coming at the aircraft. I realized that the stress level had caused me to lose most of my fine motor skills, and bullets were still coming at me.

I got the magazine in and re-engaged the enemy. I had a conversation going on in the back of my head while I kept shooting: *I am not happy. This is my first mission, and I'm going to die in the first 15 seconds! I've spent two years training for this. What kind of deal is this? I came over here to do something! This is crazy!*

I got another magazine out of the pouch and into my CAR-15.

I shot at the muzzle flashes in front of me. They would go out after I put a four or five-round burst on them, and I saw some NVA fall from trees. My magazines were coming out of the pouch and into my CAR-15 much easier now, and I racked up more kills.

I saw tracers and heard screams coming out of the jungle from the wounded and dying NVA. Then, suddenly, a blast wave followed by a loud "Boom!" came across us and almost knocked the helicopter into the trees. It was followed by several more with less intensity. All of us in the helicopter were temporarily stunned from the concussion and deafened by the loud explosions. The hooches I had seen on the other side of the ridgeline turned out to be tanks camouflaged with straw, and the A-1 Skyraiders were dropping 250-pound bombs on them. This added significantly to the noise and chaos. The A-1s were also receiving anti-aircraft fire—and they engaged those positions too.

Our helicopter started to vibrate violently because the pilot was trying to climb out of that little hole in the jungle canopy. At least we were trying to start up, but the helicopter was still taking hits and the Cobras were making more runs.

Finally, we actually lifted out of the bomb crater. As we did, the NVA shifted their fire, following us as we went up. I was learning that the NVA were an incredibly determined enemy. They would not quit! I saw a smoke grenade in the crater spewing red smoke. The red smoke meant there were no good guys left on the LZ. All aircraft were cleared "hot" for the LZ as we pulled away from the opening in the canopy. The NVA fire stopped because the Cobras blasted the whole ambush site with rockets (with 17-pound high explosive warheads), miniguns and 40mm grenades. The A-1s came in with the big stuff as the Cobras finished their last run. It was an amazing fireworks show. They destroyed the whole area to include six tanks.

As we started to fly away, I looked across at SSG Deck sitting on the other side. He looked across at me with a big grin on his face and gave me an enthusiastic thumbs up. I thought to myself, *Look at this guy! He is so excited. He thought that was the coolest thing! But man, they almost got us all!*

It was my first time to experience a level of fear that I didn't know existed. Many times, I had tried to imagine what it would be like when people started shooting at me. Of course, I knew I would be a little anxious, but I had no clue. Until I experienced it, there was no way I could even imagine a level of fear like that. Fortunately, I was able to manage the fear so I could still shoot. I did not let the fear stop me from returning fire and doing what I had to do, but it scared me. Having those two weapons right next to my head was brutal. I could tell that my high frequency hearing was steadily going away permanently, and I was burned from the muzzle flashes. You could get hurt in a lot of ways besides getting hit with bullets.

I had killed at least two NVA in the first 20 seconds—the guy down below and the first guy in the tree—I knew I took those two out and I had hit and killed several other NVA. I saved my first American's life. If Davis had fallen in the crater, he would have been gone. A second later and we would have both jumped in that crater and been gone. That was bad tactics on the NVA's part. If they had held off two or three more seconds, they could have gotten all of us and the helicopter. I earned my Combat Infantryman Badge with that action. A whole series of firsts occurred for me during that firefight.

A couple of minutes later, as I worked on Davis' legs, I thought about how glad I was that we got out of there. Then I looked down. Several streams of green .51 caliber tracers were coming up at us. Another group of NVA were trying to hit the helicopter! The tracers were bright in the darkness. Fortunately, they did not hit us. I realized that the mission was not over until you got back to FOB-1. I guessed that's why I had heard people at FOB-1 saying, "Phu Bai is alright!"

I told the door gunner to tell the pilot that we had to go straight to the hospital and drop Davis off. He needed medical attention right away. We dropped him off and flew back to the launch site to drop the team off.

Before we went into the debriefing area at the launch site, I asked SSG Deck, "I'm just curious . . . how many magazines did you empty when we were in the crater?" He said, "I emptied five, and was working on number six. I threw two frag grenades and a smoke grenade." Then he looked at me and said, "Lieutenant, you need to practice so you get faster at reloading when people are shooting at you or you're going to die." I agreed and said, "Roger that!"

The Quick Kill training I had at Fort Bragg really paid off during the ambush. There was no way I could have aimed from the position I was in.

That's part of the problem with training; you train to get a good sight picture, sight alignment, squeeze the trigger and hit the target that's not shooting back at you. Then you get in a firefight like this one and your stress level skyrockets. You trained to use those sights, and suddenly your vision changes as the stress goes up and you can't see the sights. You can't do it the way you trained. You can't reload the way you trained. Stress changes everything.

The debriefing shocked me. It was loaded with questions I had no idea I was going to be asked or had been trained to do. What was the NVA soldier wearing, in detail, that popped up and shot Davis? Did he come from the tree line? Pop up out of a spider hole? How many rounds did he fire? How many of my rounds hit him? How many rounds total did the NVA (all of them) fire at the helicopter? How tall were the trees around the bomb crater? What kind of trees were they? They continued asking for very detailed responses about everything. I finally said, "I don't know the answers to most of your questions. I was busy shooting and killing the enemy, pulling Davis in the helicopter, shooting the enemy, and staying alive by shooting the enemy. Next time I'll stop shooting and take notes about the trees and count the bullets as they come by me!" That did not go over well. CPT Washburn said SSG Willis was trying to do a debriefing and did not need smart ass answers. Deck intervened and started answering most of the questions. I made an effort to cooperate more. From that mission forward I carried a notebook to record details about vegetation, trees, soil type, temperature, rainfall, etc.

We flew back to Phu Bai the following day. I was talking to my roommate, Captain Smith, about what had happened, critiquing what we should have done before and what we should have done during the firefight. What did we do there? Were we prepared for an ambush like that? Was there anything else we could have done? I was thinking through our preparation, through what we actually did, what we could do differently next time.

My mindset was: Every time you do something, you need to be better than the last time you did it. To do that you have to practice, practice, practice. You need to understand that you will always have to adapt from your original plan. You have to have contingencies. Whatever you plan, you'll have to adapt. War is not predictable. The only predictability is that the plan will have to be adapted. And you have to be able to adapt on the fly.

Unfortunately, later that evening I shared some of my critique with the FOB-1 Commander. He was excited and said, "I told you we could get you out. If we put you out there, we will get you out. You saw how that worked, right?" I said, "Yeah, I saw how it worked. Let me share some thoughts with you, Sir."

Sequencing is important. If you are going to talk to your boss about how ugly his baby is, make sure you talk to your boss BEFORE you talk to Jack Daniels! Unfortunately, I probably had talked to Mr. Jack Daniels too much before that conversation, and I shared too many of my thoughts. People don't always want to hear someone tell them their baby is ugly. Especially a newbie. He wasn't exactly happy with some of the things I had to say because it reflected on him too. I still think most of my thoughts were correct, of course. For example, if you drop one daisy-cutter bomb out there on a ridgeline, you might as well put up a flag that says, "Hey, we're coming here soon. Get ready for us." He really didn't appreciate that comment.

After that mission, I never thought I would see my 22nd or 23rd birthdays. There was no way to survive five more missions. I also realized that being a Special Ops operator was a mindset. Only people with a certain mindset could do that job. If you didn't have it, you'd better develop what you had to the max, or you wouldn't make it—and you may get other operators killed. There was a reason they gave you an honorable out after six missions if you wanted/needed it. In reality, the 1-0 could remove you from the team before six missions. My attitude was that the NVA might get me, but they were going to pay a heavy price for me. I would take as many of them with me as I could! I would be really upset if they knocked me off with a lucky first round hit, like I heard happened so frequently. They had better get me quick, because I was going after them with everything I had. I know this sounds cocky, but that was the way my mind worked.

I learned a lot in the Green Beret Lounge between missions. I tried to pick the brains of the older, more experienced 1-0s. SFC Johnson, one of the NCO 1-0s I talked to a lot told me one night in the lounge, "When you see an NVA, you can't hesitate, Lieutenant! There is no time for hesitation. You've got to understand this, Lieutenant! Where we go, everyone is the enemy. I mean everyone! You don't have to worry about shooting a friendly by mistake. They're all the enemy! You have to understand this if you want to have any chance to live."

He chugged the rest of his drink, told the barmaid to pour him another one, and said, "And the person who shoots first has the best

*The FOB-1 Green Beret Lounge The real training center.*

76

chance of surviving. Pull the trigger. And never, ever shoot the %#$&* less than three or four times! If he is still moving, you shoot him three or four more times. Make sure he is really dead, then move to the next #@&^. You make sure they go down hard and stay down. You can't imagine how many of us have been wounded or killed by dead NVA!" I heard this same advice from a lot of experienced, battle-hardened warriors.

This was the strategy I adopted and practiced: I trained to go from the safety position on the selector switch, past fire to fully automatic faster than most people could pull the trigger with the safety already off. I practiced that over and over. I used to practice it going down to the ground. I also discovered that as soon as an AK-47 started firing, the barrel would rise. If they didn't hit you with that first or second round and you could get down, you had a chance to survive. I used to practice shooting at silhouettes on the way down with the goal of putting holes in all five silhouettes before I got to the ground. As I was dropping, I would empty a 20-round magazine in 1.4 seconds so that I would have multiple holes in all five targets and be reloading. I practiced this and other techniques, over and over and over. I realized the truth of what Deck had said, "Practice or die!"

I did my own After-Action Review (AAR) when I got back to FOB-1. I made a list of things I thought about once we returned from the mission.

## Some Firsts

- Time in combat.
- Being ambushed.
- Enemy kills.
- Unbelievable fear—adrenaline and cortisol so high I couldn't breathe, but I could shoot. In the back of my head, I thought I was going to die on my first mission. Not happy about that.
- To have that many bullets coming at me from every direction and not get hit.
- Saved an American teammate's life.
- Blood and hot brass everywhere.

- High frequency hearing loss—a lot temporary and some permanent.
- Powder burns on my face.
- Earned my Combat Infantryman Badge.
- Discovered firsthand what stress does to fine motor coordination.

## Lessons Learned

### Mission Prep

- Needed a Visual Recon.
- There was limited training for the "new guy" on team.
- Not enough range time/practice/rehearsal.
- Failed to plan adequately for an ambush.
- Incomplete training/practice/rehearsal.
- Not enough "teaching" going on before mission.
- Needed more range time (I was using a new weapon system).
- Needed Immediate Action Drill practice in an actual jungle.
- I needed more practice reloading under fire or I was going to die.
- Practice, practice, practice!

### Launch Site

- Great final mission brief with all assets.
- I should have been ready for M-60 test fire.
- Left late, long ride to insertion site, got there behind schedule (light).

### Insertion

- Very difficult to get in and out of crater in a fully loaded aircraft.
- Getting dark—raised risk of rotor strike.

### Ambush

- Triggered 5–10 seconds too early by the NVA soldier in the crater who tried to shoot me. The NVA made a mistake. Was their fear level high too?

- Enemy was not prepared for volume of fire from Cobras, the team and door gunners.
- Took too long to lift out of crater (pilot was stunned— had not been engaged this close or with this volume of fire before).
- Very difficult to lift straight up out of crater fully loaded— needed to have used two AC (split the weight).
- Helicopter was taking hits while we were in crater.
- Difficulty keeping wounded American teammate from falling out of helicopter.
- I was too busy shooting to stop Davis' bleeding initially.
- The volume of hot brass flying through the air and helicopter floor was an issue.
- The amount of blood on the floor was an issue—my hand and fingers were slick.
- Team members using Americans for cover was an issue (hearing loss and powder burns).
- Crew chief and door gunner too busy returning fire to watch rotor clearance.
- Initially, team not communicating with crew.

**Additional Lessons Learned**
- Whatever I plan, I will have to adapt. War was not predictable. The only predictability was that the plan will have to be adapted. And I have to be able to adapt on the fly.
- The enemy does not normally get a seat at the mission planning table: thus, they don't know how they are supposed to act during the mission—they tend to mess things up.
- I must control/manage my fear.
- Luck always plays a role in combat.
- Don't stop shooting. A very high volume of return fire is your best chance of survival.
- Focus on the immediate situation—too late to ask who was supposed to drain the swamp when up to your armpits in alligators!
- Must be able to do everything in the dark and under fire.

- Speed of execution and accuracy are critical.
- Know your people, their weapons and actions under fire when you select how to distribute them.
- Know how the enemy will react to your presence and actions.
- Mindset is critical to success.
- Timing is everything.
- You are part of a team.
- Practice, practice and more practice!
- I must get better every time I do something.
- I need to fix my magazines so they are easy to retrieve even under stress and with a bloody hand—attach a cord loop on middle one?

## Leadership Lessons

- Never underestimate luck (good or bad).
- I am not as good as I think I am.
- I can get injured a lot of ways besides getting hit with a bullet.
- Nothing will go as planned. I have to be ready to adapt and overcome on the fly.
- Stress changes everything.
- Never forget that I did it as part of a team.
- I can always do more than I think I can.
- Success and failure come from mindset and execution.
- If I am doing my job as a leader, I am going to get hit.
- Communication is my lifeline.
- Know my people.
- Know my enemy.
- Timing is everything—down to a fraction of a second.
- Everyone must know the 1-0/commander's intent.
- Sometimes everyone must perform on their own.
- Every time you do something, you need to be better than the last time you did it. To do that you have to practice, practice, practice.
- Combat is VERY LOUD!
- I am not out of danger until I get back to the FOB, hence the

saying, "Phu Bai is alright."

- I was upset in my first debriefing about the detailed questions I was asked. Then I had a blinding flash of insight: The volume of fire, type of weapons, how they are firing (semi, bursts or auto), etc., can tell me a lot about the force I'm up against and how to respond. I continued to learn this across missions.
- Exposure and experience prepare me for more complex learning. It's difficult to learn calculus before learning basic math.
- Knowledge and learning occur in layers.
- Never talk to Jack Daniels before giving your boss feedback about how ugly his baby is.

## Hatchet Platoon Assignment

A few days after returning from the mission with RT Alabama I was assigned as a Platoon Leader for one of our Montagnard Hatchet platoons. In addition to being the RT Alabama 1-1, I also began training with my Hatchet platoon. I found this to be quite an experience. My time with the platoon was brief because of my missions with RT Alabama.

RT Alabama began training harder and in more depth than before. Davis' leg wounds were so severe that he was evacuated back to the States. We picked up a replacement for Davis. His name was Doug Jones—the new FNG. He was relatively new and had to learn a lot about how our team conducted operations. A lot of our training was focused on getting him ready for our next mission.

# Chapter 5

## Into the Darkness

*In the darkest times, that's where you will find your greatest strength.*
—Author Unknown

*Darkness in the Garden Painting courtesy of Shiloh Brown*

Almost 50 years after the events in this book, my 8-year-old granddaughter, Shiloh Brown, will finish her picture and proudly show it to me. I will ask her what the black part of the picture is, and she will reply, "That's darkness. It's spreading around over the things in the garden." She will describe darkness as a physical thing that spreads and oozes around, slowly covering everything. That's what darkness in the jungle feels like—a dark liquid that slowly covers everything.

## RT Alabama Mission 2: Search and Destroy SOG #2 (13 DEC 68)

| Mission 2 | Team Roster |
|---|---|
| Deck | 1-0 |
| Thompson | 1-1 |
| Jones | 1-2 |
| Cowboy | Interpreter |
| Hoa | Pointman |
| Du | M-79 |
| Quang | Tail gunner |
| Quan | Alternate point |

RT Alabama's next mission was to find and destroy a battalion-sized NVA element moving south through Northern Laos to South Vietnam. Our eight-man RT would be looking for 500 NVA soldiers! If our intelligence guys could put us on the ground relatively close to them, it should be pretty easy to find a group that size. One problem might be staying alive long enough to put enough fire power on them to destroy them and still be able to escape. Not having done this before, it sounded to me like it might be a challenge. I was excited that I was going to learn how to do this successfully.

We started mission preparation: getting intelligence and weather briefings, studying maps of the areas, identifying possible insertion and extraction points, and reviewing other critical parts of the mission. An insertion date was selected. Our operations people began to put together the mission package—all the supporting elements that would be involved in getting us in, supporting us on the ground and getting us out. I was fascinated by all the moving parts. As a team, we began training for and rehearsing all the critical actions we would have to take. We practiced immediate action drills, forming a security perimeter, putting out Claymore mines (in layers), rest schedule, how to wake up team members when it was their time for security or if they were snoring, or if there was movement around us. Some of the procedures may seem simple, but when you are hundreds of miles from the closest friendly, with hundreds of enemy soldiers all around you, the fear factor is high, and nothing is simple or easy.

I talked to everyone I could find who had experience with "trackers" while on missions. I learned the various techniques used by individual and multiple trackers (signaling by "clacking" pieces of bamboo), dogs, and trackers that would herd you toward an ambush or away from LZs. I also learned how to know they were following you and techniques such as M-14 mines (affectionately called "toe poppers") to end their tracking careers. All the work I had done tracking animals during my childhood became very valuable and would save our lives on numerous occasions. I knew exactly where to put a toe popper to take a tracker's leg off; he would eventually bleed out and die. I had been training since I was a kid to read tracks on the ground and in vegetation to determine:

- The number of enemy
- Direction they were moving
- How fast they were moving
- If they were carrying a heavy load
- How old the tracks were
- If they were trying to cover their trail
- If they had dogs

I learned how to deal with dogs using CS powder (military grade tear gas combined with black pepper) and a .22 pistol with integrated silencer. (Yes, dogs were the enemy.) Occasionally, a dog would set off a toe popper by stepping on the mine or trying to dig it up. I learned how to put out frag grenades with trip wires, and on special occasions, how to replace the standard frag grenade fuse (4.5-second delay) with a smoke grenade fuse (0-second delay) with a blasting cap crimped on it so the grenade would detonate instantly. The act of deploying a grenade with a zero-delay fuse could run your stress level up. One mistake and you became pink mist!

We did a lot of planning, a lot of practice and more practice. At this point, SSG Deck was starting to listen to some of my ideas. We had been in combat together and I had more credibility now. He had seen me in action and knew I would stay calm, shoot back, and take care of team members. He also knew I was much faster at changing magazines.

## Special Equipment

Special equipment for this mission included: high powered binoculars, single lens reflex camera with a telephoto lens, additional Claymores, short time fuses with blasting caps and fuse igniters, extra toe poppers, and powdered CS mixture for the dogs. The special equipment not only added more weight to carry but required extra training.

## Travel to Launch Site

On launch day we got up early (before daylight) and loaded the RT and all of our equipment into ambulances. We traveled out the FOB-1 gate and just a little way up the road to the helipad where two CH-34 Kingbee helicopters waited with engines running. The ambulances backed up very close to them one at a time and unloaded us in two groups. There were no lights. It was very dark. No one could see us getting on the Kingbees because a CH-34 only has one door. Once inside, it was hard to be seen even with the door open. I knew we were getting deeper into the black ops world because combat troops were not allowed to be transported in medical vehicles—like the ambulances we had just ridden in. It made me feel more special since we could violate international laws.

We were using the launch site at Quang Tri, which put all our activities much closer to the Laos–South Vietnam border, the DMZ and North Vietnam. I had been to Quang Tri before and was familiar with the launch site procedure. Our launch was planned for 1000 hours that day. We had enough time to do a Pre-Combat Final Inspection

(PCFI) to make sure we had all our special equipment, and each team member had all of his personal combat equipment, including the correct ammunition and amounts, all equipment was secured and sound proofed.

We went over the mission, insertion, security halt, route, alternate extraction points, and other aspects of the mission. About an hour before launch time, we attended the Final Mission Briefing (FMB) with all the key leaders, pilots, American team members, our meteorologist, a field report from Covey who was out in the general area, frequencies, mission abort procedures, anti-aircraft fire, supporting Air Force aircraft, Hillsboro and Moonbeam aircraft, rendezvous points (RPs) and staging areas for the supporting gunships, emergency extraction aircraft and A-1 Skyraiders, emergency procedures, and other key people like the team 1-0 and 1-1. We did not expect much AAA on the way out to the AO. The insertion was expected to be quiet. Activity would accelerate after the briefing.

Soon the team stood by the insertion Kingbees, engines running, waiting for the signal to lock and load weapons and board the aircraft. The high-pitch whine of the gunships starting up, the strong smell of burned avgas from the Kingbee engines, and the copious amounts of dust and sand in the air being stirred up by the aircraft—all of this indicated the mission was a go, which brought butterflies to the stomach.

Deck gave the signal. We locked and loaded, and boarded the aircraft. Our positions inside the aircraft were different this time because the Kingbee only had one door. Deck and I were seated next to each other with our legs over the side of the floor. It was a different feeling, almost claustrophobic. I could only see out the door we were sitting in and my vision was much more restricted than in the UH-1D helicopter. We didn't have a door gunner on the other side. The Kingbee aircraft were much older than the Hueys. I didn't trust them. I was sure the Kingbee pilots were good, but it made me nervous. With a lot of vibration and noise, we lifted off. The mission had started!

**Insertion**

The flight to the insertion LZ was uneventful, but the memory of what happened on the last insertion was still burned into my brain. There was no dramatic "fall out of the sky" insertion this time. I scanned the tree line closely but saw no signs of the NVA. We landed in a small clearing of three-foot-high ribbon grass, exited the Kingbees quickly and ran into the thick jungle vegetation. I really noticed the weight I was carrying and how it impacted my movement. The vegetation was so thick I could only see Cowboy in front of me and Du behind me. I wondered how Deck was going to control the team if we made contact. If the vegetation remained this thick, some of the IADs we practiced would not work. After about 100 meters we stopped for a security halt, which allowed us to adapt our senses to the jungle environment.

We established a kneeling security perimeter and then went into adapt mode. We all listened. Could we hear any bad guys? What did we hear? We adapted to the sounds of the jungle because for the last 45 minutes, all we could hear was the loud Whop! Whop! Whop! Of the helicopter. This had created a temporary hearing threshold shift, and now we could not hear very well. Unfortunately, it would take several hours to get our hearing back to normal. Our sense of smell had also been significantly degraded from smelling the avgas from the Kingbee engines on the flight out there. This created a blind spot or dark area in our senses.

I was very fortunate to have Spidey-senses. I wouldn't be hearing any more dog whistles after our first mission, but I still had the rest of my super-senses. I would discover that I could smell the bad guys—especially if they had eaten recently. On several occasions in the future, I would sniff out ambushes. I would actually smell the enemy—their body odor, what they had eaten—and know where they were in relation to us. I could just sense their presence.

It was also very hot, over 100°F with 95% humidity. Sweat was running into our eyes, causing them to burn and our vision to be degraded. I saw leeches wiggling on the vegetation as they sensed our body heat. They were ready to feast on us. We would wake up the next morning with leeches all over us, and they would be swollen to the size of our thumbs with our blood. This was my first dense jungle experience. I was having a lot of new sensory experiences—almost to the point of being overwhelmed. I took some deep breaths and focused. RTs always started their mission surrounded. This was what I had been told and so far, it seemed to hold true.

When Deck was comfortable with the security halt, he signaled me to release the assets. I used our PRC-25 radio to transmit the day's three-letter code, Foxtrot Romeo Zulu, meaning, "Team okay, moving north" using the whisper technique. There would be no talking unless we made enemy contact. This meant all the air assets waiting at their respective RPs about 20 minutes away were released to return to their bases in Vietnam. Now we were really alone and on our own.

We had code words for various situations, for example, "Team okay, Moving North/South/East/West, Team OK, Enemy Close, RON, etc." All radio communications had to be very brief and secure. We had a code book with different codes and frequencies for each day. The NVA were always listening trying to pick up our radio signal, then triangulate it. If they had artillery in range, they would send us a "welcome message," usually a barrage of artillery fire. If artillery was out of range, they would send a large welcoming party.

If we were not in enemy contact and needed to talk on the radio, we used a whisper technique. The PRC-25/77 handset was very sensitive to a whisper. With a little practice our radio operators easily understood us. We also used a lot of "blind transmissions." We sent out coded messages at predetermined times—but not on the hour. The bad guys expected it on the hour. You knew that Covey, the Tactical Operations Center (TOC) and Hillsboro/Moonbeam would be listening for those transmissions at the scheduled times. If you failed to send a message at those scheduled times, they would know something was wrong. Covey always flew within radio range of us in the morning and at last light and put out a coded call. Two "clicks" (breaking squelch twice) on the radio handset only took a fraction of a second and let Covey know the team was OK. These techniques, and others, kept radio transmissions too short to be triangulated. If we were in enemy contact, we could talk out loud (mostly yelling) and in the clear (uncoded).

We moved as quietly as possible while avoiding trails, roads, and the tops of ridgelines. We were moving at a snail's speed of 100 meters (about 25 feet longer than a football field) an hour. It was a slow and painstaking process. We could not afford to let the NVA hear us or fail to hear them. Moving slowly also made it more difficult for the enemy to see or hear us.

We had a great point man—a very dangerous job requiring a lot of skill and guts—out in front of the team to keep us from walking up on the enemy. No surprises! In a triple canopy, thick jungle, the light is dim, even at midday. It was not unusual to be within 20 feet of the enemy when we discovered each other's presence. Most of the time we were shooting at muzzle flashes or moving vegetation. We also tried not to leave a trail that the bad guys could follow. The better the point man, the less likely we were to walk up on the enemy and die! The first 30–60 seconds after making contact tended to be very deadly because team members were often standing when the shooting started.

We also had a tail gunner rear security man. It was another very dangerous job requiring a lot of skill and guts to protect our six (rear). His mission was to make sure no one slipped up behind us. He spent most of his time guarding/looking to the rear. Each team member had responsibility for a security zone when moving or halted. Every team member was always "on," sensing the environment for the enemy—or any other threat, such as tigers, snakes, booby traps, dogs, trackers, etc. High situational awareness was critical. I had been studying and practicing personal and situational awareness for years as part of my martial arts and warrior training. Most of the time I used 4-D spheres of awareness of 10, 20, 30 and 50 meters in diameter. In more open terrain I would expand these distances. You could not let your guard down for a second!

This was an early afternoon insertion, so we had time to move a few hundred meters before eventually moving into an RON position. The vegetation was thick with a small foot path along the center of the ridge. It appeared to be primarily an animal path. We still moved over to the edge of the ridge, staying away from the trail. This provided us more concealment and security, but at a slower pace.

Our plan was to perform a fishhook maneuver when we found a good site for the night. When we found the area we wanted to use for our RON, we continued to move another 50–100 meters beyond it, then made a U-turn down the side of the ridge and came back to the RON spot on the side of the ridge. This way, if we were being tracked, we would hear the NVA go by following our trail above us, which would give us an early warning that we were in trouble. To know for sure that we were being followed and to have more time to escape, I put three M-14 toe popper mines on the trail just before it turned. Most of the time when the NVA heard the explosion from the tracker stepping on the toe popper, they assumed we were in front of them and opened fire in that direction—but not always.

As soon as we stopped for the night, we put out the Claymore mines in all likely avenues of approach. The areas to be most likely used by the NVA got extra Claymores at different distances. We also got the time fuses ready to put with blasting caps and fuse ignitors in some individual Claymores to leave behind us if we had to evacuate the RON during the night under fire. We did not carry Claymores with the blasting cap in them. If a bullet hit a blasting cap inside a Claymore, it would turn you into a pink mist!

During our pre-mission training I had convinced Deck to include a quick end-of-day briefing just before last light that included the location of a rallying point, a day and night escape plan from the RON and a reminder of our running password, frog hair. This was another addition to the team SOP that Deck agreed to establish. The running password allowed us to identify ourselves if we had been separated from the team and were running to reunite—without getting shot! The password had to be said in English. It was designed to be difficult for an enemy soldier to hear the phrase and repeat it in combat. I used a different phrase for each team I led, to include my future family.

The thickness of the vegetation in the RON site helped prevent the NVA from slipping up on us. They did not normally walk on the steep side of the ridgeline through the vegetation, especially at night. They preferred the trail on the ridgeline. In this situation each person had to straddle a tree, so he wouldn't slide down the side of the ridge during the night.

Darkness came quickly and the jungle began to swallow us whole. It closed in all around and over us, and if we were under a double-canopy jungle, it got dark even faster. We were under a triple-canopy where it was pretty dark in the daytime, but now it was night, and I couldn't see my hand in front of my face. Total darkness was spreading around and over the things in the jungle. It was like a physical thing, opaque black liquid slowly spreading and covering everything.

It was my first night in that kind of jungle. I had spent days and nights in the Florida Everglades before, but that was different for many reasons. At first, the increasing darkness made me a little nervous because even though I had night vision like an owl, I found it difficult to see. Then I had a blinding flash of the obvious (BFO): if I could not see, the NVA could not see either. A critical difference between us and the NVA was we were not moving, and they were. They could not move without making noise. If they made any noise, we would know they were out there and where they were. I was next to a big dead tree, about two feet in diameter, that was lying on the ground. I moved up close to it so I would have cover on at least one side.

I created a 4-D sphere around me, the fourth dimension being time. I started facing the ridge and then listened to identify all the sounds I could hear for 360 degrees around me horizontally, then vertically. I needed to know what was out there. What sounds did I hear? What bugs did I hear? Then I divided the area into quadrants and identified the sounds in each one. I then did the same thing going up until I knew the sounds in all four quadrants. Then I raised it up because above me were birds, monkeys and all kinds of creatures making sounds in the trees. A lot of sounds! I incorporated all this together.

The sound of silence was the trigger, which made me think of Simon and Garfunkel's song "The Sound of Silence." This system would actually wake me up if any quadrant went silent. If anyone or anything moved in a quadrant, the bugs would stop chirping. They would go quiet all of a sudden, and if they went quiet, something was out there. The silence could be deafening. This would alert me to where the creatures were coming from. It might be an NVA, a tracker, a tiger, or other large animal, but something would have caused them to get quiet. Not only was the dark becoming my friend, so were the bugs, birds, frogs and other creatures that made noise. We were all part of one big system.

The NVA could not see the team and we had area weapons, such as Claymore mines and grenades. We could set off a Claymore and all they would see, if anything, was a tremendous ball of fire and a blast wave as the 700 steel balls traveling at 4,000 feet per second shredded anyone in front of it, but they would not know exactly where we were. The team was carrying 17 Claymores! The next level of weapon was fragmentation grenades. We could throw grenades and there would be a big ball of fire and a lot of shrapnel with a 15-meter killing radius, but they wouldn't know where it came from. RT Alabama was carrying 70 fragmentation grenades! As long as no one pulled the trigger on their CAR-15, the NVA would not know where we were. I was learning to like the dark. I actually began to look forward to the darkness. I knew we would find the NVA if they were out there.

It took about 30 minutes or so for the silence that we had created setting up the RON to escalate back to normal jungle noise levels. Once everyone was down, the jungle returned to normal—except for the smell—and the RON rule was once you were down, you were down. You did NOT move again until morning. Anyone moving was a bad guy! That's one reason we carried a sharp knife. A knife did not light you up unless the bad guy pulled his trigger.

We positioned ourselves so we could reach the guy on each side to wake him up or alert him that something was happening. To wake someone without terrifying them, we gently put our hand around the back of the person's upper arm and slowly squeezed. The slow squeeze caused their eyes to open. We trained to do this so team members knew if they got squeezed, to just open their eyes—that was the only thing that moved—and then you started listening. What did you hear? It might be your turn to be on guard, or it might be that there was something out there. On my next team, RT Michigan, I would create and implement a set of touch signals for use at night.

Sometimes we dropped down to 30 percent on guard at night while the rest slept. I knew teams that let everyone sleep at night, but not me. I was not going there. We always had at least a few team members awake throughout the night. Some nights no one slept.

We had a rule that team members kept their arms through their rucksack straps at night. Your rucksack needed to go with you if you had to leave in a hurry. Our LBE never came off our body. Our weapon was always fastened to us with a cord that went through a snap-link on the shoulder of the LBE. In the RON, all team members kept their CAR-15 (or M-79) laying across their lap so they could put their hands on it easily and quietly. A knife was on your LBE where you could easily and quietly access it if you needed it. Our feet needed to be free and ready to instantly kick, fight, roll or flee. Even in heavy rain at night, we kept our feet ready to react instantly. (I still sleep with my feet free 50+ years later.) Your mind and body were always "on" even if you were asleep. Our survival and the team's survival depended on it.

Several times during the night we heard the sounds of vehicles, probably trucks, moving in the valley below us and some metallic sounds like something being put into or taken out of vehicles. Activity going on below us was definitely what made us believe we were on the fringes of the NVA battalion. At first light we had a quick snack and slowly got ready to move, bringing the Claymores in last. We had not heard any activity in the valley for two hours. Some team members and I smelled smoke from what was most likely the enemy's cooking fires. It appeared that the NVA were having a nice hot meal that morning—if we were lucky, it would be their last meal.

We were ready to move, but still down on one knee. It appeared that Deck and Hoa were having a disagreement. Hoa refused to go forward up the ridge. He told Deck, "Too many VC! Beaucoup VC!" Deck did not believe him. He replaced him with the alternate point man, Quan. I wondered what made Deck so sure it was okay to move up the ridge. I trusted Deck, but my adrenaline level jumped as we started moving. I turned up all of my Spidey senses to the max! I felt like that point in a Chainsaw Massacre movie when you knew Leatherface was going to jump out from behind a tree and start sawing people's arms off. I could still smell the smoke from the valley.

After a couple hours, we came to a small, 300-foot-high cliff that allowed us to see a piece of the valley. We stopped there, set up security and put out the Claymores. Deck, Cowboy and I moved to where we could observe the valley. We did not see any movement but saw some areas that appeared to have a road under the canopy. The air was still heavy and smoke hung just above the canopy, probably close to where the cooking fires had been. We transmitted the coordinates to Covey when he got in range.

After about an hour in this position we heard some sounds on the ridge that spooked the team. They started with their "Beaucoup VC!" comments again. Deck said, "No! Banana trees falling and deer/animals! Not VC/NVA." In my mind I wondered how Deck knew the sounds were not NVA? What was he hearing that I didn't hear? I would pick his brain to learn later. We stayed in position.

About an hour later we heard the vehicle sounds again along with voices. A lot of voices! After Deck talked to Covey, a decision was made to bring in F-4s to bomb and napalm the valley and hilltop. It wasn't long until we had two F-4s on station taking turns coming in low and hot with fangs out. They were very loud! The bombs (500-pounders) were loud and rattled our heads with the concussions. We could feel the heat from the napalm every time they dropped it. The NVA were not happy! Apparently, we had found the right spot. The F-4s not only received a lot of automatic weapons fire, but also anti-aircraft fire and secondary explosions from the ammunition, fuel, etc., each time they made a run.

Covey brought in four A-1s to follow up behind the F-4s while they were being replaced. The A-1s went after the anti-aircraft positions. Some of the team members alerted again. This time Deck agreed with them and passed the word around to get ready to repel an enemy assault coming down from above us. We would fight our way down the ridge toward the extraction LZ. Deck notified Covey we were in trouble and needed air support. About two minutes later the crap hit the fan!

A toe popper exploded and approximately 40–50 NVA coming down the ridge opened fire on us with AK-47s and rocket propelled grenades (RPGs). Quan was wounded in the arm and back by shrapnel from an RPG explosion, but he was able to move without assistance. The NVA were trying to maneuver so as to form a U-shape to force our backs against the cliff so we could not escape. We could not see the NVA most of the time, so we were shooting at muzzle flashes, moving vegetation and sounds of weapons firing. We were very close, 20–40 feet, to the NVA in thick jungle vegetation. I fired bursts of 2–4 rounds. Sometimes the vegetation opened up and we could see farther. Most of the time from the ground I could not see anything, including the enemy.

Fortunately, we had discovered them early enough that we were able to block them with Claymores long enough to run along the side of the ridge while Covey diverted the A-1s to us. Their 20mm guns tore up the ridge and the NVA, giving us time to gain a little distance. They were still firing RPGs at us, wounding Quang in the back and leg. He began yelling that he was hit and needed help. I left a couple of Claymores with time fuses behind us. They ripped a hole in the middle of the NVA assault line. This slowed the NVA while they regrouped.

The surprise Claymores seemed to have a psychological effect on them, causing them to move slower and more cautiously. As I watched how the NVA reacted to our actions, I had another BFO—the NVA were not animals, but humans. They did not want to die any more than we did.

Deck had me call Covey and request a Prairie Fire Emergency as we fought our way down the ridge. Normally, when we called a Prairie Fire Emergency everything flying that had ordnance on it and within range was diverted to the team. Unfortunately for us, another team had a Prairie Fire Emergency in progress that started just before ours. This limited our emergency assets in the beginning. A new set of F-4s had arrived on station and we had A-1s, gunships and UH-1D extraction aircraft about 30 minutes out.

We continued working the A-1s and F-4s we had until the new ones and gunships arrived. The intensity increased. Two of our guys were wounded, which significantly reduced our fire power. The NVA had the high ground advantage because we were moving down the ridge to our extraction LZ. (The same LZ we used for insertion.) The NVA knew that was where we were going. I was sure they were maneuvering a force to that location to throw a party for us. I asked Covey to be prepared to have the A-1s work over the ridge on the lower side of the LZ—just in case the NVA got there in time.

The fighting was fierce, and we were carrying Quang. I also got to see Cowboy in action. He was a real warrior! No fear. He worked with me fighting a delaying action at the rear of the team slowing down the NVA. He had experience using Claymores with time fuses and a great instinct for the way the NVA moved against us. Cowboy's experience and courage made our Claymores and C-4 charges more effective.

Jones stayed close to Deck and followed his instructions for navigating a safe route to the LZ. So far, we had been lucky in that we only had two wounded and the NVA appeared to be just on the ridge above us. We tried to move fast but we were receiving so much fire we mostly crawled, literally. The vegetation was thick and the longest distance we could see was at best 30 meters and that was in the center of the ridge. If we could keep them more than 30 meters behind us, they could not aim directly at a team member. They were just putting a lot of AK fire and RPGs where they thought we were. The same went for us firing back at them. We fired at sounds, muzzle flashes and movement. We were going through ammunition pretty fast, especially 40mm.

Covey told us that the gunships and TAC Air were still receiving a lot of automatic weapons and anti-aircraft fire. The extraction aircraft would not be able to approach the LZ until that could be suppressed. More TAC Air was about 20 minutes out. Our extraction aircraft was only about ten minutes out along with two Cobra gunships. I asked Covey to check the LZ area again for any movement. The vegetation around the LZ was thick, but he might get lucky and spot movement if the bad guys were there.

When we got about 100 meters from the LZ, all hell broke loose from our front. There were 30–40 NVA waiting on us. Now we were between two groups. The group from the LZ opened fire with a heavy barrage from AK-47s, machine guns (RPDs) and RPGs. They assaulted and began trying to maneuver around our flanks. There were several loud booms, with one of them hitting me with concussion, mud and other debris, some of which went in my eyes. I was having trouble seeing. My ruck and radio were hit with shrapnel from one of the B-40 rockets. The radio looked bad but still worked. The small wooden box of blasting caps was hit but not penetrated. Some of the C-4 was hit, but that was not a big deal.

Deck called me to his position. He wanted the A-1s to put their 20mm fire on the NVA to our front. We were about to be crushed. The first A-1 gun run got the NVA's attention and stopped their assault. They did not expect the devastation of the 20mm. The second A-1 gun run made them start to scatter. The Cobras arrived on site and worked above and below us with rockets, mini-guns and 40mm.

We continued to fight our way to the edge of the LZ and saw 20–30 NVA bodies scattered around. Some of them were still alive and had to be terminated. We were not in a position to take prisoners. Covey said the extraction ship was a UH-1C and wanted smoke. Jones threw a purple smoke grenade onto the edge of the LZ. The UH-1C identified purple. Deck got everyone ready to dash to the chopper on his command. We also turned our bush hats inside out so the bright orange VS-17 panel sewn to the inside would make us identifiable to the door gunners. We didn't want to be mistaken for an NVA trying to get to the chopper, which the NVA sometimes tried!

Deck went to the left side of the chopper with Hoa, Du and the wounded Quang. Jones, Cowboy and I took the wounded Quan to the right side. I climbed on just before Deck as the chopper was lifting off. The door gunners and all team members not wounded returned fire from the chopper. As we got about 20 feet in the air, Deck and I both threw a red smoke grenade to signal that the LZ and surrounding area were "cleared hot," meaning anyone on the ground was a bad guy. Covey was free to destroy everything there! We continued to receive fire as we climbed out. I heard a few metallic clangs as the chopper took some hits. I looked over at Deck. He gave me his characteristic big smile and a thumbs up.

As I began to give medical attention to Quang and Quan, I thought, Wow! What an adrenaline rush! I now had a better understanding of

*Cowboy and LT Thompson in the .50 cal machine gun pit, FOB-1 1968
(Picture courtesy of LT Henry Thompson)*

the emotions Deck was experiencing when he would give me a big smile and thumbs up.

As we flew away, I saw and heard our air assets pounding the crap out of the bad guys. We had found the NVA battalion and rained death and destruction down on them. Our team had also taken out a large number (100–200) of them on the ground. I continued to be amazed at how tough and deadly our little guys were in a firefight. After a short prayer, I settled down for the ride back.

We arrived back at the launch site greeted by a small cheering group. We were all excited to be back to a relatively safe area. Our medics met our aircraft and began treating Quang and Quan as they moved them to the medical tent. Now it was time to do the initial debriefing. This one went a lot better than the last one. SSG Willis had found a better way to ask me questions—and I had a better attitude toward the forest ranger questions. Later, we would fly back to FOB-1. The next day would be more debriefings and some needed recovery.

**Lessons Learned**

- Adaptation to the jungle during the security halt works for all your senses except hearing. After an hour or more helicopter ride it can take 2–3 hours for your hearing to return to "normal." After a heavy firefight it might take 16–48 hours for the hearing loss to return—or the hearing loss might be permanent.
- We did not have a jungle to train in at Phu Bai—just an open range. We needed a jungle.
- In the RON your feet need to be free and ready to instantly kick, fight, roll or flee. Even in a heavy rain at night, I kept them ready to react instantly.
- Layered Claymores are very effective. Each Claymore in a layer detonates instantly with the others linked to it. A tremendous explosion is created and thousands of steel balls fly through the jungle (and NVA) at 4,000 feet per second. For example, a layer of seven Claymores equals 10.5 pounds of explosives (C-4) and 4,900 steel balls.

- Claymores with time fuses slow the NVA's advance.
- I had a blinding flash of the obvious (BFO)—the NVA were humans too. They did not want to die any more than we did.
- Cowboy's courage and expertise really helped slow the NVA's advance. I learned a lot from him as we fought the delaying action.
- Recon Teams always start out surrounded by the enemy.
- High situational awareness (being in the now) is critical.
- Combat creates an addictive adrenaline rush.
- I had another blinding flash of the obvious (BFO): if I could not see, the NVA could not see either, and a critical difference between us and the NVA was we were not moving and they were. They could not move without making noise. If they made any noise, we would know they were out there and where they were.
- The jungle closed in around us at night.
- We used a "Fishhook" technique to move into the RON.
- I learned the dark was my friend (and used my super senses).
- Once down, no one moves!
- We used the "triceps squeeze" to wake someone up without creating a panic.
- We always slept with arms through rucksack straps, CAR-15 across lap & attached to LBE (shoulder), knife where we could get it quickly.
- At night use area weapons (e.g., claymores, grenades) only, unless no choice.
- I could not see enemy most of the time. I was shooting at muzzle flashes, moving vegetation, sounds of weapons firing. We were very close (20–40 feet) to the enemy in thick jungle vegetation. Fired 3-round bursts on full auto. Sometimes the vegetation opened up and you could see a longer distance. Most of the time from the ground you could not see team members or the enemy. It was necessary to learn to create a mental model of the battlefield, including terrain, based on sensory data and be able to operate there.

- Claymores with time fuse were a great tactic for slowing the NVA's advancement.
- Movement at nighttime was dangerous.
- The battlefield and firefights are very fast and dynamic.
- Every casualty ties up at least one or two team members, reducing your speed and firepower dramatically.
- We all need to build more physical strength and cardio to manage our loadout and other demands of combat.
- My left hand and thighs of my pants legs became my combat information center. I wrote call signs, directions, etc., on them. Information was coming too fast to mentally manage it under high stress.
- I realized that one of the benefits of being in a firefight is that my loadout (weight I was carrying) continued to get lighter as I used my ammunition, water, explosives, etc.
- High stress significantly reduces your working memory and decision-making effectiveness.
- Stress dries your mouth out. Water had never tasted so good!

## RT Alabama Mission 3: Eldest Son & Gas SOG #3 (18 DEC 68)

### Mission 3 Team Roster

| | |
|---|---|
| Deck | 1-0 |
| Thompson | 1-1 |
| Jones | 1-2 |
| Cowboy | Interpreter |
| Hoa | Pointman |
| Du | M-79 |
| Quan | Alternate point |

**Team Mission**

After a day of rest, we were assigned another mission with a short prep time. Our mission was to locate and contaminate an NVA ammunition

# RT Alabama Post-Mission 2 Training DEC 68

**Personal Fitness (w/loadout on)**

- Walking, squats, crawling, running, getting up & down, shooting, hand & arm strength, balance, climbing, makiwara board, hand-to-hand
- Hydration/Electrolytes

**Knowledge Acquisition**

- NVA
- Organization/CofC
- Food
- Sleep
- Equipment
- Superstitions

**Alabama Team Members**

- Superstitions

**Skills Improvement:**

- Tracking
- NVA Weapons
- IADs
- Firing Range
- Observation Techniques
- Treating medical trauma in field

**Equipment Organization/SOP**

- Standardizing what, where & how equipment was carried.

**Operational Terrain & Weather**

**Team Fitness**

- Exercise with loadout
- Hydration/Electrolytes
- Hand-to-hand
- Mindset

**Pre-mission Food (3-days)**

- No spices
- NVA type food

**Medical**

- IVs
- Gunshots
- Shrapnel
- Bleeding
- Tourniquets

**Stress/Fear Management**

**Data Templates**

- Vehicles
- Enemy Contact
- Patrols
- Reactions

cache near a major supply route in the eastern part of the Demilitarized Zone (DMZ) between South Vietnam and North Vietnam using Eldest Son—also called exploding ammunition, Italian Green and Pole Bean. Eldest Son was one of SOG's insidious black PsyOps programs. It was designed to invoke a deep psychological fear in the enemy. The plan called for a quick, clandestine mission to the ammunition cache while conducting a diversionary airstrike on a nearby bridge using F-4s. RT Alabama started preparing immediately for an 18 DEC 1968 insertion. We were getting into the "darker" missions of SOG right away.

**Training**

This mission would involve not only 7.62mm rounds, but also 12.7mm rounds and 82mm mortar rounds. Proper placement of this ammunition would be difficult and critical. We were scheduled to meet with a CIA operative for some specific Eldest Son training the next day. Unknown to him and us, he would also share information that would leave us, especially me, stunned!

Normally, Eldest Son insertions were accomplished using a special all-American SOG team that followed closely behind B-52 strikes, constructed hastily prepared bunkers/fighting positions, then "salted" them with the faulty ammunition. Unfortunately, two weeks prior, on 30 NOV 1968, an Eldest Son team's helicopter was hit with 37mm anti-aircraft fire and fell like a rock to the jungle canopy 3,000 feet below, exploded and burned. The air crew and seven SOG team members died that day. A Bright Light mission (mission to recover a missing team or team members) was not attempted because of the location and number of NVA in the area.

I was shocked when he shared this information. I realized that I had inventoried the personal effects of these SOG heroes, including my friend Ray Stacks, on my second day at FOB-1. This small piece of SOG had come full circle. In a week I would be inserted as part of a team to complete their mission. (See the KIAs listed at the beginning of Chapter 4. Their remains would not be repatriated until 20 years later.)

This mission would be a clandestine operation on an ammunition storage area where we would infiltrate the storage area and appear to leave it untouched. In reality, we would leave some deadly, black psychological ops surprises for the future users of this ammunition cache. The last thing I remembered as I was falling asleep that night was the image of Dick Fitts' two-year-old son, Rich, in my mind.

## Travel

We left FOB-1 right after lunch on 18 DEC 68 and arrived at the Quang Tri launch site at 1330. We were scheduled for a 1600 launch. In addition to the standard Mission Package, we would have a flight of four F-4s flying Combat Air Patrol to intercept any NVA MiGs that might try to attack us. The weather was great, not a cloud in the sky, with a 5–10 MPH wind out of the northeast. That was also the orientation (direction) of the ridge on which our LZ was located. It should be a smooth landing.

We were traveling relatively light. We would go in late in the day concurrently with an airstrike on a bridge approximately 3,000 meters northwest of our LZ, designed to focus attention away from our insertion. Once on the ground we would move quickly to the storage area and attempt to recon the site before dark. Once it was dark, we would go in, make our deposits and head back to the LZ for a night pickup (very unusual). The Air Force would pound the bridge area again with F-4s to cover our extraction. Simple plan. In and out.

## Final Mission Brief

RT Alabama would be inserted with a UH-1D helicopter with a chase UH-1D, two Cobra gunships escorting the team UH-1D, two more Cobras on station, two A-1s on station, two F-4s flying Combat Air Patrol to keep the North Vietnamese MiGs away, a FAC/Covey directing the airstrike and two F-4s delivering the strike on the bridge. All missions in the DMZ and North Vietnam required F-4 Air Cover to fend off North Vietnamese MiGs.

## Insertion

After the Final Mission Briefing, Deck conducted a final team briefing and moved to the aircraft. The takeoff was smooth, and there was no anti-aircraft fire on the way to the target. The reports coming from the AO seemed to be good. I was excited about this mission. Go in. Do it. Get out. I'd done a lot of night extractions in Special Forces and Ranger training, so I wasn't concerned about this part of the mission.

As we turned on short-final I could see the F-4s pounding the bridge and surrounding area. I didn't see any activity around our LZ. Our approach was smooth and fast. Deck gave the signal to get on the skids. The plan was for the chopper to do a touch and go. We had to get off the skids fast because it was not going to stop. We jumped off, the chopper lifted off quickly, and then it hit us—CS gas! The NVA were gassing the LZ—and we didn't bring our masks! My eyes burned and watered, and it was difficult to breathe. That light breeze mentioned in the final mission brief brought a cloud of CS gas down the long axis of the LZ. Then to make it more exciting, the NVA opened fire on us.

I called Covey and told him what was going on and that we needed to be extracted. When he came back to me, he said the air crew did not have masks either. They could not come in to get us until the CS gas had dissipated. Covey turned the Cobras loose on the wood line at the northwest end of the LZ. The CS gas had started to dissipate quickly. It appeared to be a small force of about ten NVA at the LZ. Deck made the decision to go after them. It was like chasing rabbits. It only took about 15 minutes with the help of Covey and the Cobras to terminate them. They did not seem to fight like normal NVA.

Now we had a decision to make. It was going to be dark in about 45 minutes. Our entry had been compromised. Did we continue the mission even though they knew we were there, or did we abort? I recommended that we continue the mission. If we moved fast, we could get to the storage area before dark, see what it looked like and be ready to go in by 2200. By 2400 we could be on our way back to the LZ. If we ran into any problems, we would withdraw and bomb the storage site. We could still leave our packages there. Deck agreed. He told Covey our decision and briefed the team. We moved toward the storage area at a fast pace.

We arrived at the southeast side of the storage area about 15 minutes before dark and transmitted the "onsite" code word. We did not see any security or activity inside the area. It did not have a fence around it. I heard a couple short dog barks indicating they probably had security dogs. Our plan was to take them out with our .22 caliber pistols with integrated silencers if they came after us. I also had CS powder (with black pepper mixed in) with me. If they tried to use the dogs to track us, I could really mess up their nostrils.

Cowboy and I looked around and located the areas where we needed to plant the packages. Deck agreed to let Cowboy and me go into the area as a team and insert the Eldest Sons while he kept the team ready to provide overwatch support if we got into trouble and needed extracting. We had a plan. I encoded the plan and sent it to Covey, who had returned to an orbit near the AO to be available to provide support. Cowboy got what we needed, and we all rested until 2130. I sent the "starting insertion" code word to Covey.

It was pretty quiet at that point. Cowboy and I moved into the storage area and planted the mortar rounds first. They were big and heavy. We were glad to get rid of them. Next were the 12.7mm rounds then the 7.62mm.

I thought I heard something when we were finishing with the 7.62mm plant. I turned to see a dog in the attack position about three feet from me. He launched as I was bringing my .22 pistol up, and I managed to shoot him three times in the chest. He cried out, hit the ground at my feet and grabbed my ankle! I put two more in the side of his head and it was over, but I was sure we had attracted attention. I grabbed the dog's hind feet and dragged him into the bushes. Cowboy and I moved quickly toward the perimeter, but not directly toward Alabama. We made a right turn at the perimeter and moved quickly toward the team. As we got close, I used the running password, frog hair.

I sent the "insertion complete" code word to Covey that we had completed the plant and were moving toward the LZ. The team moved quickly to the southwest, staying in the valley for 300 meters, then curved around another 300 meters to the east and up the ridge 100 meters to the LZ. Covey told me the extraction team was ten mikes (minutes) out. We arranged the LZ marking team in a T formation, with the top of the T into the mild wind in the grass with flashlights with red filters on them. The extraction chopper approached with all lights off and identified the LZ marking as Tango. I gave Covey a "Roger that" and the chopper came in. The team boarded quickly and we were off. No shots fired! I saw Deck turn his head toward my side, and I quickly gave him a thumbs up and smile. He laughed.

We were debriefed when we got back to the launch site and flew back to FOB-1 the next morning. We got our new mission that afternoon.

## Lessons Learned

- CS gas was one of those things that we didn't plan for. It was such a rarity for the NVA to use it; we just didn't do it on this mission. Sometimes we would carry CS grenades and CS rounds for the M79 (40 mm grenades). If we carried CS, then we carried the masks too. If you used CS gas, you had better have a mask or you were going to be as bad off as the NVA, because without fail, the winds would change and it was going to come right back on you. Then you'd be in trouble.
- The new RT Alabama SOP—carry M-17 protective masks. I carried the rule to my future teams.
- Always plan for the unexpected.
- Train for night movement. RTs rarely move at night unless they are trying to escape. We need more training.
- We can execute a night raid.
- We can execute a night extraction.
- The dog at the ammunition cache was an adrenaline rush.
- Animals are the enemy too.
- A dog can take several hits from a .22 unless the bullets hit the right place—so can an NVA.
- This was a Demilitarized Zone (DMZ) operational area which meant that the rules were a little different. NVA MiGs were a possibility. The DMZ itself was considered a much more sensitive target politically.
- After this mission I started carrying an Eldest Son AK-47 magazine with me on most missions (unless we were using AK-47s). I was required to keep detailed notes on where and how I deployed it as an Easter egg for the NVA to find—and

maintain its security to prevent US and SOG members from accidentally using it.

- The first group of NVA ran from us! We were very aggressive, hunted them down and terminated them. They were guards. They were not the normal NVA warriors we fought.

**Post-Mission Training**

- Continue fitness training. For the most part, the team did not like it or want to do it. I began to camouflage it into mission pre-training by having the team carry their loadout weight for most of our training. I found them to be very strong for their size. They had been carrying a similar weight for a long time.
- We continued working on all IADs and standard operating procedures.
- The team members were not happy about the eating and hydration procedures but did it anyway.
- We did IAD practice on the range, expanded medical training, and focused more on hydration and dealing with dogs.
- We began to spend more time on situational awareness and natural night vision training.
- We spent time talking about and training to be more aggressive.

# RT Alabama Mission 4: Christmas Road Interdiction SOG #4 (23 DEC 68)

### Mission 4 Team Roster

| | |
|---|---|
| Deck | 1-0 |
| Thompson | 1-1 |
| Jones | 1-2 |
| Cowboy | Interpreter |
| Hoa | Pointman |
| Du | M-79 |
| Quan | Tail gunner |

## Background

We were approaching Christmas, 1968. President Lyndon Johnson called a cease fire in Vietnam for Christmas Day. The North Vietnamese claimed they were doing the same. There would be 24 hours of neither side shooting at one another. This had been going on for several years, with numerous violations by the North Vietnamese each year. In SOG, we had heard about the cease fire. No one thought it would apply to us. The cease fire would give the enemy a "free day" to move more troops and supplies from North Vietnam, Laos and Cambodia into South Vietnam.

On 21 DEC, SSG Deck and I were called into the FOB-1 Operations Center and told that RT Alabama was the next team up and for us to get ready to launch on the 23rd with the plan to stay at least through the 27th. This meant we would be deep inside Laos and near large concentrations of enemy on Christmas Day. I learned that the cease fire did not cover countries outside of the two Vietnams. No Christmas turkey dinner this year!

Our mission was to make sure that the NVA in our area of operation did not get a free day. We were to move to an observation point where we could observe and interdict supply traffic on a major shipping route from Laos into South Vietnam.

## Training

We began planning and training right away for our new mission. We planned to take a seven-man team. Quang's wounds would not be healed enough to go on this mission so he would remain behind to rest and heal. Quan would be ready to go. The team would be Deck, me, Jones, Hoa, Cowboy, Du and Quan. We would be using high powered binoculars, an SLR camera with a 900mm telephoto lens to photograph the traffic before we destroyed it. This equipment was new to our team, so we needed time to play with it both day and night. We also continued to do our regular team training, incorporating lessons learned from our last mission. We had a lot to do in a short period of time.

We trained a lot on IADs, photography, hiding the glare/reflection of the binoculars, our day defensive positions, RONs, Claymore rigging and placements, and navigating in that type of rugged terrain. Everything we planned to carry was evaluated for its usefulness. Weight was critical. I changed my food to a mixture of PIRs (Project Indigenous Rations) and LRPs. Rice, meat, fruitcake and the cereal bar became my primary food during missions. This gave me a lighter and less noisy way to eat. I also added Lomotil to create a little constipation—an antidiarrheal, antiperistaltic agent. It will stop you up! Didn't want to get caught with my pants down. But it has side effects!

Special Forces, and especially SOG, had its own "Q" (from the James Bond lore). Our indigenous forces (Vietnamese and especially the Montagnards) were getting diarrhea from eating US rations. Ben Baker wanted to create a ration that the indigenous forces could eat. He went to the US Navy and was told it would cost millions to create such a ration and take 2–3 years to complete the project.

Baker used $250 of his own money and within eight weeks, completed the Project Indigenous Ration (PIR). He found a private company willing to manufacture the meals for $1.00 apiece. He placed an order for 30,000 meals. By the end of the Vietnam war, his organization, the US Army Counter Insurgency Support Office (CISO), had sent over 66 million rations for use by the US and its allies.

I also made a "scoop" out of the bottom of the thick plastic bag in the PIR. I could use this to dip rainwater from the low places on my small, indigenous poncho to fill my canteen and to get water from streams. I found many uses for this scoop across time.

### Visual Reconnaissance (Aerial)

One tool the RTs had, in some cases, was a Visual Reconnaissance (VR) of the AO. The 1-0 and another team member, usually the 1-1 (assistant team leader/radio operator), would fly to the AO and observe and photograph the area from the air. The VR had to be designed not to call attention to the AO. This meant that the VR aircraft would only be in the AO a few minutes, as if crossing the area enroute to another location. This meant the 1-0 had to look quickly and get a lot of good pictures.

The VR aircraft would typically be a small O-1 with a Vietnamese Air Force pilot. Sometimes we would fly with a US Air Force FAC in an O-2 (push-pull aircraft). And in 1969 if you were really lucky (or not!) you might get to ride in an OV-10. When you flew with a FAC, you were going along on his mission of putting in air strikes near your AO with a couple of passes over your area. The FAC constantly flew a zig-zag path to make it more difficult to hit with anti-aircraft fire. It was sickening, literally. When he found his target, he would dive down to fire WP rockets to mark it as a target for the F-4s to hit. I knew my stomach would be in my throat. The pilot would dive right into the anti-aircraft and automatic weapons fire. Disney would never build a thrill ride that came close to that!

After firing two rockets, he would pull out of the dive and head almost straight up. The g-forces would crush me into my seat! I could not move. When he leveled off the ascent, my stomach was back in my throat again. After a few of these target-marking episodes, almost everyone who had flown with the FACs had the contents of their stomachs all over them and the aircraft. Fortunately, these missions only lasted 4–5 hours.

Deck scheduled a visual recon of our AO for Day 3 of our mission prep. This involved flying out to our area in a small Cessna fixed-wing aircraft with a Vietnamese Air Force pilot. I was not excited about this, but it would give us a chance to see the area from the air. I really hated sitting in the back seat. It was too difficult to get in and out of—especially in an emergency. Most of our time in Laos would be spent in areas other than ours. We didn't want to give away our AO. It would also give us a chance to get used to our big cameras. We took pictures of the LZs in the area, the ridgeline, cliffs and portions of the road that were visible. We could see some cliffs on the ridgeline we planned to use for observation. These could possibly support our mission. We even got to see an Air Force FAC working airstrikes with F-4s along the supply route.

The flight was rough, and the little plane bounced all over the sky. Deck and I were both on the verge of vomiting in the plane. In addition, we heard a lot of automatic weapons fire pass by us. The NVA knew we were up to something and really wanted to shoot us down. I was glad to get back to Da Nang! Unfortunately, this was the least

*Conrad "Ben" Baker Deputy Director of CISO*

| Long Range Patrol Ration: Example | Project Indigenous Ration: Example |
|---|---|
| Freeze-dried meal: *Chicken stew* *(8 meal types)* | Rice, 18 oz, pre-cooked, dehydrated |
| Accessory packet: *(instant coffee, cream substitute, sugar, salt, candy-coated gum, toilet paper, matches, 4 cigarettes)* | Dried fish or meat (5 types) |
| | Dehydrated Asian vegetables |
| Compressed fruitcake or chocolate bar | Sauces or spices |
| Cornflake bar | Vitamin pill |
| Tootsie rolls | |
| Oatmeal cookie | |

*LRPR vs PIR Rations*

brutal of all the VRs that I would conduct across the border. A Kingbee picked us up at Da Nang and flew us back to FOB-1. I was nauseated the rest of the day.

Our small photo lab at FOB-1 did a rush job on the film (it was all black and white in those days) and we used the pictures with the team that afternoon to plan our route, observation locations and alternate LZs. We did detail planning and then conducted rehearsals based on the data we had gathered.

## Launch Site

Before daylight on 23 DEC 68 our team was covertly loaded on CH-34 helicopters and flown to the Quang Tri launch site for a launch at 1000 hours. We did an equipment check and reviewed our five-day plan and IADs. It seemed like we were spending a lot of time at Quang Tri.

During the Final Mission Briefing we learned that the weather forecast was great for the next five days with only a few scattered showers predicted, mostly at night. We should have good conditions to interdict the highway. Everything was falling into place for a successful mission. Soon we were lifting off and flying away into the black hole.

## Insertion

Our FAC/Covey took up a position at a rendezvous position near the insertion area. Cobra gunships escorted the insertion aircraft to the landing zone and watched over us during the insertion, ready to provide close air support instantly if we made contact. Fortunately, the insertion went smoothly. We moved approximately 150 meters and made a security halt. After approximately ten minutes of adaptation, we had not detected anything unusual, so I sent that day's "Charlie-Two-Alpha" code to Covey that meant, "Team okay, moving east." The terrain was rugged and rocky with relatively thick vegetation which slowed our movement. On the positive side, the rocks provided a lot of cover if we made contact as we traveled toward our first planned observation point. Cover stops bullets. Concealment does not.

We spent an uneventful rest of the day slowly moving toward our first observation point where we could observe traffic flow on the large road that went through the valley. When we got to the small cliff, we did our normal fishhook maneuver to come back to the cliff. At the cliff, we did a security halt while Deck, Cowboy and I crawled forward to recon the site and determine the best way to secure the observation position. Then we brought the team forward, set up security, Claymores and toe poppers, and made sure everyone knew our different escape routes. It was very dangerous being up against a cliff. We could easily be surrounded with no escape except over the cliff—and that would be certain death. We emphasized to the team that we could not let the bad guys slip up on us.

Just as we were finishing our briefing, Du leaped forward and crawled quickly away from his position, making a lot of noise and startling the whole team! Quan, who had been next to him did the same thing. Du gave the signal for snake. I crawled carefully over to where Du had been and a saw a black and yellow Banded Krait, about five feet long with a highly toxic venom. The Banded Krait was one of 22 varieties of venomous snakes in our area. If it had bitten Du, he would have died before we could have gotten him out. Fortunately,

Yellow and black Banded Krait (Bungarus fasciatus) venomous and deadly. © Tom Charlton.

*Yellow and black Krait*

114

this type of snake is primarily nocturnal, and bites during the daytime are rare. I pinned it down with the butt of my CAR-15, cut its head off and tossed both pieces over the cliff. We did not want it crawling back into our site at night and biting someone—or the team spooked all night because they thought it might be back. I didn't mention that it probably had a mate somewhere close by.

It did not take long to spot activity on the road. Within about 30 minutes after reporting the activity, a pair of F-4s came out of nowhere and began pounding the vehicles and traffic on the road. It was exciting to watch, but we knew it wouldn't take long for the NVA to suspect that there was a team in the area—and that they were probably using the cliffs.

## First Night

About an hour before dark, we made the decision not to use the observation site as an RON. We didn't want to be against the cliff. We had been there long enough that we might have been detected, and the team was still spooked by the snake. We brought in our Claymores and toe poppers, moved to a rocky area with thick vegetation and set up our normal security. We did not have a view of the valley from this site, but it provided us much more initial protection and better access to escape routes.

We heard lots of activity in the valley during the night. The NVA were using the cover of darkness to recover their dead and any materials and vehicles they could salvage. New vehicles arrived and passed through the area headed south along their route to South Vietnam. We sent regular reports, but there were no air strikes during the night.

It rained for about an hour starting around 2330 hours. The temperature was in the low 90s and the rain felt cold. I used my small poncho to try to stay partially dry, with little success. I did however manage to catch some rainwater that I was able to scoop out and drink. The rain made it much easier to move undetected through the jungle because the sound of the rain masked the movement sound and made the ground, vegetation, leaves and sticks quieter when you stepped on them. All of this also made it much easier for the enemy to slip up on our position unnoticed. All team members remained awake while it was raining to help detect enemy movement and to reduce reaction time if we were discovered.

Sound traveled faster and longer when the air was damp. Any metallic sound or voice traveled easily. If we were in a static position or moving, we had to be careful not to bump our weapon against a tree or rock. The NVA often gave themselves away because they tended to carry their pots and pans on the outside of their rucksacks. These sounds often gave us advance warning. The team knew to be careful and listen for the NVA to make a mistake. Around 0245 hours we heard a small group move up the ridge.

## Day 2

As daylight dawned on Christmas Eve, all team members were alert and listening for the enemy. It wasn't uncommon for the NVA to attack at the Beginning of Morning Nautical Twilight (BMNT)—the last vestiges of darkness were still present, but the enemy could see for a short distance around them. This enabled them to move relatively quietly and accurately and get very close to us before we could see them. Throughout history, dawn has been a common time to attack. We also knew that in general, humans tended to be the sleepiest between 0300 and 0600 hours. We knew that BMNT that morning would occur at 0555 hours outside the jungle and approximately 0635 under the jungle canopy. We planned to begin moving to our new observation position around 0700 if everything seemed okay.

We had been moving for about 20 minutes when we heard the "clack" of two bamboo sticks hit together approximately 200 meters down the ridge and off to the east. Forty seconds later we heard a response clack that seemed to be the same distance but on the west side of the ridge. We had two trackers leading an NVA group up the ridge looking for us and attempting to flush us out of hiding so they could find us. This was not a good sign. To make it worse, we heard a couple of dog barks. I scattered some CS powder around the path we took as we moved toward the new observation point (OP). This would definitely slow the dog down once it got CS powder up its nose.

It took about an hour to get to the vicinity of the new OP. During that time, we continued to hear the bamboo clacking. They were still behind us. It was mid-morning and we had lost a lot of observation time.

We did not go to the next cliff as planned. We continued up the ridge past the cliff and found a rocky spot near the steep side of the ridge where we could put an observer in a tree. Between the sounds from the valley and what the observer could see from the tree, we could give Covey enough information for the Air Force to act on. We did a fishhook and came back to the rocks. I put out toe poppers and CS where we turned to go back to the rocks. We set up our defensive position and put Du in the tree. He was excited to get off the ground and away from any more snakes. I didn't mention the varieties that liked trees.

It did not take long for Du to start sending back information that we relayed to Covey. By 1130 the first airstrikes started hitting the area hard. This increased the NVA effort to find our location. The clackers were coming closer. I was concerned the dog might hear us, run ahead and move directly to us, missing the CS. I moved away from the team where I could have a better view of the approach the dog might take. I had been in position about 30 minutes when I heard the dog coming toward us. I knew his handler and trackers could not move that fast.

My Hi-Power .22 LR with integrated silencer pistol was ready. He knew where I was and was running directly at me. I waited until he was almost on me and hit him with four shots that put him down. The first one hit him in the head. He did not make a sound. The handler did not know which way the dog went in the thick vegetation and knew he could not call for him.

Soon we heard the trackers, handler and a small group of NVA go by us and continue up the ridge. That was close! We decided to stay where we were for our RON. It did not appear to be a suitable location for what we were doing. The trackers did not find us when they went by, so it was best not to move just then. It was almost dark, so we prepared for the evening, expecting more rain.

The traffic increased during the night and the F-4s made a lot of strikes in the dark. So far this had been a successful mission. The NVA were not getting a free day in this area. Santa was delivering a lot of presents to the NVA on Christmas Eve! It was a noisy night, but worth it. We had some heavy rains on and off, but the weather was clear in between.

### Day 3 (25 DEC) – We're Busted!

It was Day 3—25 DEC 1968 (Christmas Day)! We moved from our RON site back to the third and most distant cliff to set up our observation. It had rained hard during the night, and the terrain was slippery. We had to be careful. We observed a lot of traffic just after we got in position and reported it to Covey. In less than 20 minutes we had F-4s pounding them. We were able to provide targeting data for about two hours before everything appeared to have been destroyed.

The rain came back in, and we decided to take advantage of it and move away from the cliff. The search parties were coming closer to us each time they came by. It was early afternoon and we decided to take a break for a while. We put out two layers of Claymores, and I put out four toe poppers and two frag grenades with instant fuses and trip wire. There were some strange trees in that area. I don't know what they were called, but they almost looked like big rockets with fins. The roots came out of the ground and grew up the tree maybe 2–4 feet like rocket fins, 2–3 inches thick in most places. We were taking a break, and I thought I would lie down between the roots, and no one would be able to see me unless looking at just the right angle. I kept all my equipment on while we were taking a break.

We had been on the mission for three days. The Lomotil had done a great job of keeping my pants up, but an urgent time had come. I could go in my pants or take a chance and drop my pants. I chose the latter. The ridge dropped off steeply for a few feet on the other side of the tree. I felt like that was the safest place to go. I left my ruck and squatted behind the tree. After depositing three days of poop and covering it, I felt like a new warrior.

I quickly returned to my position between the roots and laid back against my ruck. Two minutes later we heard a toe popper explode, a loud scream, and almost simultaneously, a second toe popper explosion, followed immediately by a barrage of AK-47 fire. Some of it was in our direction, some of it in other directions. They didn't know exactly where we were, but in that first barrage, three AK-47 rounds came through the root on my left side and tore my shirt as they went across my chest and through the root on my right side. I had just exhaled. If I had just inhaled, the bullets would have taken the top of my chest off when they came across me. They grazed me just enough to draw blood. It was obvious that the roots were providing just concealment, not cover. I had to get behind the tree. I jumped behind the tree with my ruck (75 pounds) trailing me in my left hand.

I heard another toe popper go off followed by a loud scream, then the grenade I had left in that area with a trip wire. All the AK fire shifted toward our position now. They were trying to flank us with a group of about 20 NVA maneuvering around to our right to push our backs against the cliff. The grenade I had put on my side exploded and slowed their flanking movement. We had a full-fledged firefight going on with more NVA coming down the ridge.

Deck gave the command to detonate the first layer of Claymores. It was a tremendous explosion as seven Claymores exploded simultaneously. It was raining debris, dirt, pieces of trees, rocks and body parts. A bloody arm landed right in front of where I had been lying between the roots. A thick smoke and smell (strangely familiar) covered the jungle. It temporarily stopped their assault, but the automatic weapons fire picked up again. It was easy to tell that the group was a lot smaller because of the lower volume of fire, but more NVA were coming.

As soon as the team got near my position and below me, I was getting ready to set off the other layer of Claymores when a B-40 rocket hit the tree in front of the one I was behind. Fortunately, my ruck was still setting on the edge of the bank and provided me some protection. It was riddled with small shrapnel. I ducked behind the tree and set off the last layer of Claymores. This group only had five Claymores (7.5 pounds of C-4 with 3,500 steel balls), but it ripped a hole in the NVA assault. They were stunned—physically and psychologically. I don't think the NVA believed we had more Claymores to set off. I also got another taste of the impact of adrenaline. When I came out from behind the tree, I had to grab my rucksack with my left hand. It

*The Rocket Tree*

weighed probably 75 pounds and I'm not a big guy, but I tossed that rucksack around like it was a pillow. I took it with me as we fought our way down the ridge and toward the LZ, but I paid for it later on. After we got extracted, I realized I had pulled muscles in my shoulder because they just weren't designed to handle that much weight. But I had so much adrenaline pumping through my system I didn't notice at the time.

Cowboy had dropped off with me and was providing overwatch fire as I scampered down to him. Deck and Jones were leading the team down the ridge toward the LZ. The rocky terrain was providing us some cover, but the NVA were able to take advantage of it too. As soon as the first toe popper exploded, I had notified Covey that we were in heavy contact and a Prairie Fire. Usually, Covey could have assets on site within 30–45 minutes. But it was Christmas Day, a holiday, and not a lot of assets were just hanging out nearby. It was a good thing that we notified Covey right away. We needed Close Air Support (CAS) and gunships immediately. We knew it would be a while before things would calm down enough to get the extraction ship in.

The NVA were not stopping. Cowboy and I went into a delaying technique with Claymores on time fuses that we were becoming pretty effective at using. The NVA appeared to have run right up on the first delayed Claymore based on the screams and yelling that we heard. Cowboy said, "VC angry!" My response was, "Good! That means we're really hurting them!" We left another one as we ran to catch up with the team. We were shooting a lot of them, but it seemed that it was taking 2–3 hits to put them down. Cowboy said, "VC take drugs!" He must have been correct because they were hard to stop. I noticed that three hits on automatic had a lot more knock down power than three fast, individual shots. When I hit them on auto they dropped immediately. I made a mental note to remember this for later. Covey told me he had a couple of SPADs with 20mm and napalm 20 minutes out. I updated our situation.

We were still receiving a lot of fire into our area as we caught up with Deck. I updated Deck on what Covey said and about the problem putting the NVA down. We had a steep grade to go down to the LZ and no protection once we got there. We decided to stay where we were in the rocks. Suddenly, things got quiet. Too quiet! They were up to something. We decided to put out four Claymores on the most likely avenues of attack. We redistributed ammunition and moved our extra frag and WP grenades out of our rucks. We were expecting a heavy assault to begin any minute. You could hear a pin drop! Then, at a very low volume, I heard . . .

"Bravo Six, this is Covey."

"Six, go."

"SPADs (A-1s) are here. Mark your position with smoke and tell me where you want the 20 mike mike."

I threw a smoke grenade and said, "Roger, smoke out."

"Sandy Lead (the lead A-1) identifies yellow."

"Six, Roger. Make first run northwest to southeast 100 meters northwest of smoke. Danger close!"

"Roger. Keep your heads down!"

I heard the engines on the A-1s whining as they built up speed on their way in, then the automatic weapons fire toward the planes, followed by the chatter of each plane's 20mm cannons spitting out the HE rounds. That was followed by the exploding rounds. Some were going off in the trees and some on the ground. Shrapnel was flying everywhere, as were tree limbs, dirt and mud. I could hear people screaming. Within seconds, the second A-1 opened fire. We could tell from the screams that the rounds had found some of the NVA. They knew it was now or never. The gun runs effectively triggered the NVA assault on our position. We thought there were 20–30 of them left. It was closer to 200.

One thing I had learned is that if you are not moving, you are dying because the NVA are maneuvering into position to cut off your escape. The NVA had managed to move so that they had us flanked on three sides. The only way we could escape them was to run into the open LZ. They were assaulting. We set off four of our remaining seven Claymores to slow their assault. Four simultaneous Claymore detonations and 2,800 steel balls traveling 4,000 feet per second is devastating to an assaulting force. It made the survivors stop and think about coming after us.

I told Covey what was happening.

"Covey, this is Six. Have one SPAD put napalm where it made its first gun run and the second to drop his napalm flying northeast to southwest 100 meters north of the smoke. This is danger close. Do it now and come back around with guns in the same place!"

"Covey, Roger. You guys take cover and take a deep breath. It's going to get very hot instantly! The gates of hell are about to open!"

"Six, copy that!"

Meanwhile we were being hit with a hail of AK-47 and RPD (machine gun) fire and B-40 rockets. We returned fire and lobbed frag grenades from behind the rocks. It was so smoky you could barely see. When we heard the planes getting close, we each threw a grenade, took cover and took a deep breath. The air was about to be so hot it would fry the inside of your lungs.

The fire ball, heat and smoke were tremendous, and the napalm sucked all the oxygen out of the air. Air was available, but it was hot, smoky and choking and had no oxygen. We could see NVA running around like human torches covered in fire and screaming. It reminded me of the Jody call that started with, "Napalm, napalm sticks like glue . . . ." We took out all the torches we could see as fast as we could. It was the humane thing to do. We could hear a lot of NVA screaming that we couldn't see. The terrified survivors were running back up the hill. Once you have seen the gates of hell open, you do not want to see it again!

We were still receiving a lot of fire from the south.

"Covey, this is Six. That was fantastic! We are still receiving fire from the south. Make one more napalm run 100 meters south of the smoke flying northeast to southwest, danger close!"

"This is Covey, Roger. We also have four gunships five mikes out."

"This is Covey, napalm 30 seconds out. Take cover!"

The napalm was once again surreal. The screams! The choking, super-heated air! The smoke! The smell of burning and charred flesh! We took out the human torches we could see. A couple of our guys could not take the smell and could not hold back the vomit.

"Covey, this is Six, that was great! Creedence Clearwater Revival should be here! The devil is on the loose! Have the SPADs make another run on each side of us with the remainder of their 20 mike mike and put the last napalm 200 meters up the ridge from our position."

"Covey, Roger. Gunships are on station and extraction bird is ten mikes out."

"This is Six, Roger. When the devil ships leave, have the gunships work around the LZ as we move down to the LZ. I'm popping another smoke so they know for sure where we are. Smoke out."

"Covey, Roger. Gunslinger lead identifies green."

"Roger that. We're moving."

Going down the steep part of the embankment I slipped and went feet first into a big pile of fresh elephant poop. It was all over my boots and pant legs, and it was ripe with a very strong odor. This was literally a crappy day!

Once we had suppressed most of the fire, we were able to bring in an extraction ship. As we were lifting off, still under fire, Deck and I both threw a red smoke grenade—meaning the LZ was "cleared hot," take out all living creatures. Covey worked the area over as we pulled away.

"Covey, this is Dynamite. We really appreciate your help. We could not have made it without you! Thank all of your assets for us. See you back at the ranch."

"Roger that, Dynamite! You guys did a great job today!"

As soon as we got far enough away from the LZ, and most of the NVA fire had shifted away from us, I looked over at Deck to see his big smile and thumbs up. He wasn't smiling, and there was no thumbs up! I thought, *Crap! He must have been hit.* I crawled across the guys to get to him, grabbed him by the shoulder and asked, "Deck! You okay?"

He slowly looked up at me and said, "Lieutenant, I'm done! This was my last mission." Then he looked away. I went back to my position in the helicopter. A lot of questions popped into my mind. I would talk to him more about this when we got to the launch site.

When we reached the launch site, I immediately went to him. "What's going on?" I asked. He said, "I've completed my mission requirement and I'm going to move to a different job when we get to CCN. I would appreciate it if you wouldn't say anything about it. I'll tell the team when the time is right."

We did a quick debrief and flew back to what was left of FOB-1. We got there after dark to find the Mess Sergeant had saved our Christmas meal for us—steak, if I remember correctly. It tasted really good. But the best part was that FOB-1, even almost totally closed, did not forget about us. Phu Bai was alright! But this was the end of Phu Bai, FOB-1. It was being closed as an FOB and the teams distributed around the other FOBs. We would be the last team out.

RT Idaho with John Stryker Meyer ("Tilt") and Lynne Black ("Blackjack") had barely managed to escape from Laos that day too and had already been transported to CCN. RT Alabama would rest that night and fly to CCN the following morning.

I had been on four missions with RT Alabama in less than a month. We were in heavy contact and a Prairie Fire Emergency each time. I learned a lot from Deck, the firefights, Covey, Close Air Support (CAS) from all types of aircraft, and others I talked to during that time. I felt confident that I was ready to lead a team. SSG Deck agreed and gave me a 1-0 recommendation. I was going to miss the team and Deck, even though he was going to CCN with me. He would be leaving the team for a non-operator role. I was being assigned to a different team as a 1-0. I was excited about having my own team but had grown close to Cowboy and the others. Deck and I would still see each other from time to time, but we would both be busy in our new jobs.

CCN was a much larger compound than FOB-1 with lots of people, teams and activity. I had heard that they were experiencing issues between some of the officers and NCOs. A lieutenant had been killed on the mountain, and they endured frequent rocket and sniper attacks. I was sure I would have to make adjustments, but it would be an adventure.

**Lessons Learned**

- If you can be heard, you can be found. If you can be found, the team can be killed.
- A three-round hit on auto had much more knock down power

than three rapid single shots.

- Leeches are bad, but snakes can kill you. Du would have died if bitten.
- If you are not moving, you are losing the battle—you are in the process of dying.
- Claymores on time fuses stunned the assaulting NVA. It made the survivors stop and think. They are human. They don't want to get shredded.
- When napalm explodes it really does make you think the gates of hell have opened.
- When you are under a jungle canopy it's hard to tell where the napalm cannister will explode and where the napalm will land after falling through the trees.
- Napalm was a very scary and powerful weapon—the NVA hated it.
- The encounter with the banded krait helped me make the decision to carry a KA-BAR as my primary knife. A little extra distance between my hand and the snake's fangs would have been nice. The KA-BAR would also give me more ability to "hack" if I need to cut limbs (wood or bone).

# PART 3

# Chapter 6

## Command and Control North (FOB-4)

*CPT Welch's DEROS Party CCN 1969 (Picture courtesy of Russ Mann,
FOB-3, FOB-2 1968)*

*Without the uniforms, it could be a college frat party picture. Hard to
believe their job was so desperately dangerous that only being wounded
was a good thing. They had the power to call down death from the sky.
They operated in small teams far from friendly forces. Alone in hostile
environments. Yet here they are with young happy faces. I've always told
people the most dangerous men I knew were really nice guys when they
weren't working.*

—Russ Mann, FOB-3 & FOB-2, 1968

## Teammates/Friends KIA/MIA JAN 69

SSG James M. Hall, KIA JAN 1
SP4 Wayne L. Hawkes, KIA JAN 1
SSG Michael J. McKibban, KIA JAN 1
SSG Gerald F. Apperson, KIA JAN 8
SP4 Bill F. Williams, KIA JAN 8

FOB-4 at Da Nang transformed into Command and Control North (CCN) in late 1967. It had only been in existence for about 18 months. This was a top-secret base belonging to MACV-SOG. It was structured with the typical military headquarters organizations: Command, S-1 (Personnel), S-2 (Intelligence), S-3 (Operations), S-4 (Supply), Medical, Meteorological, Aviation, etc., plus Recon Company (with approximately 20 Recon Teams of 9–12 Operators each and Hatchet Force Companies (with approximately 200 commandos each).

Recon Teams at CCN were assigned targets in the northern part of southeast Asia. The Hatchet Force Companies/Platoons were assigned larger targets requiring more firepower and staying power.

CCN also managed Marble Mountain with its two Combat Outposts (COP). People had been killed on the mountain as well as inside the caves. The COPs were attacked in some manner almost every night. The mountain provided an impressive "light show" most nights with red and green tracers, explosions and flares.

CCN was a large site located on the beach in Da Nang. The South China Sea was about 100 meters outside the perimeter wire on the eastern side of the compound. The south side was only 200 meters from the base of Marble Mountain which jutted 450 feet straight up out of the sand. CCN was one big sand lot. It was hit frequently by rockets, mortars, sniper fire and occasional sappers. It was critical that everyone knew where their defensive position was and how to safely get there when the siren went off—usually in the middle of the night!

The American mess hall had better food than you would expect in a war zone. The indigenous population of CCN had their own mess hall serving ethnic food. The ethnic groups (Vietnamese, Montagnard, Chinese Hmong, Laotian) had their own eating schedules.

Unfortunately, the groups did not like each other. Everyone in the camp was armed and if you did not space out the feeding of the ethnic groups, it could easily result in a firefight in the mess hall.

## Recon Company

When I arrived at CCN, CPT Welch was the Recon Company CO, and Campbell was the First Sergeant. I was welcomed to Recon Company, processed in quickly, given a "Get out of jail free" card and assigned as 1-0 of RT Michigan.

CPT Welch, the Recon Company commander spent about an hour with me asking about my background, experience and my goals. He was a black belt in martial arts and told me he wanted us to incorporate that into team training. We seemed to get along well.

## RT Michigan Prep

RT Michigan had a reputation as a solid team and had lost its last two 1-0s. Unlike RT Alabama, RT Michigan was a Montagnard team. Montagnard is a broad term left over from the French colonial period in Vietnam that refers to tribes (mountain people/dweller) living in the central highlands of Vietnam. They tended to be a little smaller and darker than the Vietnamese and had their own languages (tribe dependent). They grew up in the jungle and were very skilled at living and fighting in the jungle environment.

In my experience with them, the Yards did not like the Vietnamese. I would need to adapt from the Vietnamese culture and superstitions to that of the Montagnards. For example, on day one, Bargewell (the team 1-1), a few team members and I were walking along the street in front of Recon Company when Chung the Yard next to me reached over and gently took my hand. Bargewell saw the shocked look on my face and quickly said, "He will be insulted if you don't hold his hand. He is offering his respect and friendship to you as the new 1-0. It doesn't mean anything else." I continued to walk down the street hand-in-hand with my new mercenary Yard friend. I had a lot to learn.

### RT Michigan Team Members

| Name | Position |
| --- | --- |
| LT Henry Thompson | 1-0 |
| SP4 Eldon Bargewell | 1-1 |
| SSG Joe Nash | 1-2 |
| Cantua | Interpreter |
| Camba | Pointman |
| Hieng | M-79 |
| Acat | Tail Gunner |
| Aita | Alternate Point |
| Chung | Alternate Tail Gunner Scout 1 |
| Scout 2 | |
| Scout 3 | |

Nash had some team experience but had joined Michigan the day before me. Eldon Bargewell was the 1-1 when I took over as 1-0. He was a Specialist 4th Class (SP4) at that point and already had a solid reputation. I had asked about Bargewell before I went to CCN. Everyone I talked to said, "Bargewell is a very good Operator." I also

*Recon Company Sign CCN 1969*
*(Picture courtesy of LT Henry Thompson)*

found out that he had been asking about me.

I asked him the first day what he had found out. He said, "I talked to SFC Jones—and I have total faith in him—and he said Thompson is the only Lieutenant I've ever met that you can give a map and compass to and he can give you 10-digit coordinates to where you are standing. He can navigate to anywhere you want to go—and he's been proven under fire on several missions. You just don't find Lieutenants like that." Bargewell said that was good enough for him.

I was impressed with Bargewell right from the beginning. He was very knowledgeable and a great Operator. He had been at Khe Sanh with a team during the siege of Khe Sanh. They were hammered for 77 days by a massive NVA force. Bargewell had recruited some of the RT Michigan team members. This was a Yard team and they all liked him and had a lot of respect for him. He was a smart guy. Everything about him said warrior. I figured if he didn't get killed, he was going to be a legend in the Special Ops world at some point. Sure enough, Bargewell remained in Spec Ops, SOG, Rangers, Delta and SOCOM throughout his career and retired as a Major General and Special Ops legend. We remained friends until his death on April 29, 2019.

At the Operations Center I met with the Operations Officer who managed the area that RT Michigan would most likely be operating in and got as much information from him as I could. I wanted to know what the AO was like, what types of missions were most common there, other teams that operated in this area and how soon he thought we would receive a mission. He would not tell me about other teams but did share about the AO. I knew I would get a lot more information once we were assigned a mission.

I began to sketch out my plan for building the team trust required for becoming the 1-0 of RT Michigan. I had a lot to learn about Yards. They were different than the Vietnamese I had been working with. My network consisted of Bargewell, Nash and other 1-0s of Yard teams. It was going to be interesting.

## Team Training

I had learned a lot from my onboarding with RT Alabama and how things worked in combat. My plan for integrating into Michigan was much better focused than with RT Alabama. I needed to assess RT Michigan's performance baseline and that of the individual members. I would begin working from there to turn a good team into a great team. All the components and talents were present. They just needed to be fine-tuned.

I used my first day with RT Michigan to get to know each team member, including Bargewell and Nash. I spent time on the range learning how they had been taught to do different IADs, the commands to initiate them, how they moved, what they did when they stopped— enemy, break, security, etc.—hand and arm signals, how they used Claymores and toe poppers, handled wounded, how they set up and secured an RON, what they ate, how they ate and a layout of the equipment they normally carried. I took detailed notes, and in some cases, pictures. I needed to know where they were in terms of basic

*My "Get out of jail free card" or*
*"One of the most dangerous men on the planet. Give him whatever he*
*wants." (Picture courtesy of LT Henry Thompson)*

operations. I tried not to look shocked with some of what I saw them do. I would have to be very careful how I went about modifying their tactics and teaching new ones.

That evening I ate dinner with Bargewell and Nash to find out their thoughts about the team and its members, which gave me an opportunity to learn about their knowledge, philosophy and beliefs as they answered questions about the team. When I got back to my room, I captured key thoughts about the team and my 1-1 and 1-2. I realized I had a lot of work to do and could be given a mission at any time.

I met Bargewell and Nash for breakfast to talk about the day's activities and get their buy-in. I laid out a general plan for the next few days that would address some of the issues they were concerned about and how we could take a really good team to the next level. They added some great ideas and suggestions of their own. We were coming together quickly as a team. They seemed to go along with how I wanted to do it.

That day we would focus on basic tactics, modifying some of the IADs and doing some live fire on the range. The next day would be a continuation and expansion of our operating procedures and live fire. By the end of the week, we would be practicing all of our tactics and SOPs in the jungle on Monkey Mountain. I thought, If we're lucky, we might even find some targets that shoot back!

One of the most important SOG Rules I had learned with RT Alabama was you have to practice, practice, practice. One of the most critical skill sets we had to know was the trauma ABCs: 1) Clear the airway to keep the breathing, 2) Stop the bleeding (many SOG members died from bleeding out), and 3) Control for shock. (Today ABC stands for Airway, Breathing and Circulation.) I scheduled a training session on each of these with the CCN medical team. The team was okay with this training until we got to use the Ringer's solution. I made everyone practice putting in an IV. I went first with Cantua inserting an IV in me. Then I did him.

When we went on a mission, we were out there for so long that the Americans carried a 1-0 medical kit. This kit included medications. All other team members carried an indigenous medical kit, Ringer's solution, field bandages, tourniquets, and triangular bandages. When someone got hit and died, most of the time he died from bleeding to death. If we could get the bleeding stopped in time, the person might have a chance to survive.

My thinking was—especially after my first firefight when I was having a hard time getting a magazine loaded in my weapon—I don't want one of my guys trying to put a needle in my vein for the first time while he is being shot at and have him jabbing the needle all over my arm while I'm lying there bleeding to death. It was also very important to know how and where to apply a tourniquet. It's more difficult than it looks even if people are not shooting at you.

Practice was important, so we swapped partners and did it again. Then again. Going forward, we would do this training before every mission. Yes, the medics supervised us, kept us sterile and cleaned us up after we finished. We could not afford to get an infection.

The best way not to bleed out was not to get hit in the first place. I had been trained from day one in the military that, if you can be seen, you can be hit. If you can be hit, you can be killed. It made sense to spend some time on being "invisible" in the jungle. We even created a signal for "be invisible" to keep invisibility top of mind. Invisibility training is about how not to be heard, smelled or seen (visually). There were no spices or sauces in meals, and to the degree that we could, all meal containers were opened before the mission (no tearing, wrinkling or any other container noise—no metal cans from American rations).

This was not popular, but the team agreed to the rule. We actually did some practice to be sure we could open what we planned to carry quietly. We also replaced the snaps on canteen pouches with wooden buttons. Silence and no smell were critical. During the last three days before a mission there were to be no showers or soap—and wear the fatigues you were going to wear on the mission after they had been washed in plain water. Later we would add eating a similar diet to the NVA during the last three days. What you eat has a lot to do with fecal matter smell. RT poop needed to smell like NVA poop. During our pre-combat inspection everyone (including me) had to jump up and down to make sure nothing made noise.

We also practiced effective camouflage (no red scarves, unpainted smoke or white phosphorous grenades, or bare metal on LBE, etc.). We practiced movement techniques, e.g., lateral movement is the easiest to spot. Even when moving directly toward the enemy, if you turned your head from side-to-side looking for them, your face would give you away. "Everything that gives you away gives the enemy away."

The NVA seemed to like to use dead foliage to camouflage themselves and their positions—especially ambush positions. I demonstrated to the team what foliage does when it is not getting enough water—it turns the bottoms of the leaves up trying to collect more water. The bottoms of leaves tend to be a lighter shade than the tops. This lighter shade is very obvious when next to leaves with the tops facing up/out. I think the team members knew this but had not thought about it in terms of camouflage and trying to hide. Now they would be on the lookout for vegetation that did not match.

We spent time on the range practicing with Claymores, learning to set them up in "layers" and detonating them simultaneously. I explained what a powerful weapon Claymores were and that I wanted each person, except the point man and M-79 gunner, to carry at least two (7 pounds) and most likely three (10.5 pounds) Claymores instead of the one they had carried previously. This would give an eight-man team approximately 24 Claymores, way beyond what the "normal" SOG team carried. They also knew that the blasting cap had to be kept separated from the Claymore until it was deployed—and if they recovered the Claymore, they had to take the blasting cap out of it.

We trained on using the Claymores (and two-pound blocks of C-4) with time fuses so the 1-2 and tail gunner could more effectively delay NVA who were chasing us. I also showed them what happens when you set a WP grenade up against the front of a Claymore. Stunning! But you had to make sure you were far enough away from it when it detonated. It was best if the Claymore/WP were in front of a tree facing the NVA. I trained everyone on how to use the delaying tactics and let the team experience how long a 15-second and 30-second time fuse burns. It sounds obvious, but they needed to experience it a few times before combat. You don't realize how short 15 seconds is when you have to get away from a Claymore with bad guys shooting at you so the concussion doesn't knock you unconscious or kill you.

I also told the team that I wanted most of us to increase the number of frag grenades we carried from five (4.4 pounds) to ten (8.8 pounds) for each person except the point man and M-79 gunner. With an eight-man team we would be carrying approximately 80 fragmentation grenades. We carried a lot of area weapons for their large killing radius with shrapnel going out in all directions. Plus, these weapons could kill more enemy at one time than a single bullet from a rifle. The M-79 gunner carried fifty rounds of 40mm (25 pounds) and each team member carried eight rounds (four pounds) for a total of 98 rounds of High Explosive, buckshot, CS gas, smoke and flares mixed in based on mission requirements.

### Monkey Mountain

When I asked Operations where I could train my team in a relatively safe jungle environment, the closest and best option was Monkey Mountain. This area was located on a peninsula, almost an island, across from the Da Nang Bay. We could actually see it from CCN. MAJ Sims in Operations said he could get a couple of Kingbees to drop us off on a little beach area and we could walk up toward the lighthouse and stop to train where we wanted to. We would need to be careful to watch for Viet Cong who occasionally found their way to the Mountain. This was exciting!

I got with Bargewell and Nash and set up a morning insertion with an evening extraction the following day. This would give us almost two days of light and one night to practice. The team was actually more excited about it than I thought they would be. The next day was a good training day at CCN followed by packing for our simulated mission. We planned to take the whole team and full combat load to see how we handled the weight.

It was a simulated mission. We ran from the Kingbees into the jungle, moved 100 meters and stopped for a security halt. Then we processed our movement and what we got from the security halt—smells, sounds, tastes, etc. Aita said he could smell a cooking fire from the lighthouse even though we were a half mile away. They were cooking fish. That started a lot of fruitful discussion.

### RT Michigan Pre-Mission Training
*(All team members)*

| Name | Position |
|------|----------|
| LT Henry Thompson | 1-0 |
| SP4 Eldon Bargewell | 1-1 |
| SSG Joe Nash | 1-2 |
| Cantua | Interpreter |
| Camba | Point |
| Hieng | M-79 |
| Acat | Tail Gunner |
| Aita | Alternate Point |
| Chung | Alternate Tail Gunner |
| Scout 1 | M-79 |
| Scout 2 | Gunner |

Then we moved up the mountain practicing our invisibility, stopping often to demonstrate techniques. The Yards had jungle skills and readily shared them. They were beginning to see how we were becoming a better team. It was a very hot and humid trip up to the lighthouse. When we got to the lighthouse, we conducted a surveillance of the area. After moving 300 meters away from it we did a debrief of what we learned and discussed how we would attack it, take a prisoner from it, etc. It was a good tactical discussion that got the team thinking about tactics. We also got in a lot of practice with all of our hand and arm signals.

We moved farther down the ridge and found a good RON site while it was still light. The team moved in and set up the RON site complete with Claymores. Then we did a walkthrough of likely avenues of approach, how the NVA might attack the RON and how we would defend it and escape to a RP during darkness. We practiced using the running password, Hens Teeth. We occupied the RON position and went through "wake ups," and other security procedures during the night. We ate shortly after first light and used the rest of the day to practice IADs, tactics, fighting back on different types of terrain, delaying actions, carrying wounded, etc., until time came for the choppers to pick us up. We used the pickup as a simulated extraction under fire complete with smoke.

When we arrived back at CCN we did a debrief and AAR of our "mission" and what we had learned. Everyone, including Bargewell and Nash, seemed pleased with the outcome of our training mission. The AAR has unanimously been one of the most useful tools for all the military and civilian units I have worked with over the last 50+ years.

The team was ready. The next morning, we received a Warning Order for our first real SOG mission together. I was pumped.

## RT Michigan Mission 1: Walk-In SOG #5 (12 JAN 69)

*A team is more powerful than a group of individuals. Synergy: 1+1>2.*
*Leadership creates the synergy that transforms individuals into a team.*
—Henry L. Thompson, Ph.D., 1970

### Mission 1 Team Roster

| Name | Position |
|------|----------|
| LT Henry Thompson | 1-0 |
| SP4 Eldon Bargewell | 1-1 |
| SSG Joe Nash | 1-2 |
| Cantua | Interpreter |
| Camba | Pointman |
| Hieng | M-79 |
| Acat | Tail Gunner |
| Aita | Alternate Pointman |

My first mission as 1-0 of RT Michigan was to provide assistance to a Hatchet Force Platoon, led by my friend CPT Glen Jordan, that would be interdicting a resupply route. RT Michigan would be operating across the road from the HF providing security, and if necessary, reinforcements. The operation would begin with an insertion of the Hatchet Force Platoon (45–50 people). RT Michigan would conduct a clandestine insertion in a unique manner.

The plan called for RT Michigan to be inserted into Laos by "walking across the border" from a 101st Airborne Division company temporarily positioned at the border. Our plan was to dress like members of the 101st and fly into their company area on a resupply helicopter, as if we were replacement troops coming to join the fight.

They put us inside the perimeter but in a "hot" section. The Company First Sergeant said, "You'll need to dig in." All of my guys looked around and said, "We no dig!" I said, "You need to dig fighting positions. You're out here with a conventional unit, and bullets will be going everywhere tonight. The 101st guys have not seen you. You may be mistaken for VC/NVA in the dark tonight! You need to dig in." It was a good thing we did because the company got hit hard that night. It was nice to be able to get down in a hole and let the company fight it out with the bad guys.

While the team was digging fighting positions, Bargewell and I met with the Company Commander, a platoon leader whose men would be on the water resupply the next morning, and their Forward Artillery Observer (FAO). I laid out our plan on a makeshift sand table solely with "need to know" information. I included phase lines (PL). For example, PL Snake, meant we had crossed the river. What surprised the 101st coordination team the most was when I said, "I want you to pre-plan and register 81mm mortar, 105mm and 155mm howitzer artillery targets at these coordinates (marked on the sand table). Name this one Target Monday, this one Tuesday, then Wednesday, Thursday and Friday, respectively. All the targets together make up Target Weekend. Preset all the targeting data now. If we get in trouble, I'm just going to call the name of the Target and 'fire for effect' (to fire three rounds from all the artillery guns as fast as possible) or 'adjust fire.' I'm not going to give you coordinates. You must have these already pre-planned and registered. When I say 'Tuesday,' I expect to hear the rounds coming." I had never been close enough to the border to have friendly artillery on SOG missions before. I would have NVA artillery fired at me on several occasions. It was not a good feeling. This was going to be great. I planned for it. I planned targets throughout our

AO. The company coordination team was surprised at the detail of our plan, even the Company Commander. They had not heard anyone plan targets like that before. We did it all the time in Ranger training. (Two years later, a fellow Ranger Instructor would tell me that a friend of his who had been a Company Commander told him about a Special Forces Lieutenant who gave him the most impressive mission briefing he saw during his tour in Vietnam.)

The next morning, just after first light, RT Michigan mixed in with the water supply team members, dressed like them with steel helmets, flak jackets, etc., and went down to the river to retrieve water. When we got to the river, we changed into our "Batman suits" and gave the water team our helmets and flak jackets. They put them in bags and carried them back up with the water while we crossed the river (South Vietnam–Laos border) into the jungle on our mission, hoping that the NVA did not realize we had entered Laos.

Jordan's Hatchet Force Platoon had been inserted much farther out in the valley late in the afternoon the day before. Our insertion was different than normal, but a cool way to do it. And it appeared to have worked.

We moved quickly but stealthily away from the 101st. We had a long way to go. I called in the PL "Snake" to the 101st FAO and Covey. I was moving behind Camba, the point man, Bargewell was in the middle of the formation and Nash at the rear in front of Acat, the tail gunner. I liked to keep the Americans spread out to make it more difficult to get all three of us at once. The terrain was thick and mountainous. We wanted to get at least 200 meters before we did a security halt. We needed to adapt to the jungle environment. Fortunately, we didn't have to get rid of the sensations of an hour plus helicopter ride. We found a place at 225 meters that gave us the security we wanted and far enough away from the river not to hear it. The jungle settled down around us and we adjusted to our new environment. I looked back at the team and gave the signal that we were moving out. Bargewell and Nash gave a confirmatory head nod.

Camba began to pick a route through the thick vegetation with the least lateral movement relative to where the enemy might be. I had spent a lot of time teaching the team about being invisible in the jungle. Lateral movement made you visible very quickly. Over the years, SOG lost a lot of point men and tail gunners. Being invisible wasn't just about sound. Camba was already good at invisibility and was getting better quickly.

We continued to move until we got close enough to the road to hear any traffic on it. We set up our security, Claymores, etc., and began listening and reporting to the HF platoon by radio. I gave Covey our PL for the day one observation point. After about an hour we heard a group of 20–25 NVA pass by us moving rapidly up the ridge. All indications were that they did not know we were in the area. They seemed to be focused on the HF and did not notice us. The enemy's movement in the area seemed to be limited to the main trails running along the center of the ridge lines.

At about 1630 we decided to look for an RON site. There were trails everywhere, some more traveled than others. We found a site that provided us the best combination of concealment and cover in the area. Bargewell and Nash wanted to stay back down closer to the river. I told them that would put us too far away from the HF. The site we had found would provide what we needed for the night. Claymores were the key. Neither one of them had been on a team that carried the number of Claymores (20) and frag grenades (70) we were carrying. I could tell there would be techniques we would be using that would make them uncomfortable until they saw them work. We set up and put the Claymores out in two layers like we rehearsed during pre-mission training.

Just after dark, the NVA fired a half dozen mortar rounds at the HF. Fortunately, we could hear them clanging and banging around as they did their fire mission. The mortar rounds hit outside the HF perimeter and did not cause any physical damage to the HF but did scare them. They knew more would be coming. Bargewell and I got under my poncho with a red pen light and looked at the map. We estimated their position relative to Target Wednesday. I called Covey and the 101st FAO.

"Covey, Xray Five. Stay two clicks southeast of Wednesday, over."

"Covey, Roger. We are clear."

"Eagle 26, this is Xray Five. Fire mission, over."

"Eagle 26, Roger. Send it."

"Xray Five, from Target Wednesday, direction 350, drop 200. Fire for effect, over."

"Eagle 26, Roger, stand by."

"Eagle 26, rounds in the air."

"Eagle 26, Splash, over."

"This is Xray Five, rounds on target! Great work. Thanks."

In a matter of less than two minutes, we had sent a fire mission to the 101st Airborne company FAO and had nine rounds of 105mm high explosive in the air descending toward the location where we had made an educated guess that the NVA were firing from. They were seconds away from getting a dose of their own medicine. The loud sound split the relatively quiet jungle when the rounds hit. Their launch site was out in the relative open. The rounds were close enough to the NVA to kill and wound some of them. The survivors grabbed what equipment they could, along with the wounded, and moved out quickly. I thought they figured that the HF had made a lucky guess. We did not hear any more firing at the HF during the night. The movement in our area did, however, begin to increase around 0100. We went to 100% alert and enjoyed two hours of steady rain.

## Day 2

We started day two having had almost no sleep because there was so much NVA movement in our vicinity after midnight. Fortunately, we were in an area, although close to some trails, where the NVA would have to step on us to find us. We just had to be quiet and not move. Just before first light, the HF was hit with a mortar barrage followed by a hard-hitting ground attack that included machine guns and B-40 rockets. The mortars were firing from an area too far from our location for us to pinpoint their position. The attack against the HF lasted about an hour inflicting some casualties, but the NVA suffered more.

When the HF contact was over, I asked Covey to look for and send me any potential mortar sites he could find in range of the HF. There were a few small clearings and openings in the canopy that would allow them to fire their mortars. I plotted these and sent them to Covey and the FAO so he could register these as targets. We would be ready for them that night. I also told Covey, the HF and FAO that I planned to engage movement on the ridge with artillery during the day, a form of harassing and interdiction fire (H&I). We would try to slow their daylight movement on the ridges under the canopy. Thus, Covey needed to remain two clicks (2,000 meters) SE of Target Wednesday to stay out of the line of fire.

The HF planned artillery targets on the road for use that night. It was going to be a busy afternoon and long night. Cantua said the team was not happy about being in the middle of so many NVA moving around and us attacking them with artillery. "VC will start looking for us. Not good!" I asked Bargewell to help calm Cantua and the team down. I don't think Bargewell and Nash were happy about what we were doing either. They had not been on a team playing such a deadly cat and mouse game!

We decided to remain in our current RON position for the morning and see what kind of movements the NVA made. I could see that everyone was getting tired and anxious. Just before noon, we heard a relatively large group of NVA (we counted 52) coming up the ridge, talking and making noise as if they did not suspect a team was in the area. I alerted Covey to stay clear and gave the FAO a Fire Mission with a standby and requested it be with the 155mm howitzers because they had a much larger killing radius than the 105mm and I wanted to crush this group immediately. I needed to wait until the NVA moved far enough past us that the artillery did not drive them back down the ridge into us.

I was getting ready to say, "Fire for effect," when they stopped moving. Their trailing element was less than 25 meters from us. They had stopped to eat. They spread out on the ridge with at least two of them 20 feet or less from the team! I put the artillery strike on hold. They were laughing, talking, banging pots and pans, building some small cooking fires and acting like they were going to spend the day there.

This really spooked the team. No one could move, cough, sneeze or make any sound. We were frozen in place—mannequins! And we were hungry and thirsty and needing to pull leeches off, scratch an itch and breathe. Fifteen minutes went by, then 30, then an hour, and they were still there. What were they doing? Did NVA take siestas after lunch? I gave Cantua the signal of, "What's going on?" He signaled back "sleep." Crap! We had 52 NVA taking a siesta 20 feet from us! I alerted Covey and turned the radio off. We could not afford for it to make any noise or movement.

After about 15 more minutes they began stirring around. Finally, they were going to leave! We could hear them talking, banging and clanging around. Then the two closest to us began talking to each other, turned and began slowly to walk toward us—without their weapons— and stopped at the edge of our thicket, a couple of feet from Camba, and began to pee into the bushes—on Camba! I was sure they would either see him trying to move away from the pee or he would shoot them. Either way, it was going to be the seven of us against the 52 of them.

In the back of my mind I remembered that a couple of months back, CPT Jordan's RT had counted 252 NVA walk through their ambush site, designed for 20 people, and more were coming, when an NVA turned and peed on one of Jordan's Yards. Yards hate Vietnamese. The Yard promptly shot him. Jordan had no choice but to initiate the ambush and have all of his team make a run for the extraction site. The NVA were so stunned by the violence of the ambush that it was a full five minutes before they began to return fire. Covey counted over 80 dead NVA on the trail.

We all had our Claymore clackers in our hands ready to detonate them if we were detected, just before we scampered down the hill. I would be saying, "Fire for effect, danger close." Fortunately, Camba had the patience of Job. They did not see him, and he did not shoot them.

The two NVA, laughing and joking, turned, walked back to their gear, put it on, got back on the trail and were soon moving up the ridge. The 155mm howitzer was known for firing a "short round" (a round that doesn't quite make it to the target) occasionally. Fortunately, we were not on the gun-target line. If a round was short, it wouldn't drop on us. I gave everyone the artillery signal and for everyone to get down. The team had not used artillery fire before. I could tell by the look on their faces they were scared. Bargewell and Nash were uncomfortable.

"Covey, Xray Five, stay clear."

"Covey, Roger."

"Eagle 26, this is Xray Five, fire for effect, danger close, over.

"Eagle 26, Roger, shot, over."

"Eagle 26, splash, over."

In a few seconds I could hear that familiar sound of artillery rounds screaming toward the earth from high above. Even if you heard them, you could not get away! Then the whole jungle exploded sending trees, boulders, dirt, body parts and shrapnel flying through the air. And right behind that came the second volley. I doubted that any of them were still alive, but if they were, they would be really angry and running for their lives. They did not know if a third volley was coming.

"Eagle 26, outstanding! Right on target. Estimated 52 dead NVA." I turned to the team and said, "VC dead!"

I sent a coded message to Covey and Jordan, "That's 52 that won't bother us again." We moved closer to the road and found an RON site. Everyone was tired, and the team seemed to be even more spooked. They were saying, "VC know we here. They look for us. Too many VC." This was the team's first mission with me. They knew Bargewell was crazy. Now they knew there were two crazies on the team. The RON site provided us some cover and a concealed escape route. We layered our remaining Claymores. We did not put out toe toppers and trip wires because if the NVA hit those, they would know we were there. Our plan was to let them walk through our perimeter and not react unless they stepped on someone. We were going to be at 100% alert all night. Time for the Americans to dig into their med kits and get something to keep the team alert and eyes open. I shared with Cantua. Within about 20 minutes all of our eyes were the size of saucers. Our biggest problem would be staying still.

The team was not only listening to our surroundings, but for the sounds of mortars firing. We needed a distance and direction. Bargewell, Nash and I had our compasses ready to shoot an azimuth as we estimated the distance. I had already shot azimuths on the map from our location to the potential mortar sites Covey had found during the day. When I shared the potential mortar locations, distances and azimuths, Bargewell and Nash thought I was 150–200 meters off on our current location. I assured them there was no way I was off more than a few meters. I described what was out in front of us and told them we would go down to the road the next morning and they would see I was correct.

Now it was time to slowly take the rice ball with mutton mixed in it out of my pocket and enjoy my evening meal. I would have a little water to wash it down and it would keep my stomach from growling during the night. It was good and filling. We were at 100% alert. No one was sleeping. Covey did a final check, and I keyed the hand set twice to let him know we were okay. I had sent our location to him shortly after we were down for the night—we hoped.

We heard a little movement, but not much until 2237. Vehicles were moving on the road near one of our targets. I called Eagle 26 and put artillery where I estimated them to be. Jordan reported seeing what appeared to be burning vehicles on the road. Then it was quiet again.

At 0138 we heard the mortars fire on the HF. Bargewell, Nash and I agreed on an approximate distance and azimuth. I had Eagle 26 send them a 105mm welcome packet. No more mortars from that location. At 0230 we heard what sounded like a large group of NVA (50–75) moving up the ridge. We didn't want them to feel left out, so I had Eagle 26 deliver a 155mm welcome packet to them. I think it got their attention. We could hear screaming, yelling and some gun fire from that area. They were obviously not happy with their welcome packet.

You just can't satisfy some people. No more movement from that area the rest of the night.

At 0310 we heard more mortars fire on the HF. Bargewell, Nash and I agreed on an approximate distance and azimuth. I had Eagle 26 send them a 105mm artillery welcome packet. No more mortars from that location!

## Day 3

It had turned into a long and busy night. We were all very tired, but we knew they had to realize a team must be on this side of the road and would be looking for us when it got light. The rising sun would give us a new day to show what we could do. Our plan was to lay low in the morning to see how the NVA were going to respond. It didn't take long. Around 1000 we heard a dog bark once about 900 meters from us. They were trying to pick up our trail or have the dog hear us. Fortunately, the wind was coming from his location toward ours. This would make it more difficult for him to hear or smell us. And we had not been in the area the sound came from. We continued to lay low and silent.

## Unrequested/Compromising Resupply

At 1410 we heard bad news from Covey.

"Xray Five, this is Covey. The launch site is sending a helicopter to resupply your water, food and batteries. Your mission has been extended. The chopper is ten mikes out. You will need to identify your location, over."

"This is Xray Five, Not going to happen! I say again. No way! We have bad guys all over us. We cannot mark our location or receive supplies. Send it away!"

"This is Covey. I sent your response to Quebec Tango 6. He said it's coming. Get ready to receive it. Sorry about that."

"This is Five. I'm not marking our location."

"This is Covey, the chopper has been ordered to drop the supplies at your last known location."

"This is Five. You know this is going to create a Prairie Fire! You better start lining up assets. They are going to be on us like a chicken on a June bug."

I got Bargewell, Nash and Cantua together and told them what was about to happen. It was not a pleasant conversation, and probably too loud. In the end, I told them we could not stop our position from being compromised and we needed to at least try to hide the supplies so the NVA would not find them when they came looking for us. We would not have much time.

In about five minutes we heard the "whop, whop, whop" of a helicopter approaching fast. It was also accompanied by sporadic gun fire. Suddenly, it was about 50 meters east of us and boxes were falling through the canopy. The chopper left as quickly as it came. More sporadic gun fire. Based on where the boxes hit, I decided to split the team into an overwatch team and a recovery team. I took Nash, Cantua and Camba with me to recover the boxes. Bargewell kept the rest of the team in an overwatch position to protect us while we frantically gathered the boxes, put them in a thickly vegetated area and covered them with leaves. We carried the water back to the team and quickly distributed it. We knew we had to get away from that area as quickly as we could without compromising ourselves.

## Enemy Contact

"Covey, this is Five, moving south fast. We can hear them coming. We need air support here now! Calling artillery."

"Covey, Roger. Gunships 20 mikes out. Working on SPADs. Are you calling a Prairie Fire?"

"This is Five, soon."

"Eagle 26, Xray Five, fire mission, over." "Eagle 26, send it."

"This is Five, from Target Friday, direction 265, add 200, fire for effect, over."

"Eagle 26, shot, over." "Eagle 26, splash, over."

"This is Five, outstanding. More to come."

We were moving fast toward an area that we could use for an extraction LZ. Suddenly, Camba signaled, "Halt. Enemy!" Just as we stopped, a barrage of AK fire came at us, hitting Camba. He went down in the vegetation. Cantua yelled, "Camba hit!" I yelled "assault front!" We needed to get on-line and assault beyond where Camba went down so we could get him. As we got near Camba, we found RPGs were coming at us. We had to get Camba and start moving backwards. There were at least 20 or more NVA. As we were fighting and trying to withdraw, I worked my way over to Camba. He was bleeding badly. Bargewell was trying to stop the bleeding. Bargewell personally recruited Camba when he was at Khe Sanh. He knew

Camba's family. "Covey, this is Five, we're in heavy contact with 20 or more NVA. We need help. Have at least one red head (code for wounded). I'm declaring a Prairie Fire Emergency, over." I shouted over the background heavy volume of gun fire and men yelling.

"Roger that. Can you send up a flare? We don't know exactly where you are."

"Roger, stand by."

"This is Five, flare up, identify." "This is Covey, identify blue."

"This is Five, Negative. Negative! That is not us. Hammer it! Sending up another one." (Heavy volume of gun fire and men yelling in background.)

"This is Covey, identify red."

"Roger that. Stand by. Artillery coming in. Eagle 26, Xray Five, fire mission, over."

"Roger, send it."

"From target Friday, direction 270, add 250, adjust fire, over."

"Eagle 26, Roger. Shot. Over."

"Covey, this is Five, make first gun run northeast to southwest 100 meters northwest of our flare after artillery fire for effect impact." I shouted over the gun fire, explosions and yelling.

"This is Covey, Roger."

"Eagle 26, direction 255, drop 100, fire for effect, over."

"Eagle 26, shot, over. Eagle 26, splash, over."

"Covey, this is Five, run the guns, over. Rounds on target. Great job, 26."

"This is Covey, guns are hot, over."

"Five, Roger. Run them now!"

The NVA had cut off our route to the possible LZ. And their numbers were increasing. We made it into some rocks. They were trying to flow around us. Bargewell had Camba's bleeding under control and gave him Ringer's solution to get some of the volume back in his blood.

"Covey, this is Five. This is as far as we can go. Run the guns again. Same place. We need a string extraction if you can get it here fast enough. These jokers look like a giant amoeba flowing around their dinner. I want to give them indigestion. I really appreciate Quebec

Tango's resupply of food. He should be here with us to enjoy it, over."
I was sure QT6 could hear what I was saying, even with the heavy
volume of gun fire, explosions and men yelling in the background.

## String Extraction

"Covey, Roger. Guns coming back around. Working on strings. SPADs
here in five mikes."

"Roger. Getting ready."

"This is a thick canopy. Not sure they can get the strings through."
"Roger. I'll notify Casper Five."

Extraction on strings through double canopy jungle was rough.
We would be dragged through the limbs of the trees and treetops. The
aircraft would always start to go forward before we were above the
canopy and then we were being dragged through it.

"This is Casper Five. We are here to do some fishing. Ready to put
four lines in the water. The McGuire rigs have been removed. Watch
for the sandbags."

"Xray Five, Roger. Move 12 o'clock 40 meters and 3 o'clock 20
meters."

"Roger. Moving. Taking fire. Might not be able to stay. You guys
hurry up."

"You're over the fish bed. Drop the lines."

We were receiving heavy fire and the extraction aircraft did not want
to stay over us long. The "strings" would be 120-foot-long nylon ropes
with a sandbag on the end of each to get them through the canopy. If
they left the McGuire rigs on the ropes, they would hang in the canopy.
This meant we had to use our nylon utility ropes measuring 12 feet to
make Swiss seats while lying down and getting shot at then hook on to
the ropes while we were lying on the ground. While this was going on,
four people would not be returning fire at the NVA. Bargewell's first
group to be extracted were tossing some of their loaded magazines in a
pile for my group to use. We were quickly running out of survival time.
The hourglass had almost run out of sand. I really didn't think there
was much of a chance that my group would get out.

I put Bargewell, Nash, Camba and Acat on the first aircraft's strings. I wanted the two Americans, Camba and Acat out! I couldn't help the group get hooked up because the NVA were starting to charge our position. I was shooting some of them within ten feet or less of our perimeter, and some even inside our perimeter! My magazine ran out just before one of them jumped over my rock and landed on me. I terminated him with my KA-BAR to his neck, hitting his carotid artery, as he landed on me. We were receiving a heavy volume of fire. The NVA realized what we were trying to do and were really trying hard to kill us and shoot the helicopter down. It wasn't every day they got a chance to shoot at a helicopter 100 feet in the air and not moving! We had to be careful not to use our grenades up too quickly. We were going to be fighting for a while!

"Casper Five, you have four fish. Go! Go! Straight up FAST. Have your door gunners flood the Willie Pete you are about to see," I shouted over the gun fire, explosions, Yards and NVA yelling.

"Roger."

I threw a white phosphorus grenade as far as I could toward the main body of the NVA. WP grenades were big and heavy and had a large bursting radius. I had to get it far away from me before it exploded, which was not easy while receiving a heavy volume of fire and idiots diving on me! The WP grenade created a dense white smoke with small chunks of WP landing on and burning through the NVA. The dense white smoke provided some concealment for Bargewell's group and acted as a choking agent burning the NVA's lungs.

"Casper Five, this is Xray Five, Take them straight up, over!" "This is Casper Five, we're taking hits! We have to get out of here." "This is Xray Five, have your door gunners move their fire 25 meters north of where they are currently firing, over." "Casper, Roger!"

The door gunners continued to return fire. I could see the red tracers coming down to the ground, and I was on the radio trying to adjust the door gunner's fire, because I could see where the NVA were on the ground. I was trying to get Cantua and Hieng ready to hook on to the next set of ropes—if there was a next set. I returned fire at the NVA as I talked to Covey to tell him where I needed the gunships to make their runs while I was dodging bullets. I saw that Camba, Nash,

Acat and Bargewell were getting beat up going through the tree limbs. I couldn't help them now. They would have to survive the ride to the fire base.

"Covey, have the guns make a run on the east and west sides of Casper Five going from north to south. Danger close, over."

"Roger. Keep your heads down. There will be some 40 mike mike mixed with guns."

"Five, Roger."

I had maxed out at multi-tasking, writing call signs and azimuths on the palm of my hand and the right thigh of my pants as new players arrived! In the back of my mind, I knew that I had to replay Bargewell's scenario again as I tried to get myself, Cantua and Hieng out with almost no fire power on the ground. Two of the fun things SOG 1-0s got to do were to be the first person off the aircraft into the firefight and the last one off the ground during the extraction. But that was what SOG 1-0s did. First in, last out, or FILO—a manufacturing term I would learn many years later.

Bargewell and his part of the team were through the canopy and out of sight. Now the enemy fire really picked up. The NVA knew it was just me and a couple of Yards. They were flanking us and trying to get in a position to overrun us. I used the grenades the departing team members left for us. Even if we were not preoccupied with tying a Swiss seat on and trying to get hooked up and out, we would not have enough firepower to fend off the number of NVA who now had us surrounded. The extra grenades we brought had literally been life savers, but they were almost gone. People used to ask me why I carried 50 magazines of ammunition. I did it for situations just like this. I tossed some of my magazines to Cantua because he was out of ammo. I tossed my last bandoleer of 40mm ammo to Hieng, my M-79 gunner. I always kept the M-79 gunner if we had to split the team so I would have the additional firepower of the 40mm grenades.

I only had a couple of frag grenades left and the NVA were getting ready to assault again. I got out my two-pound blocks of C-4 and inserted the blasting caps that had been crimped on the time fuses with fuse igniters. I only had one Claymore left. I set up the Claymore facing the direction of the most NVA, unrolled the wire and put the clacker under the rope on my hip so it would be fastened to me, and I could reach it to detonate the Claymore. My plan was to set it off just before I got to the end of the wire (100 feet) as I was lifted up. Even if none of the 700 steel balls hit anyone, it would distract them for a few seconds. I also left an Eldest Son AK-47 magazine in the magazine vest of one of the dead NVA I had shot inside our perimeter. I'm sure one of his buddies took his magazine and had an exploding brain day when he used the Eldest Son magazine.

The gunships were keeping most of the NVA back from us, but a few were moving closer to us. They wanted to literally hit us and maybe the helicopter as we were being lifted up. I had always told my guys, if you are not moving, you're dying! And here we were. We couldn't move because we had to wait to be lifted up on strings through the canopy. Our death seemed to be rapidly approaching.

We had only three courses of action at this point: 1) Try to survive getting lifted out on strings—if the pilot was willing to try while receiving so much fire; 2) Try to break contact and disappear into the jungle and hope to be found alive in a few days; or 3) Make a stand here until we ran out of ammo, then throw a red smoke grenade indicating that the gunships and A-1 Skyraiders were "cleared hot" to totally destroy our current location and take out as many NVA as they could. I didn't like the third option!

I decided to have the gunships make two more passes, but much closer to our position, and have the extraction ship follow right behind them. We would fasten to the ropes as fast as possible and give the clearance to lift us out. I would provide covering fire while assisting Cantua and Hieng in hooking up. If I had time and was able, I would fasten on. If I couldn't for some reason, (wounded, dead, too much fire) I would send Cantua and Hieng out, stay behind and implement course of action two or three.

"Xray Five, Casper Four, we are dropping ropes now." "Roger. One is hung in the canopy."

Fortunately, we only needed three. Cantua and Hieng hooked on to their ropes while lying on the ground behind the rocks. The gun runs were just about on top of us, and they took out a few of the guys who had crept up on us. I didn't have to help Cantua and Hieng very much, so I just provided covering fire.

"Casper Four, Xray Five. Take us up now! Straight up!"

I told Casper Four to lift off as I was still trying to fasten on to the rope. I was holding on to the rope with one hand and trying to fasten on with the other while it was starting to drag me. Cantua and Hieng were lifting off the ground when an NVA jumped up and grabbed Hieng by the ankles. Above the noise of the gunfire and explosions I could hear Hieng and Cantua calling me for help, "Trung Uy! Trung Uy! Trợ giúp! Trợ giúp!" (Lieutenant! Help!) My rope was about ten feet

**LT Dick Thompson, RT Michigan 1-0, Landing at Fire Base, 1969**

**Thompson**

*Lt Henry Thompson and wounded team members landing on strings at a Fire Base 1969 (Unknown photographer. From LT Thompson's private collection)*

longer than Cantua's and Hieng's ropes, and I was still on the ground. I instinctively put a four-round burst in the NVA, then thought, wow. We might have had a prisoner! I managed to get linked in with a death grip on the rope just as it tightened up and started to lift me off the ground. It pulled me off balance and I fell over, bounced off a rock and lifted off the ground exposing me to all the NVA. They shifted their fire toward me. I could hear the rounds cracking by me and feel pieces of rock hitting me that were chipped off by bullets. Fortunately, I was being initially pulled into thicker vegetation and up making it more difficult for them to see me.

We were taking a lot of fire. I felt two really hard hits to the back— one in the radio and one in the upper left chest. It knocked the breath out of me. It really hurt but I did not think the bullets penetrated me. I was still alive, and that was good! As I neared the end of the Claymore cord, I detonated it. I was almost directly above it. It was very loud and actually took out some of the NVA and stunned me a little.

I was having difficulty shooting accurately, or even into the right place, because I was twisting and turning and hitting limbs. I dropped two of the blocks of C-4 with 15-second time fuses. They made a lot of noise. Now, the NVA were behind me, and it was difficult to shoot in that direction. I could tell both Cantua and Hieng were hit because blood was dripping down on me. I had no idea how badly they were wounded. Both seemed to still be alive. I tried to radio Casper and Covey, but the PRC-25 radio, which had been hit by two AK-47 rounds, would not work. I tried to use my URC-10 survival radio, but it had been hit with a large piece of shrapnel and was not working. It was covering my heart. I was very fortunate that it stopped the shrapnel. At least that part worked. But this left me with no way to communicate with the helicopter or Covey.

It was a long ride back to the first safe place to land the helicopter. And to add to the fun, we flew over several anti-aircraft positions. But it felt good to be off the ground. We were soaking wet from all the sweat, but the air going by us felt good—at first!

Now we had to get past the anti-aircraft fire. Suddenly, I was freezing. We were flying at 7,000 feet—AGL (Actual Ground Level), not sea level—hanging on the end of a rope and freezing to death (we were used to 100 degrees/100% humidity, not 75 degrees with a 100 MPH wind.) And it just kept getting better. I looked up. I was swinging back and forth, and my rope was rubbing on the edge of the floor of the helicopter. We were at 7,000 feet to avoid some of the anti-aircraft positions along the route. We had a long way to go, and I could see that my rope was starting to fray from sliding back and forth on the edge of the floor. Were we going to get to a place where they could set us down before the rope broke? This ran my arousal level up a little. I was shivering, my teeth were chattering, and I could feel my legs going to sleep because the Swiss seat was cutting off the blood supply to my legs. I knew that when we got to a safe place to set down, I wouldn't be able to use my legs. Someone would have to pick me up and put me in the helicopter.

We planned to set down at an Artillery Fire Base just across the border. Bargewell and the first part of the team had already landed, been put inside their helicopter and were continuing toward the launch site. This was a real treat for the fire base guys. They never got to see a helicopter with people hanging underneath on ropes. And never, ever did they see helicopters coming from the Laotian side of the river, especially not with people hanging under them. Medics were standing by to treat Cantua and Hieng as soon as we landed, along with a couple of people to carry me to the helicopter and put me inside.

As soon as I got near the ground, two members of the fire base caught me and began asking me if I was okay as they moved me to the helicopter. One wanted to know if we were the people they were providing fire support for over the last couple of days. I said yes and thanked them profusely. I told them they saved our lives and to make sure they passed our thanks to all the members of the fire base and that they did not see us!

As soon as Cantua and Hieng were ready, the rotor RPM increased, the aircraft began to vibrate and as we were starting to lift off, I saw a soldier running toward the aircraft holding his hand high in the air holding something. He thrust it up to me just as we started moving. He had taken a picture of our aircraft coming in with one of those new

Polaroid Instant cameras! I grabbed the picture at the last second, and yelled, "Thank you!" as we flew away. Over 50 years later, I still have that original picture and have no idea who gave it to me.

Fortunately, Cantua had flesh wounds to the side and arm. Hieng had been shot through the thigh, but it had missed the bone and artery. Nothing too serious. They would both live to fight more battles. As we flew back to the launch site, I thought to myself, just another day in SOG. But then I remembered, the day was not over!

## Mission Debrief

I was not happy about the resupply. CPT Welch, the Recon Company Commander, had flown to the launch site to be part of getting RT Michigan out, to talk to me before I talked to MAJ Sims, and to attend the debriefing to make sure things (me) did not get out of hand. He told me before we went inside to stay calm, remember I would be talking to a Major and not to hit or shoot anyone. And to make sure the team did not either. He said we would discuss what happened with LTC Warren, the CCN Commander, when we got back to CCN that evening. LTC Warren would deal with the launch site commander. I still expressed my displeasure about the resupply during the debriefing. RT Michigan's location was confirmed to be where I said it was.

When the debriefing was over, the real news came. MAJ Sims said for me to get the team ready to go back out; they were going to reinsert us at first light! I almost lost it. CPT Welch immediately stepped in and said, "They have three people wounded! The team can't go back out at first light. We would have to find, equip and fly four replacement Michigan team members from CCN up here tonight. None of the current team members have slept for three days. It's not possible to put Michigan back out in the morning. LTC Warren is not going to approve this! And you need to extract the HF before they get overrun by the NVA." There were some heated words between CPT Welch and MAJ Sims.

I assembled the team and told them the launch site wanted to send us back out at first light. Cantua said, "Team no go back out. Too many VC. Too many team wounded." Bargewell, Nash and I got together to discuss the situation. While we were talking, we heard a single gunshot. Acat had shot himself in the foot while cleaning his weapon! He could not go back out. I don't believe it was an accident. His story of how it happened was flaky. I think it was a show of team solidary, that they were not going back out the next morning.

After about an hour, RT Michigan's mission for the following day was cancelled and the decision was made to extract the HF at first light. Now it felt like just another day in SOG. But we still had to fly back to CCN the next day after we picked up the Yards from the hospital. The hospital and treatment of Yards was another story for another time.

## After Action Review Summary

### Wounded Team Members

| Member | Type of Wound |
| --- | --- |
| Camba | Bullet through left shoulder |
| Cantua | Bullets through arm and side |
| Hieng | Bullet through thigh |
| Acat | Accidentally shot in foot |

- The insertion into the AO went as planned and we were successful in our mission until the unexpected/unneeded/insane resupply. The mission ended at that point.
- Using mortar and artillery support from the 101st was great for the mission and a literal life saver. It worked great. Too bad we didn't have this type of fire support on all missions.
- Extra frags, Claymores and ammunition were also life savers.
- The extra weight did not present a significant problem, but we needed to work on a fitness program like I had started with RT Alabama.
- The team really did a great job with security halts, movement, security, RONs and eating.
- Our weakest area was putting on Swiss seats lying on the ground under heavy fire. It took much longer to put the seats on in this situation compared to the way we had trained. The

loss of firepower during these periods almost allowed the NVA to win. We had to train and look for other solutions.

- We needed to evaluate our med kits (American and Indigenous) to determine what and how much we needed to have with us. One compression bandage per person was not enough. When you had a wound with an entry and exit point, or multiple wounds, you needed more bandages. We needed more medical training and practice with techniques like inserting IVs under fire. Bargewell did a great job, but all of us needed to be at least that good. We scheduled additional medical training with the medics the following day.

- One wounded team member and someone to assist him reduces the fire power of a six-man team by 33% or more. It also significantly slows the team's speed and ability to maneuver.

- We needed more practice in the three combat fundamentals: shooting, moving and communicating, especially in thick jungle vegetation.

- We needed to add/define more single word "contact" commands.

- For example, "assault" always meant forward, toward the enemy. It also meant to become much more aggressive. Go after them. Hunt them down and terminate them. I could always add "left" or "right" if I wanted to maneuver around the enemy.

- We needed to practice fighting techniques, e.g., grenades, C-4, smoke, WP during string extraction.

- Fear is one of the most powerful emotions we have in our arsenal. It can stop us in our tracks, make us run away, or like General Patton said, "Go through the enemy like crap through a goose." Respect, control, manage and use fear to defeat the enemy.

- If you are not moving, you are dying.

- Everything—movement, smell, etc.—that gives the NVA away gives you away—eliminate what you sense from the team and "sense" the NVA.

- When we get low/on the ground we can't see each other or the NVA.
- If you don't get low, you get hit.
- We had to work on functioning as a team even when we couldn't see each other—have a mental 3-D picture of the battlefield.
- Don't keep shooting from the same place—shoot and move or they will take you out.
- There are always multiple people shooting at you, or at least in your direction.
- Keep shooting. Keep moving.
- Redistribution of ammunition is very important.
- Practice throwing grenades from the prone position—especially WP (because it is heavy).
- Consider the impact of the following on your senses—vision, hearing, smell, touch and taste: Avgas; smoke; gunpowder; dust; dirt; mud; rock chips; rain; sweat; thirst; pain; bleeding; heat; cold; hot weapon; fear; stress; wounded/dead teammates; a teammate's blood/guts/brain matter in your face.
- My radios literally saved my life by stopping bullets. My URC-10 survival radio over my heart stopped the deadly piece of shrapnel.
- There tends to be a pattern in our mission cycle.

*Team Mission Cycle Pattern*

## Post-Mission Training

### RT Michigan Post-Mission 1 Training JAN 69

**Person Fitness (w/loadout on)**

- Walking, squats, crawling, running, getting up & down, shooting, hand & arm strength, balance, climbing, makiwara board, hand-to-hand
- Hydration/Electrolytes

**Knowledge Acquisition**

- NVA
- Organization/Chain of Command
- Food
- Sleep
- Equipment
- Superstitions

**Michigan Team Members**

- Superstitions

**Skills Improvement**

- Tracking
- NVA Weapons
- IADs
- Firing Range
- Observations Techniques
- Treating medical trauma in field

**Equipment Organization/SOP**

- Standardizing what, where & how equipment was carried.
- I enhanced my Ka-Bar's role in survivability by wrapping a piece of OD parachute cord around the handle with fishing line and two hooks under the cord.

**Team Fitness**

- Exercise with loadout
- Hydration/Electrolytes
- Hand-to-hand
- Mindset

**Pre-mission Food (3-days)**
- No spices
- NVA type food

**No Soap the last three days**

**Medical**

- IVs
- Gunshots
- Shrapnel
- Bleeding
- Tourniquets

**Operational Terrain & Weather**

**Situational Awareness Training**

**Invisibility**

**Communication During Contact**

*My actual, well used, Ka-Bar (7-inch blade) from my SOG days with survival handle modification. Note the "blood groove in the blade." (Courtesy Henry L. Thompson, Ph.D.)*

## RT Michigan Mission 2: PW Snatch SOG #6 (20 JAN 69)

### Mission 2 Team Roster

| | |
|---|---|
| LT Henry Thompson | 1-0 |
| SP4 Eldon Bargewell | 1-1 |
| SSG Joe Nash | 1-2 |
| Cantua | Interpreter |
| Pua | Pointman |
| Rapun | M-79 |
| Chung | Tail gunner |
| Aita | Pointman |

The team was banged up pretty badly from the last mission. Cantua was adamant that he was okay and would be going on the new mission. Camba, Hieng and Acat would not be healed in time to go. All who were physically able would, however, be allowed to participate in most of the Pre-Mission Training (PMT). For this mission, the team would be me, Bargewell, Nash, Cantua, Aita, Chung, Rapun and Pua.

### Mission

Our new mission was to conduct a prisoner snatch from area Oscar 8. We had an insertion date of 12 JAN 69. That would not give us much time to prepare.

## Mission Prep

The more I learned about and experienced SOG missions, the more security conscious I had become. I was so concerned about Soviet satellites watching us train for our missions in the big open area next to CCN that I requested and received a satellite fly-over schedule. I also scheduled time on Monkey Mountain to allow us to train in terrain similar to our target area—and out of sight of satellites. We would actually conduct live fire ambushes to make sure there was only one "hole" in the kill zone (KZ) and we did not put too much C-4 in the hole.

The KZ of an ambush is set up so that no one who is in this area should survive when the ambush is initiated. The hole in a KZ is used in a prisoner snatch or high value target acquisition to prevent killing one to two enemy soldiers. This hole normally has a blast wave running through it to knock the potential prisoners unconscious.

We spent every day practicing and working on the weak areas described in the AAR plus mission specialties. The three primary snatch techniques were raid, ambush and stealth, and there were variations of each. An example of one other technique was to follow closely behind a B-52 strike. Most NVA who were still alive were usually stunned from the concussions and relatively easy to capture. If they were not dead or stunned, they were not happy and intent on taking their anger out on the team.

First, we would walk through our basic mission plan with the team from start to finish. The next day we would begin to get specific and practice what we were going to do with priority going to the ambush snatch technique.

Bargewell, Nash and I continued our discussion of the mission over dinner in the mess hall that evening. All three of us would look for other teams that had conducted snatch missions, intentionally or not. Sometimes you just stumbled upon an opportunity. We also discussed that, with the exception of Cantua, Nash and I had no combat experience with the other Yards because they were not on the previous mission. Bargewell shared what his experience with them had been up to that point, which was helpful. After dinner we set off to see what we could learn from other operators with experience.

## Next Day

The next day, Bargewell, Nash and I spent the morning planning the details of the mission while the team was preparing and cleaning their equipment. We gave the ambush snatch technique priority because we had a better chance on this mission of setting up an ambush than using the other two techniques. Oscar 8 was known for its density of NVA activity, thus, finding a group on a trail we could ambush was highly likely. The difficulty with operating in Oscar 8 was trying to get out after you were detected. Oscar 8 had a reputation for making whole teams disappear without a trace. Teams went in and were never heard from again.

To make things more difficult, the NVA in this area would do anything to stop us from getting out with a prisoner—to include killing the prisoner of war (PW) themselves. The potential prisoner would be terrified and would fight to the death to prevent being taken. We could expect him to kick, bite, headbutt, scream, yell for help, and use anything he could find as a weapon, to include taking one of our knives, pistols, grenades, etc., and using it against us. He would kill himself before surrendering. So, while catching an NVA was difficult, keeping him alive was even more difficult, and getting him back to the launch site alive even more so.

To get out with a prisoner required all the tactical pieces, e.g., Covey, gunships, TAC Air and extraction ships to be in place before we initiated the capture. Then with deadly surprise and violence of action we would stun, secure, drug, head-bag, gag and move the PW to the extraction LZ as quickly as possible. His ultimate level of fear would cause his blood to be replaced with pure adrenaline. At that point, his physical size would bear no resemblance to his extraordinary physical strength and lack of ability to feel pain. He would fight and delay us every step of the way. Anyone involved in subduing and/or transporting him would look like they had tangled with a mountain lion.

What all this meant to us was that we had to plan, train and prepare ourselves mentally for the process of bringing our prisoner—and our team—back alive. This was not the same as shooting and killing an NVA. This was hands on, up close and personal "killing" of a human being psychologically while fighting to keep him alive biologically. It would be an experience none of us would likely forget for the rest of our lives.

We had to find a well-traveled trail that we could watch for a couple of days to determine the frequency of use, how many people were traveling together, how they were armed, their spacing, security, etc. We would set up an interlocking, detailed, deadly and stunning ambush with a hole in the KZ. No bullets would be fired into this hole, but there would be a demolition charge aimed to fire a blast wave through it more than capable of rendering anyone in the hole unconscious—unless we used too much C-4! The rest of the NVA in the kill zone would die instantly.

I would initiate the ambush when the lucky person was in the hole. Specified team members would leap into the hole to handcuff, gag, head bag, drug (with morphine syrettes), search and begin moving the prisoner toward the extraction LZ. He would be questioned along the way. From the initiation of the ambush until we were moving should take less than two minutes. This meant practice, practice and more practice—day and night. If we were taking more than one PW it would take longer. If we had only one PW and had to stop severe bleeding, it might require us to spend longer in the kill zone. That would be very dangerous, and maybe even deadly for some or all of our team members. The ambush and follow-on actions would be an extremely high stress event with a constant flow of life and/or death decisions in rapid succession. Past experience told me that almost nothing would go as planned.

We would actually set up three ambushes. The middle one would be for the PW. The first and third ones would be for any reaction forces that tried to come from up and/or down the trail to help the middle group. These two ambushes would be mechanical with no people at the sites. We could not allow any NVA to catch us in the kill zone securing the PW or searching the bodies of NVA killed in the ambush. We would detonate any remaining explosives in all ambush sites as we left for the LZ. We would not have time to recover the explosives and could not leave them for the enemy to use against other teams.

Our training and practice at Monkey Mountain would include how to handle a conscious or unconscious PW and multiple PWs. We would not take more than three PWs. All other NVA would be dead. The PWs would most likely be temporarily or permanently deaf from the explosions. This would hinder our initial and later interrogations. We had to make sure that none of our team members had permanent hearing loss. Shielding them from the blast waves was critical.

Every team member had a specific job to do and had understudies/backups for their job. Team members were cross trained in several jobs. It was possible that we might have wounded and/or dead team members. We had to be prepared to handle those casualties in addition to the PW(s).

As stated earlier, every contingency required practice, practice and more practice. The stress level would be so high and the decision times so short that we could not make a mistake. We had to be able to do everything blindfolded and in the dark. The three ambushes would actually be set up in the dark.

Some of the special equipment included daisy-chained Claymores—when one goes off, all in a chain detonate simultaneously—with extended detonator wire, specially rigged C-4 charges, head bags, morphine, medical gear, handcuffs, gags, ankle ropes for PWs, pre-tied Swiss seats for PWs, etc. We needed extensive practice for each phase of the PW capture—from setting up the ambushes to knowing what each team member was carrying and how to find it on his body in the dark. A personal change I had made for this mission was to wear Army-issued leather gloves with half fingers (I cut the fingers off). I wore them during all practice sessions to get used to them and finalize my decision to wear them. The gloves would give my hands more protection against thorns, critters, leeches and especially the heat coming from the hand guard on my CAR-15. In heavy firefights the hand guard became too hot to hold bare-handed. I had talked to a number of operators and 1-0s to get the pros and cons and was eager to see whether the gloves worked for me.

After lunch we met with the team and laid out our plan. The team members had a lot of questions, some of which would be answered as we demonstrated some of the actions and techniques. We rehearsed the ambush in the company area in between Soviet satellite flyovers. We did not want the Russians to see and recognize what we were planning. We spent the rest of that day focusing on the execution of the ambush and PW recovery and transport. Then practice, practice and more practice! The next morning Nash would continue the practice sessions while Bargewell and I conducted a visual reconnaissance of the AO.

## Visual Reconnaissance

Bargewell and I left out of Da Nang airfield at daylight in an Air Force O-2 Sky Master observation aircraft (the push-pull type) to fly a VR of the Oscar 8 AO. We planned to make one pass over the target area taking photos as we flew over enroute to a fake area that we would pretend to check out. It was a somewhat cloudy day, and the air was very rough. As we approached the AO the NVA welcomed us with fire from a couple of .51 caliber machine guns. A round hit the right wing flap and another came through the floor hitting the pilot in the leg. The pilot was bleeding badly, in a great deal of pain and struggling to control the plane. We were all over the sky—which actually made us more difficult to hit. Meanwhile, the rounds were still coming up at us. Another round came through the cargo compartment just behind Bargewell and out through the top of the plane causing the rear engine to shut down. I said to Bargewell, "I think I have seen enough for today!" He agreed.

I took my belt off and used it as a tourniquet to slow the pilot's bleeding. We could not afford for him to become incapacitated or die. Once I got his bleeding slowed, I sent out a "Mayday" and notified the control tower of our situation and approximate location. I assisted the pilot in turning the plane back toward Da Nang, keeping it from flying in circles. In about 45 minutes we were joined by an Air Force OV-10 Bronco to help guide us back to the airfield—or see where we crashed if we didn't make it.

The pilot stayed conscious most of the time and was able to imitate a landing when we got to the airfield. It was not pretty. We hit the runway at an angle so hard that it caused the left side landing gear to collapse on impact. The plane skidded before going off the runway into a grassy area and stopping. The fire crew was there almost immediately to get us out of the plane and foam it. The pilot was taken to the hospital and lived. I was glad to be alive and have my feet back on the ground. I think Bargewell was too. So much for the recon!

## Monkey Mountain Pre-Mission Training

We arrived back at CCN in time to have lunch with Nash and bring him up to date on the VR. He briefed us on how the morning rehearsals had gone and what he thought needed a lot more work. We agreed that the afternoon would be a combination of more rehearsals and preparing our equipment for our 1000 hours insertion on Monkey Mountain the next day for live rehearsals. We planned to use the flight to Monkey Mountain as a practice insertion. We finished lunch and went to work. The next day we made a practice insertion, movement and security halt, then went "admin" to review the flight, insertion, movement and security halt. This included things we had worked on before, e.g., being invisible, including our new hand signals and one-word commands, enhanced sensations, etc. Then we picked a section of the trail that went to the lighthouse to talk through the ambush setup and execution. After that we set up the ambush and simulated the execution, PW recovery, attack by NVA reaction forces from both directions and movement of the PW. We took a break for lunch, then went back at it making slight modifications to our techniques as we executed.

Just before dark we moved into our RON. About an hour before daylight, we moved back to the trail and set up the three ambushes in the dark, the way we planned to do during the mission. At first light we were ready to execute the ambush. We simulated an ambush using the C-4 and taking a PW and discovered we had set up too close to the C-4. We were literally stunned! A few team members were so stunned that by today's standards and terminology, they might have qualified as having a traumatic brain injury (TBI). Bargewell, Nash and I were stunned, but seemed to be OK.

After recovering, we practiced movement and extraction with one PW and multiple PWs. This had proven to be a worthwhile trip that pointed out some areas that needed a lot of work before going live. I felt like we needed another trip to Monkey Mountain, but there wasn't enough time before the mission.

Back at CCN we got a couple of RTs to provide "bad guys" for our simulated practices and American operators to provide critique, general observations and questions. CPT Welch also observed our practice sessions. I kept the team training day and night, going over and over different contingencies until I felt like we were close.

## Launch Site

The Final Mission Briefing (FMB) was very similar to the others I had been in, with the exception of the insertion helicopter pilot offering to provide me with a headset, and that all the extraction assets had to be in range and ready to react when the PW capture was executed. Something else that made this mission different was that we would be in Oscar 8, a notorious hot bed of NVA, anti-aircraft guns and automatic weapons fire. Bargewell and I had already experienced some of this when we flew the VR.

Wearing the headset would allow me to hear all the radio traffic among the different aircraft, know where they were and what was happening at the LZ. Having all this information allowed me to feel and be more in control. It was a game changer and would be SOP for me on future operations. Why did I not think of this before?

It was a long flight to our insertion LZ. Fuel would make the various aircrafts' on-station times short, meaning that we would have a very short window for the capture and movement to the LZ. All aircraft would be on runway alert—the pilots and crew in their aircraft and ready for takeoff as soon as I transmitted "Xray Yankee Foxtrot," meaning the capture was imminent. The four Cobras, four SPADs (A-1s) and two F-4s would launch immediately to their rendezvous points (RPs) near the extraction LZ, or if necessary, straight in to provide air support under Covey's control. Additional gunships would be on standby in case they were needed. The four extraction aircraft (two primaries and two backups with a medic on each backup) would head for their RP near the extraction LZ to wait for clearance to approach the LZ. Everyone knew there would be a high anti-aircraft threat once the NVA knew the team was on the ground.

The next Covey coming on shift would be on standby during the operation in case we lost the primary Covey (low fuel, shot down, etc.). The Hillsboro/Moonbeam would be monitoring—and relaying if necessary—all communications. Medical personnel would be on standby at the launch site in addition to RT Rattler as a Bright Light team (a quick reaction force) in case we were lost (all killed, MIA, disappeared, etc.).

During the final mission briefing (FMB) I shared that our O-2 was hit with .51 caliber fire during our attempted VR. The NVA out in that area were not happy people. We needed to be prepared to take some heavy fire on the way in and out of the AO. Everyone agreed.

*RT Michigan Traveling to Helipad. Bargewell and Cantua in picture.*
*Note Ringer's solution can behind their necks.*
*(LT Thompson's private collection)*

## Travel to LZ

This was my sixth launch from Quang Tri. I was very familiar with the process, the people, and what the initial route to the border was like. Even though I wore a head set and could hear all the radio traffic, I felt a little more anxious than normal. I think it was because the PW capture process had so many moving parts and so many opportunities for things to go wrong. The team had been thoroughly trained for what we had to do. I knew the Coveys and had great confidence in all the support aircraft units and crews. This was an exciting mission. I just needed to relax, take some deep breaths, focus and enjoy the ride.

Covey was enroute to the RP and would arrive in Oscar 8 prior to the two Cobra team escorts and the team on two UH-1H helicopters. Two additional Cobras would be at the gunship RP, TAC Air (two A-1s) would be on station at the TAC Air RP, and two F-4s would be on station at their "fast mover" RP ready to support us if needed.

## Insertion

The team insertion was smooth and uneventful. We did not receive any fire on the way into the AO or LZ. We quickly jumped off the insertion helicopters, ran into the edge of the jungle, made a quick head count, rapidly and silently moved into our traveling positions and began to move forward. Everyone knew to focus on being invisible. I gave the signal to remind them.

As the backup helicopters arrived at their RP, two .51 caliber machine guns opened fire on them. Their Cobra escort immediately went after the gun positions with mini-guns and rockets. When they had expended their ordnance, the two A-1s came in with napalm, ending the ground fire from that area.

## Security Halt

We moved about 100 meters and found a site for a security halt. Everyone moved into their security posture and began to adapt to the jungle environment. I immediately noticed a difference in my hearing. The headset provided a significant amount of hearing protection. I hit the ground with almost all of my hearing ability. The difference was dramatic. The jungle was thick and the trees were tall. After about ten minutes the team felt "one with the jungle," and no signs of the enemy had been detected. I sent the code to Covey for "Team OK. Moving southeast." Covey clicked twice acknowledging receipt. I also knew that those two clicks meant I had just released all the assets from their RPs to fly back across the border to their units. We were now all alone except for Covey off in the distance.

The terrain was thick; it was slow going and definitely leech city. Leeches were everywhere! The jungle seemed too quiet. We knew NVA were in the area, but where were they? We worked our way along slowly, trying to stay invisible. We used our newly developed hand signal for "be invisible" to help the team keep invisibility top of mind.

## RON 1

Soon we found a well-used trail and set up an observation position to monitor the trail traffic. After observing it all afternoon, we only saw one group of three NVA on the trail. We moved from this site and eventually found another trail that appeared to be well traveled. I made the decision to move into an RON and watch this trail again the next day. The RON site was relatively close, but a safe distance from the trail. We set up for the night. After the site was secured and we were set for the night, I sent Covey the RON code word and grid coordinates. Oscar 8 was a place that demanded a lot of respect. That night we would maintain a minimum of seven of nine team members awake all through the night based on the reputation of this AO.

In addition to the RON site being full of leeches, the temperature was dropping. The ground was wet and cold. If that wasn't bad enough, it rained like a cow peeing on a flat rock for about two hours, followed by a steadier rain for another two hours. I had one small indigenous poncho that covered about half of me, so I was soaked and freezing. It was so cold I feared the NVA would hear my teeth chattering. When you are used to 100-degree weather and the temperature drops to 80 degrees and you are soaking wet, you freeze. It was a miserable night! A night like this was perfect for the NVA sneaking up on us and taking the team out before we knew they were on us. That night required extra vigilance. I would sleep with one eye open!

At 0210 it was raining hard, and we heard movement near our RON between us and our outer layer of Claymores. They were not on the trail but moving along the side of the ridge directly toward us. I estimated there were four of them stumbling through the thick vegetation. They might be a team looking for us with a large NVA group waiting on the trail. We went to full alert with all team members awake and ready to respond. I sent a whisper message around to Bargewell, ".22. My lead." I was ready with my .22 High Standard with integrated silencer. Bargewell had a .22 and would not fire until I did. I wasn't sure we could get all four of them in the dark without at least one of them firing a shot. Team members knew not to stand up because Bargewell and I would shoot anyone standing and they were ready with their knives. We did not want to fire a CAR-15 if we could avoid it. Firing an unsilenced weapon would end the PW mission and probably get all of us killed. Everyone's hearts were in their throats and pure adrenaline was running through our veins.

The four-man NVA group walked/stumbled within less than two feet of stepping on Chung and kept going. All of us were holding our breath. I had Chung's NVA in my sights. If he had stepped on Chung, I would have dropped him and with the help of Bargewell, taken out the other three. The team members would have silently finished them as they hit the ground. Holy crap! What a rush! No one got their heart rate back to normal the rest of the night. We had avoided a mission ending event by less than two feet! Cantua told me later he heard the NVA talking. They had strayed off the trail in the heavy rain and were trying to get back on it.

Fortunately, we made it through the night undetected—except for the leeches. We were covered in big fat ones. I had three the size of my thumb on my face and one had managed to get inside my shirt and attach to my side. The fastest way to get a leech off, besides a match, is to put a few drops of insect repellent on its head. I was concerned about the team using insect repellent because of the smell, but we had to get the leeches off.

The rain stopped before first light and we remained at 100% alert before BMNT ready for an attack, if it came. Everything seemed secure, but we had heard some noise coming from the vicinity of the trail just after first light. Then it was quiet again.

### Day 2: Observation of Trail #2

After we ate, we moved quietly into an observation position near trail #2 at 0700 and put out five Claymores. At 0750 a group of six NVA came up the trail from the small valley below. They seemed relaxed, AK-47s slung on their shoulders and talking in low voices. From all outward appearances they didn't think anyone might be in the area. This was a good sign.

About two hours later, another group of six came up the trail with the same low level of security as the first group. A light rain had started, and they didn't appear to be happy about getting wet. None of them had any type of rain gear. They continued up the ridge at a steady pace. The observation process also allowed team members to get some sleep during the day. Sleep was rotated so that two members at a time slept with a buddy/sleep monitor next to him in case he began to move, talk or snore. Everyone except Bargewell and me got at least an hour of sleep during the observation. My belief, based on my training and limited combat experience was that sleep loss was detrimental to successful performance during combat—especially for leaders— because lack of sleep made our brains foggy and slow. Bargewell and I would get extra sleep that night. In the 1980s I would become an Army Subject Matter Expert on sleep loss and its impact on leadership and performance in combat. In 2001 my work would be used to increase performance during the Gulf War.

This type of regular movement activity, six to eight NVA every two to three hours, continued throughout the day until approximately 1700. All activity stopped at that point. We used the relatively consistent group separation during the day to make three-man recons 100 meters up and down the trail starting about 15 minutes after a group passed. We sketched out what ambush sites #1 and #3 looked like and how we planned to set up the ambushes.

## RON 2

It appeared that we had found our PW capture ambush site. The trail produced ideal ambush targets approximately every two hours beginning around 0800. We moved to a new RON site that better supported establishing the ambush sites before first light the next morning. Once we set up the RON, I sent our new location, the code for "ambush, 0800 and grid coordinates" to Covey as he made his evening check in. The capture mission package would be in position no later than 0800 ready to respond as soon as we triggered the snatch.

Each team member put on his Swiss seat before dark and slept in it, even though we didn't plan to use them. (We had three pre-made Swiss seats for PWs. I had never tried this as an actual mission before, but we were ready to find out if we could force a seat on a PW.) Putting our Swiss seats on now was one less thing we had to do in the dark the next morning—or under fire like last time. The weather was projected to be clear with light winds by 0800. At that point, everything was a go.

The temperature was much warmer. The team would be able to get some sleep but would still maintain seven of nine awake even though it wasn't raining. We couldn't afford to take any chances! We had to be prepared for another lost group of NVA. At 0430 we would go to 100% alert, use 15 minutes for adaptation, then move to the ambush sites, establish the ambushes, settle into position and wait. I would send the code word indicating we were in position as soon as the ambushes were ready. This would trigger the assets to launch toward their respective RPs.

At 0745 I heard the sound of silence. No bugs. No birds. No lizards. Then I smelled spices. A group was coming! I heard the footsteps of NVA coming up the trail, and my heart rate increased. All team members and Covey were alerted, and we waited for the lucky one to step into the hole. Everyone was holding their breath. To our surprise, there were only three people in the group. We had not seen a group this size the day before. No one moved. No one made a sound. They might have been a point team for a much larger group. I made the decision to let them go through the ambush. After a few minutes, the bugs and birds started making noise again. Everyone exhaled and relaxed—just a little.

After about 30 minutes Simon and Garfunkel were back. I heard silence coming from down the trail. No bugs. No birds tweeted; they were actually flying away! That had not happened with the small group of NVA. A larger group was coming. Were they too large for our ambush? I heard sounds from down the trail, footsteps and low mumbling sounds. Now I smelled them, they had eaten recently. They were getting closer. Adrenaline caused my heart to race. I could see the lead person! I put my head closer to the ground. He was in front of me looking from side to side as he walked. I was afraid he could hear my heart. Just then, a leech jumped on to my cheek and I almost flinched. I didn't dare move or I would die. The leech was cold and slimy.

This group was much larger than the last one, the largest group we had seen. They were spaced further apart than the other groups. I was located in the center of the ambush. My first job was to initiate the ambush unless the group was too large or detected us. I counted 12 NVA walking through the "hole" and saw and heard many more coming. This group was much too large! I felt the leech bite into my cheek. I ignored the leech and decided not to initiate the ambush.

Suddenly, I heard a group of NVA open fire at ambush site #1. Something scared them and they had opened fire, randomly spraying bullets to both sides of the trail. Some bullets were coming our way! The sounds were all AK-47s except one light machine gun. They had a machine gun! The sound of the NVA in ambush site #1 firing spooked the NVA in our ambush site. It was decision time. I had no way to warn our team to close their eyes because they were about to get hit with a blast wave and debris. It was too late!

I simultaneously detonated the Claymores in site #1 and the main ambush site. The detonation was massive! Seven Claymores, five frag grenades, four pounds of C-4 and automatic weapons fire from the team. I was stunned by the blast wave from the explosives. Debris, branches, leaves, rocks, dirt, smoke, a blast wave and sound hit me in the face and blinded me! The smell of gunpowder and smoke was choking. I couldn't hear! I jerked the leech off my face.

*Wait! The team wasn't firing! Why weren't they firing? Were they knocked out? Temporarily stunned?* The 6-10 NVA not in the KZ were firing in random directions. Then some of the team began firing. Now the surviving NVA knew where we were and directed their fire on us. They were gaining fire superiority and we couldn't let that happen. I emptied two 20-round magazines (eight seconds total counting reloading) and tossed a frag grenade. I had to get everyone returning fire quickly!

I yelled, "NASH, TAKE 'EM OUT!" Nash, Pua and Rapun focused their fire on the NVA and threw two frag grenades and a WP grenade at them. Bullets were flying in all directions! The WP grenade produced a shower of white phosphorous chunks that fell on the live NVA burning them severely and creating a very dense, white choking smoke. It looked like some of the chunks were going to hit us, but they didn't. The smoke provided temporary concealment of the KZ and some incapacitation of the NVA. Nash, Pua and Rapun fired into the dense smoke and into the KZ.

Most of the team dashed on to the trail to make sure all NVA except PWs were dead and searched. Two of the three NVA that had been in or near the "hole" were on their hands and knees. The third was trying to stand up. Bargewell got there first and quickly body slammed the one trying to get up (PW1), then pounced on another (PW2). I took the third (PW3). Chung and Cantua jumped on the PWs as soon as they hit the ground, got the handcuffs on them, drugged, gagged and head-bagged them while the other guys were finishing off NVA in the kill zone and searching them. Aita was standing in the KZ providing security.

The clock was ticking. We had to get out of the KZ! Suddenly, the first small group of NVA that had gone through the ambush came running back down the trail and opened fire on us. Now we were the ones in the kill zone! Aita was hit immediately in the abdomen and went down. I was on the ground wrestling with PW3 and was splattered with Aita's blood. He began yelling, "Hit! Hit!" I turned and shot one of the three with a four-round burst. Cantua quickly terminated the other two, then sat on PW3 while I dragged Aita out of the kill zone. He was bleeding badly, and his intestines were hanging out. He was in tremendous pain and screaming. I slowed Aita's bleeding and got his intestines contained against his abdomen. I injected him with morphine and got on the radio. Cantua maintained control of PW3.

"Covey, Charlie 5. Alpha India (ambush initiated). One brunette (wounded), three Papa Whiskies (prisoners). Heavy contact. Moving to Lima Zulu (LZ), over."

"Roger, Charlie 5. Two Cobras five mikes out. Echo Hotel (extraction helicopters) standing by."

Some NVA ran up the trail from site #1 through the smoke and put out a heavy volume of fire. Nash, Pua and Rapun were in the KZ searching bodies when the group coming up the trail put fire directly on them. Chung was kneeling in the KZ returning fire on the group coming through the smoke. He got two of them before getting hit in the left shoulder and going down. Chung yelled, "Hit! Hit!" Pua threw a frag grenade at the NVA, then grabbed control of PW1 that I had while emptying a magazine on the new arrivals. Rapun grabbed PW2.

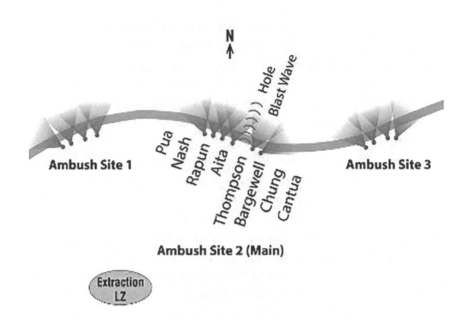

*Mission #2: PW Snatch Ambush Sketch*

Nash dragged Chung off the trail, continued to return fire and threw a frag grenade. Then he started working on Chung.

Crap! There were a lot more of them than we thought. And they were not happy.

"Covey. This is Five. We have another brunette."

As the PW and search teams left the KZ, I tossed my Eldest Son AK magazine next to a dead NVA, certain some "lucky" NVA would pick it up later. I could hear the clock ticking in my head. We had taken too much time in the KZ. The NVA force was much larger than we thought and determined to take back the PWs. We were running out of time!

We had three PWs handcuffed behind their backs, gagged, head bagged, drugged and secured with ankle ropes (an eight-foot rope tied to one ankle) so we could jerk their foot and cause them to face plant if they tried to run.

A fourth group of approximately 25–30 NVA came up the trail and engaged Nash and Pua. Pua was rapidly firing 40mm high explosive rounds at the NVA causing them to take cover. This fourth group seemed to be increasing in number. We tried to escape down the slope toward the LZ, but they were gaining on us. We couldn't move fast with the PWs fighting us every step of the way to slow us down. They kept throwing themselves on the ground and fighting to prevent us from getting them up and moving. Bargewell carried Aita. Nash assisted Chung and returned fire.

I yelled to Nash to help Pua put out some Claymores with time fuses to slow down our pursuers. I took control of PW3 from Pua. He put out a Claymore with a time fuse. A group of NVA ran in front of the Claymore KZ just as it detonated. It ripped a hole through their assault line and shredded them. While they were trying to regroup, another Claymore detonated, hitting a few more of them. The second blast really increased their fear of chasing us—but they did it anyway! They moved slower, however, and were hesitant to get too close to us. Pua put several 40mm rounds in and around them in rapid succession to slow them down.

"Covey, Charlie 5. Where are the snakes? We need them now!" "They are just coming on station. Where do you want them?" "Identify my flare." I yelled over a large explosion from an RPG in the background.

"Covey, Roger. Identify red."

"Roger. Put the guns and 40 mike mike 100 meters north of my position. Run from northeast to southwest."

"Covey, Roger. 30 seconds out. Get your heads down!"

I yelled to my team, "COBRAS COMING IN! EVERYONE GET DOWN! PROTECT YOUR HEAD!" Some of the bullets were stopped high up in the trees along with some of the 40mm, but most were getting through and hitting some of the NVA. It was difficult for bullets to get through triple canopy.

"This is Five, good run! Good run! Do it again!"

There was a loud boom and a flash that Covey saw from the air. Nash made his way to Rapun and PW2 to see how badly they were injured. He yelled, "The PW2 is dead! Rapun has shrapnel in his leg and arm. Bleeding. Can't walk. I've got him!"

"Nash, make sure PW2 is dead and leave him. We've got to go!" I yelled back. "This is Five. Crap! They just took out PW2 with an RPG. And we've got another brunette that can't walk. Wait. Out."

"This is Five, marking my position again. ID color." "I've got a white flare."

"Roger that. Make the run 50 meters south of my position flying east to west. DANGER CLOSE. DO IT NOW!"

More bullets and 40mm got through the canopy this time and did some damage. It became very smoky and hard to see. The NVA were still creeping toward us, and we were taking some of them out with single shots. Pua was working magic with Aita's M-79. He was pumping the HE rounds on to the NVA.

"This is Five, that was close, but right on. I need napalm. Now!"

"Roger that. I've got two SPADs three mikes out with napalm. Where do you want it? You copy, Five? You want it deep or wide? Five, you copy?"

The NVA had massed about 20 meters out from us and were assaulting. "TAKE COVER! THEY ARE ASSAULTING! THROW SOME GRENADES! SWITCH TO AUTO! PUA, PUT SOME

40MM ON THEM!" I shouted.

They were dropping like flies, but more were coming. I was firing from behind a tree and just as I finished a magazine, I saw an NVA five feet from Cantua, whose weapon was empty, and PW3. I drew my Colt 1911A1 .45 caliber pistol and shot the NVA soldier twice. The impact of the bullets literally picked him up off the ground and threw him backwards. Wow! A .45 hits hard!

"DON'T LET THEM GET AWAY! KEEP FIRING!" I reloaded and got a couple more as they were retreating. So did Cantua. "Cantua, lead us to the LZ."

"I'm a little busy, Covey!" I finally yelled back over the heavy volume of gunfire, explosions and me yelling something about the NVA's ancestors in background.

"This is Five. A group of NVA just made the final assault of their lives. Put the first napalm 150 meters south of my position flying east to west. Danger close! Don't. Miss! We are moving toward the LZ." I shouted, "MICHIGAN! GET DOWN! NAPALM 20 SECONDS OUT!"

The napalm hit in the trees, but a lot of it came to the ground—right on the NVA! If it gets on you, it won't come off. It just sticks and burns. The smoke was so thick under the canopy, our eyes were burning, and we couldn't see and were having trouble breathing. The smell was sickening. Pua and PW1 were both throwing up.

I accidentally pressed the push to talk button before I finished talking to the team. "CHECK AMMO AND REDISTRIBUTE! Sorry, Covey. It's a little chaotic down here. Put the second napalm 100 meters east of my position flying south to north."

"Roger. Second napalm 30 seconds out. Get on the ground with something between you and the napalm ASAP!"

I yelled, "MICHIGAN ON THE GROUND! NAPALM 20 SECONDS OUT! COVER YOUR HEAD!"

Most of this one came to the ground. It was on the NVA, but almost hit us! This stuff scared me. "TAKE OUT THE TORCHES!" I shouted. The napalm had burned away a lot of the vegetation making it easier to see the NVA and shoot them. I kept saying to myself, *This is the humane thing to do.*

"WOW! That stuff is hot! We've got human torches running around."

"Five, get down. Third napalm 30 seconds out!" "Roger that! It's barbeque time!"

"MICHIGAN, GET DOWN! NAPALM 20 SECONDS OUT!" Another good drop right on the NVA. The smell of over-cooked human flesh, smoke and low-oxygen air makes you want to vomit. I watched as Cantua and Chung began throwing up.

The napalm stopped the NVA's advancement toward us. We grabbed our PWs, Bargewell picked up Aita and Nash picked up Rapun and made a run for the LZ before the NVA regrouped and came after us. We were only about 200 meters from the LZ. I had put the last napalm between us and the LZ to clear a path. It definitely did that. Quite a few of the charred bodies were still burning as we moved through the area. The smell was gross. There was little oxygen in the air making it difficult to breathe and it was very smoky and burned our eyes. We were sweating so much that it was running into our eyes making it even more difficult to see. We moved as fast as we could with two PWs fighting every step and three wounded team members, two of whom were being carried. We were all soaking wet from the heat and humidity, running, fighting and dragging PWs. We were dehydrated, thirsty, exhausted, running on pure adrenaline but getting closer to the extraction LZ.

When we were about 100 meters from the LZ, we hit a wall of withering AK, RPG and RPD fire. BOOM! BOOM! The heat and blast wave from the RPGs temporarily blinded us. We found the RPD to be a devastating weapon too. The NVA had anticipated that we were going to the LZ and sent a group there to welcome us. They arrived at the LZ after the napalm. They weren't tired. The RPD was tearing the jungle up! RPGs were firing at us. Boom! Boom! Bullets, debris and shrapnel were flying everywhere. It was very smoky. The sound of the RPD with its 100-round belt was overpowering the sound of AKs and shredding everything around us. We could not put our heads up to shoot back. The NVA machine gunner would have to change ammunition drums soon. Plus, we were ordering a present for them.

"MICHIGAN! GET DOWN! USE SINGLE SHOTS!"

"Covey, we are in heavy contact on the south side of the LZ, got any more napalm?"

"This is Covey. Yes. Where you want it?"

"I want the center of mass to be 30 meters north of the tree line on the south edge of the LZ. Fly east to west. Danger close! Actually, very close! Don't miss!"

"Roger that. Stand by."

"This is Covey. The gates of hell will open in 30 seconds. Get down!"

"Roger!"

"MICHIGAN! GET DOWN! NAPALM 20 SECONDS OUT! DANGER CLOSE!"

During those 20 seconds an NVA fired an RPG close to PW3 and hit him with shrapnel and peppered me with small shrapnel! I could feel the heat and blast wave from the RPG. Cantua was with PW3. The PW3 was bleeding badly. I couldn't do anything for him until after the napalm strike. The napalm hit very close resulting in most of the team receiving small burns. This stuff was really scary to use. One miscalculation and the entire team would be crispy critters! I scrambled to my PW3 and began trying to stop the bleeding. I looked up and saw a torch coming toward me.

"CANTUA, TAKE OVER!" But not just any torch. This one was dragging an RPD by the barrel! I hit him in the chest with a three-round burst from my CAR-15 and the torch and machine gun were gone. All future generations that could come from him were instantly erased.

Wow! My pants leg was on fire! I tried to pat it out, but it just spread and got on my glove. Now my glove was burning too, and it was hot! I grabbed a handful of mud, and my glove went out. I rubbed the mud on my pants leg and put the flame out. It lit up again. I put more mud on it then realized my shirt sleeve was burning. Again, I rubbed mud on to put it out. Napalm was hard to extinguish!

"This is Five. That was a little closer than I expected. It fried the bad guys, but we may have gotten a suntan through our clothes! We might even have some burns. We are ready to go home. Can you get us out of here?"

"Roger that. We have two birds on final approach escorted by Cobras. Stand by for extraction."

"Roger. We will be wearing orange hats. Expect a lot of ground fire. Standing by."

"MICHIGAN TURN YOUR HATS ORANGE!" I yelled to my team. "The first load will be Bargewell, Nash, PW1, Aita, and Pua. There will be a lot of ground fire. We have to load fast or they will leave us. Keep the PWs secured!"

PW1 resisted getting on the helicopter until Bargewell punched him in the jaw. He staggered and dropped to his knees. Bargewell grabbed him and threw him in the helicopter. It seemed like it took a long time to load the wounded. My job was to provide supporting fire. Bargewell and Nash were doing a great job loading the wounded without injuring them more. They were finally in and lifting off. I could hear the metallic clangs of bullets hitting their chopper.

The second aircraft was on short final. I had the wounded PW3, Cantua, Chung and Rapun with me. We were receiving a lot of fire, but our PW3 was not resisting. Cantua and I helped the others get aboard and we lifted off about two minutes after Bargewell's aircraft. The ground fire was still coming at us, and the helicopter received several hits as we were leaving. I dropped a red smoke grenade. The Cobras were ripping the area around the LZ apart with miniguns, 40mm and rockets. SPADs were working more napalm, 250-pound bombs and 20mm machine guns higher and lower on the ridge trying to interdict the flow of troops up the ridge and suppress the ground fire. As I watched the fireworks show around us, I took a deep breath, let it out slowly and thought, we just might make it out of here.

"Covey, this is Five. Thanks. We really appreciate everything you guys did for us today. Outstanding job! We'll take care of you back at the ranch."

I sat back to relax. A few minutes later I was looking at Bargewell's helicopter in front of us and thinking that although the team was banged up pretty badly, it was a successful mission. We got out with two prisoners. Then—it happened! I saw a body fall from Bargewell's helicopter. I had on a head set so I was able to ask our pilot how high we were, and would he ask the lead aircraft what happened. He told me that we were at 2300 feet AGL and apparently the prisoner got loose and dove out of the helicopter still handcuffed and head bagged. He was last seen as he disappeared headfirst into the jungle canopy 2300 feet below traveling at somewhere between 160–180 MPH!

Now we had one PW3 left and he was steadily bleeding. I had tried everything I knew to do. The bleeding had slowed, but I couldn't stop it. He was hit with several big pieces of shrapnel in the head, chest, side, arms and legs, and a ton of little pieces elsewhere. The floor of the helicopter was covered with blood. He was slowly bleeding out. I had already put one IV of Ringer's solution in him and started the second. He was getting weaker, no longer able to talk. I couldn't let him die. Fortunately, we had gotten some information from him before he was hit.

We flew straight to the 95th Evac Hospital Emergency Room helipad to get the wounded treated. When we arrived at the 95th ER our unconscious PW3 was rushed to OR. About 20 minutes later one of the surgeons who had been working on him (PW3) came out to tell us he died on the table. They did all they could but were unable to save him. This was both depressing and frustrating news.

The most important thing now was the condition of our team members.

### RT Michigan Injuries

| | |
|---|---|
| Thompson | small shrapnel, 1st & 2nd degree burns |
| Bargewell | small shrapnel, 1st & 2nd degree burns |
| Nash | small shrapnel, 1st & 2nd degree burns |
| Aita | bullet in abdomen |
| Cantua | 1st & 2nd degree burns |
| Chung | bullet in shoulder, 1st & 2nd degree burns |
| Rapun | shrapnel, leg & arm |
| Pua | 1st & 2nd degree burns |

**After Action Review Summary**

- The only thing the VR did was confirm the NVA were out there and could hit a small plane with 51 caliber machine guns.
- The pre-mission training was critical, especially what we did on Monkey Mountain. We needed to rehearse in Monkey Mountain's jungle whenever possible.
- The Final Mission Briefing and insertion package were outstanding.
- The team performed very well on the ground prior to and during contact.
- Adequate sleep is critical for excellent performance under fire—especially for leaders. Leaders tend to be reluctant to sleep—almost seeing it as a sign of weakness. Sleep loss makes our brains foggy and slows decision making. Chemicals like caffeine, dextroamphetamine, etc., give us an alert foggy brain.

**The Ambush:**

- The terrain did not allow us to be a safe distance from the Claymores and C-4 in the main site. We were hit with a lot of debris and blast, even though the Claymores and C-4 were in front of trees. We were all slightly stunned and blinded by the effects of the explosions.
- Our view of the KZ was partially blocked by vegetation.
- We needed a larger team to handle three PWs and wounded team members.
- The NVA came very close to taking us out at the KZ and during the ensuing fight to get to the LZ.
- Several valuable documents and maps were recovered from bodies in the KZ.
- We began an immediate interrogation of the PWs starting in the KZ while they were being secured. Only one PW had any partial hearing. The other two had ruptured ear drums.
- Four pounds of C-4 combined with the blast effect of the Claymores might have been too much. Three pounds would probably be more than enough to have staggered them.

- We needed at least one Claymore (with WP in front of it) about 20 meters down from the KZ on each end to help provide security against reaction forces.
- Needed more practice securing a violently resisting PW loaded with adrenaline.
- I had no way to alert the team that I was going to initiate the ambush. I hoped that they knew I would when they heard the gun fire at ambush site #1. We had not practiced for this situation.
- Needed more practice carrying different types of wounded under fire. We were not ready for Aita's abdomen wound. Bargewell did a great job, but we should have trained for this before the mission.
- Need to reinforce training on when to fire semi vs. automatic.
- More practice on redistributing ammunition (magazines, 40mm, frag grenades and Claymores).
- Trying to communicate during a firefight, especially if we are trying to escape, is very difficult. Need to have the Americans in the right places and them relaying commands.
- Bargewell and I carrying silenced pistols provided a way to salvage the mission if the "lost" NVA had stepped on Chung. The silenced pistol became part of my standard loadout on all future missions.
- We need more medical training, especially controlling bleeding.

**Psychological**
- We need to stay busy between missions. Inactivity allows fear to creep in.
- There is a direct relationship between time between missions and level of fear.
- We need time to heal, physically and psychologically, between missions.
- We need time between missions to correct problems and train for the next one.

- The physical and psychological effect of wearing a headset was stunning. In addition to providing real-time battlefield information, it also gave me the ability to:
  - Adapt the insertion plan while we were still in the air
  - Have more control of the insertion
  - Manage fear
  - Focus and relax
  - Be fully in the game before arrival at the LZ
  - Preserve hearing—now and in the future

## Napalm:

- Napalm puts the fear of God (or maybe the devil) in the NVA. It is the most horrible, cruel, terrifying, physically and psychologically damaging weapon in our arsenal. It creates a lot of human torches—enemy soldiers covered with burning napalm blindly stumbling around as they are being consumed by fire. The enemy survivors, if there are any, never get over the screams, smells, pain, lack of oxygen in the air, choking air, smoke and visual images they see. The experience is literally burned into their brains/minds.
- The team that delivers napalm never gets over the experience. Calling it in scares me because I know the slightest miscalculation by anyone in the process can cause it to hit the good guys. All of the team received some burns this time. But sometimes you have to choose to save the team at all costs.
- Napalm opens the gates of hell. It makes the survivors think twice about attacking the team. It also makes them use the tactic of hugging the team. They try to get close enough to the team that you can't use napalm, airstrikes or gunships.

## Lessons Learned

- Wearing gloves provided my hands some protection, but not enough to overcome the heat generated by emptying 32 magazines (20x32=640 rounds), mostly with automatic bursts.
- The .45-caliber pistol (M1911A1) demonstrated outstanding

knock down power at close range, but it was heavy, the ammunition was heavy and it only has a seven-round magazine. I will consider carrying it again. (Even if I carry the M1911A1, I will still carry the silenced pistol).

- The team needed to have more than one M-79. We would carry an additional sawed-off version (so we would still have the CAR-15) as a minimum on future missions.

- The PWs fought us the whole time and really slowed our movement, especially under fire. They also made loading the aircraft more difficult. Bargewell had to knock his PW out to get him on the helicopter—and he still managed to get loose and jump out of the helicopter at 2300 feet.

- We recovered a lot of valuable NVA documents, maps, etc.

- This was a very mentally and physically fatiguing operation—start to finish.

- We needed more physical training.

- Bargewell seemed to be fascinated by the fire power of the RPD. He played with one during post-mission training and decided it was too heavy and awkward to carry on an RT mission. I could tell he had not given up on the idea.

- Bargewell would eventually begin carrying a modified (no bipod and a shorter barrel) RPD as his primary weapon. His RPD would play a major role in the firefight in which he won the Distinguished Service Cross. Bargewell would pass on this particular RPD to 1LT Ken Bowra, a SOG 1-0, who would not only become a SOG legend, but also, like Bargewell, a Major General. I should have told Bargewell I wanted to use the RPD. Maybe I would have been a MG. On second thought, no. I don't think it was the gun.

SSG Nash was moved to another team after this mission to be a 1-1 on a team with only one American.

# RT Michigan Marble Mountain Security Mission with Cousin Carl 25 JAN 69

There are five Marble Mountains near Da Nang, each named after one of the elements: Kim (metal); Thuy (water); Moc (wood); Hoa (fire); and Tho (earth). The highest is Thuy, which set approximately 300 meters outside the southern side of the CCN compound defensive wire. Marble Mountain, as we called Thuy, rose almost straight up out of the sand for over 450 feet. It forms a saddle with a peak on each end. If the bad guys could get on one or both of those peaks, they could fire directly into the CCN compound. That is exactly what they tried to do on 23 August 1968 when the compound was overrun.

After that, CCN kept an RT on each of the peaks all the time. RT Michigan's mission would be to man the combat outpost (COP) on the eastern most peak (COP 1) for ten days. RT Georgia had been on the western most peak for about five days and would be replaced by another RT in five to eight days.

*Marble Mountain (Thuy) from inside CCN. A Combat Outpost on each peak. (Courtesy of LT Henry Thompson)*

## Marble Mountain Team Roster

| | |
|---|---|
| LT Thompson | 1-0 |
| SGT Bargewell | 1-1 |
| Cantua | Interpreter |
| Hieng | M-79 |
| Camba | Pointman 1 |
| Pua | Pointman 3 |
| Acat | Tail Gunner 1 |
| Chung | Tail Gunner 2 |
| Rapun | M-79 |
| Aita | Pointman 2 |
| SGT Hudson | Straphanger |

## Travel to COP 1

Just after first light we exited the CCN compound through the rear exit in full combat gear and made our way along the beach very carefully. Before arriving at the base of the mountain we were met by a three-man escort team from RT Coral. Their job was to show us the way to approach the mountain and point out the hazards to watch for— booby traps, mines, ambushes, etc. We passed through the edge of a small village and followed the trail up to a plateau to the Pagoda where the monks lived. From there the trail changed dramatically. It was very steep and rough with loose rocks, and it was difficult to climb, especially while carrying so much gear.

Eventually, we arrived at the top and were greeted by the RT Coral 1-0, SSG Jason, his 1-1, SGT Mulberry, and his team. They were excited to be getting off the mountain. It was only a little after 1000 hours and already 100 degrees. No trees grew on the mountaintop, just sun and a light breeze coming off the South China Sea.

SSG Jason and SGT Mulberry gave us an operations and tactical briefing as they walked us around the COP perimeter covering the topics below:

- Snipers
- Defensive Positions

- Rules of Engagement
- How/when/where the enemy attacks
- Coordination/communication with COP 2
- Interlocking fires
- Food/water/ammunition resupplies
- Daytime security patrols
- IEDs/booby-traps
- The heat and humidity
- Don't forget the snipers

Our mission was to defend the COP and not to allow the VC or NVA to get in the COP. Our secondary mission was to support COP 2 on the other peak in the event the enemy tried to take it. We could see the RT Georgia team members moving around about 300 meters across the plateau. SSG Jason got RT Georgia's 1-0, SFC Saunders, on the radio and I talked to him. Bargewell knew him, and I had seen him in the CCN compound but never had actually met him.

*LT Thompson and SGT Eldon Bargewell on Marble Mountain, COP 1 near CCN, 1969 (Picture courtesy of LT Thompson)*

Bargewell tested the landline that had been strung high above the saddle between the two COPs. This provided a secondary and private means of communication between the COPs. The TOC monitored all of our radio traffic and kept the CCN Commander apprised of what was happening on the mountain. Note: There would come a time in the near future, during the heat of battle, when I should have remembered that what I was saying on the radio was being monitored by a lot of people, including the CCN Commander.

## Day 1

Once we settled into our defensive positions and notified the TOC that we had control of COP 1, RT Coral left the COP and started their hike back to CCN. All Michigan team members began fortifying their defensive positions and checking fields of fire, aiming stakes, ammunition, grenades and flares, getting ready for the enemy to test our resolve that night.

What the team found most interesting, however, was the latrine. They found it very funny to watch each other use the apparatus. It gave a new meaning to being totally open. It was a wooden platform with a commode seat mounted over a hole on the edge of the cliff with the seat/hole extending beyond the edge of the cliff. When you used the latrine, your waste matter dropped 200 feet straight down to some rocks. Getting on and off the latrine was a challenge. It took some getting used to both physically and mentally. You also did not use it at night—snipers.

A little after 1500, Hieng was welcomed by a sniper when one tried to pick him off. Two rounds ricocheted off a rock about 12 inches from Hieng's head. That was close and a little earlier than we expected. We did not see the sniper's location, but we all got the message. The bad guys were out there and intended to take us out! We were also learning about bullets ricocheting off our mountaintop of stone.

The sunset was beautiful from the COP, but it was the lull before the storm. Around 2030 we came under heavy fire from the small plateau between us and COP 2. This gave me an opportunity to play with my M-60 machine gun. I engaged the enemy with a heavy barrage

*Marble Mountain COP 1 200-foot-high latrine*
*(Courtesy of LT Thompson)*

of 7.62mm fire and was joined by an M-60 on COP 2. It was nice not to have to carry the heavy M-60 (23 lbs) or the ammo (30 lbs/1000).

As we returned fire, it lit up each of our defensive positions. Now the NVA knew exactly where our positions were located. A second NVA group located almost directly across from COP 1 engaged our positions from the mouth of a small cave approximately 40 meters away. This caused us all to get down until Hieng put two 40mm HE rounds in the mouth of the cave followed by a flare to light up the inside. The cave went silent and stayed that way the rest of the night. So did the plateau. I'm sure the guys watching the movie inside the compound continued to enjoy the main feature while we played with the bad guys nicknamed "Charlie."

After the attack ended and my adrenaline began to wear off, I was able to process what the experience was like physically and psychologically. I made a list to discuss in the AAR I planned to do the next morning.

**Day 2**

During the AAR we noted that the sandbags around our positions had not fared well during the attack. Bargewell put in a request for 50 full sandbags, along with more ammunition, to be delivered by lunch. We also discussed the following:

- We were not only "trapped" on the small mountain peak with our backs against a cliff, but also in most of our fighting positions, especially mine. My position was on the primary route of engagement. I had a view of the entire battlefield. This gave me great fields of fire, and I had a machine gun, which made my position the primary target for the NVA. They could easily see my position and some others on my side of the peak making it easy to attack us in the dark.

- I was mostly confined to my position once the attack started. To escape from my position once I began to fire would totally expose me for 15–20 meters. Moving to another place on the peak would greatly reduce my ability to see and control the battle. I had a ringside seat for the entire battlefield. I had become so used to shooting and moving that my position and the peak felt almost claustrophobic. We could not maneuver. Being pinned down in heavy fire and not being able to raise my head above my sandbags was almost like being underwater at night—no visibility. I elected to remain in this position for a few days to see how it worked for me.

- Another problem we had to work out was internal communication. Bargewell and I both had a PRC-25. This allowed us to talk to each other, COP 2, TOC, helicopters and gunships—but not the team members. We had to yell to the team over a very loud environment of guns firing, explosions, etc. We kept Bargewell just over the backside of the peak which gave him mobility to get near each fighting position and check their status and give instructions. We became better at how we communicated as the days went along.

- We did an AAR each morning to learn and improve our ability to destroy the attackers and keep team members safe.

- In hindsight I find it difficult to believe that we did not wear helmets and flak jackets in this static position.
- Our M-79s played a critical role in our defense. Shooting the 40mm grenades from the peak extended their range significantly. Being in a static position allowed us to stockpile 40mm ammunition and include CS gas and smoke rounds along with a lot of HE rounds. During attacks, Hieng and Rapun would create a 40mm rain on the NVA. Bargewell would just order more the next day.
- We knew we had a lot to learn about best practices on the mountain and went after it aggressively like the team was learning to do with everything else. I had the best 1-1 I could have had in Bargewell, and we were in the early stages of what would become a 50-year friendship.

*Marble Mountain, COP 1 Fighting Position*
*Transistor radio on right side*
*(Courtesy of LT Henry Thompson)*

Day 2 was a hot, slow day. Fortunately, the COP had its own transistor radio (see the right side of the picture. This allowed us to tune in our one station, the Armed Forces Vietnam Network (AFVN), Saigon, hosted by DJ Pat Sajak (yes, later to become the famous "Wheel of Fortune" host beginning in 1981). He was the AFVN host from October 1968 to December 1969. Every weekday at 0600 he would shout those famous words, "Gooood mornnning, Vietnam!" This boosted our morale and helped us keep up with the latest music in the States.

The snipers returned around 1630 and played with us until 1800. The snipers liked to attack before it got dark enough that we could see their muzzle flashes. We had a break for a couple hours, then a small attack just to let us know the NVA were thinking about us.

## Day 3

Another beautiful sunrise, a cool breeze and an afternoon that would bring me a big surprise!

Around 1100 on Day 3 the TOC called and said I needed to report to the Recon Company TOC—a visitor was waiting for me. That was all they would say. I took Cantua and Hieng and we made our way down the mountain. I was in total shock when I saw who was waiting for me. It was my cousin Carl. Remember Thompson's Rangers? I knew he was in country on his third tour in Vietnam but did not expect to see him while I was at CCN. I especially did not expect to see him inside a top secret SOG compound that few people outside of SOG knew existed. How did he know I was there and how did he talk his way into a restricted compound? He had always amazed me with what he could do.

He said he had a few days leave from Golf Company, 75th Rangers and came up to see me. I explained that my team was securing COP 1 and I had to go back up there, but if he didn't mind getting shot at while he was on leave, I could show him a good time. He was all in. We ate in the mess hall then went to the supply room where he signed for a CAR-15, some tactical gear, ruck, LRPs, ammo, an IV of Ringer's solution, a poncho and liner. He declined the helmet and flak jacket and we headed up the mountain. It was great to see him and serve in combat for a few days together like we did when we were kids. I would have felt better if he had taken the helmet and flak jacket because this time the bad guys would be shooting back with AK-47s and RPGs.

The enemy did not disappoint us. They attacked several times during the night. I think they knew we had a new person with us on the mountain and wanted to welcome cousin Carl to Thuy.

## Day 4

We did our normal AAR as we ate breakfast. It was good to have Carl's perspective on what he observed and his recommendations.

After our AAR, the boredom of Day 4 set in. Being confined to a 40-foot-in-diameter mountaintop in direct sun, plus 100 degrees and high humidity got old fast. It was time to do something. I rounded up Carl, Cantua, Camba and Pua and told Bargewell we were going to clear some caves, starting with the one across from us. I noticed that Camba and Pua did not seem to want to go and had a conversation with Cantua. When I ask Cantua what was going on, he said they didn't like caves. They went anyway.

We did not find anyone in the cave across from us but did see a lot of dried blood. When we went into one of the lower caves, we surprised two NVA. Carl put one of them down right away, then we started dodging our own bullets! We were educated on what happens when you start shooting in a stone cave—ricochets! Each bullet was bouncing off two or three walls before it stopped. After a few minutes we got the hang of it and took out the other bad guy. We searched them and left their bodies outside the cave and returned to COP 1. Camba thought we should put the two NVAs' heads on stakes as a warning to the other NVA. I told him to re-sheath his knife. We were not going to do that. He and Pua were not happy.

We had some sniper fire during the early evening, but no attack that night. We managed to get a little more sleep than normal.

## Day 5

In our AAR, we spent time processing shooting in stone caves and how to use ricochets to our advantage. The team had also heard about the

Marble Mountain shootout with the NVA in 1968, LT Dan Thompson was tasked to take his Hatchet Force Platoon up the mountain to find a hole in the top of the mountain that could be used to retrieve three Americans and six indigenous commandos—all wounded and trapped inside the grotto with no way out—and to retrieve LT David Lenchner's body. Dan found a hole and was able to rescue the nine wounded personnel and recover LT Lenchner's body.

Knowledge of this incident was what caused Camba and Pua not to want to go in the caves the day before. Cantua did not tell me that when I asked what was wrong, so he and I had a private talk about the need to tell me everything.

Bargewell ordered more sandbags, ammunition and food. A Kingbee delivered the supplies just before lunch.

About 1400, Hieng and Camba asked if they could make a quick run down to the village. Hieng said they would be back in an hour. Carl and I went with them to keep them out of trouble. We looked around the village a little and got a range of reactions—from amazement to fear. The villagers weren't used to seeing SOG members up close. We found a small restaurant and stopped for a snack. Carl had learned to speak Vietnamese pretty well. Not sure what we ate, but it was very hot! I'm sure Carl knew but did not tell me. Hieng and Camba disappeared while we were eating. When they came back, they had a live chicken— sans feathers.

We went back up the mountain and enjoyed an early chicken and rice dinner. When we finished our meal and made our final security inspection of the mountaintop, it was about time for the snipers to say hello. It was a beautiful sunset, even with the snipers.

Around 2200 hours our friends came back and primarily attacked COP 2. We were able to provide fire support for them. It was a relatively easy night for us. A little target practice without much return fire. I think Carl was disappointed.

## Day 6

A really hot and boring morning. But you never knew what excitement the day could bring.

About 1300, Hieng and Camba asked if they could make a quick run down to the village. "No trouble," they said. Hieng said they would be back in an hour. Bargewell agreed and I said they could go, but they had to take Cantua, Pua and the radio with them. Twenty minutes after they left, we heard two CAR-15 gunshots followed immediately by Cantua on the radio saying, "No problem. We come home." Bargewell said, "They've done something. I can hear it in Cantua's voice."

After about 15 minutes we saw them climbing up the last and steepest part of the trail. They were carrying something. When they got on top, I could see they had a bloody sandbag with something heavy in it and blood dripping from the bottom of the bag. Bargewell asked Cantua what was in the bag. Cantua became angry during his discussion with Hieng. He turned to Bargewell and said, "Monk dog. They eat." Bargewell almost lost it. He shared some very heated words with Hieng using Cantua to interpret them. Bargewell was not happy with them. They had killed the monks' dog and were going to eat it!

The evening meal was dog and rice. Bargewell, Carl and I had LRPs. Actually, Carl and I did have a small portion of dog and rice with our LRPs—just to maintain the team bond. We were living the dream. A belly full of dog and snipers shooting at us while the latest hits from America blasted in the background, knowing all along that this was the warmup act for what was coming later that night. And the attack did come. Just another day in SOG.

**Day 7**

AAR: We spent time on no heads on sticks and no eating monks' dogs. Even though the Vietnamese ate dogs on a regular basis, RT Michigan was not going to take people's dogs and eat them. Today we were going into caves again and were going to be careful where we shot. I wanted them to avoid hitting the big fancy buddhas. We didn't need any more trouble with the monks.

We decided we would spend the hottest part of the day searching caves, especially the big ones with the big carved buddhas in them. The monks were not happy when they saw us going into their main areas. Unfortunately, we did not find any bad guys, but it was a lot cooler than being outside in the sun.

Just before our evening meal of LRPs for the Americans and PIRs for the little guys, our sniper friends returned. Then a small attack. Not very exciting.

## Day 8

AAR: We had not found any NVA in the caves but did notice that the monks and Vietnamese were acting suspicious. Bargewell and Cantua picked up on it right away. Something was up—or coming.

The wind and hard rain started about an hour before daylight. There was no way to stay dry or warm. We had planned to go back in the caves that day but decided to stay in the COP.

The snipers started early that afternoon, taking us by surprise. The first round hit Pua in the arm. Nothing serious, but I'm sure it hurt. I called the TOC and had them send a chopper to pick up Pua and have him treated. He was back in a couple of hours.

We tried to stay behind cover as much as we could but staying covered reduced our ability to see what was happening around us. The increased sniper activity combined with the weather made Bargewell's and my Spidey senses go off. I called SSG Saunders on COP 2 on the landline and shared our concern that this had the makings of a CCR Bad Moon Rising. He said they had the same feeling. I called the TOC and shared my concerns about what might be coming.

Just before dark, the sniper fire stopped. Everything got quiet—except the wind and rain. Both COPs were on full alert and looking for any sign of movement. I told Carl to mentally prepare for a heavy attack that night. I had passed that same information to the TOC and asked them to have the mortar crews on alert and ready to fire flares for us. Bargewell had already distributed extra hand flares and frag grenades to the team. The rain stopped around 1930 and the wind slowed a little. Cantua was scanning with the starlight scope, but the night was so dark he couldn't see very far.

Just after 2100, a large group of NVA opened fire on both COPs with AK-47s and RPGs from the back side of the plateau. A couple of B-40 rockets went over our COP and down toward the CCN compound but hit short of the defensive wire. I called for flares from the mortar crews. At the same time this was happening, the Marine compound on the other side of the village was attacked. We could see a heavy exchange of fire. The Marines called in 155mm artillery to help defend their position.

With our COPs lit up by the flares, the snipers decided to join the party. Then a second group of NVA opened fire from positions much closer to us. They had used the dark night to slip in closer than normal. We were definitely slugging it out with them. After about 20 minutes while communicating back and forth with SSG Saunders on COP 2 over the radio, I slipped in a comment that if we had a case of beer, we would be having a real party up here.

A few minutes later a 155mm artillery "short" round landed next to one of the Marine barracks and leveled it. Fortunately, everyone was on the perimeter in their fighting positions. You do not want to be on the artillery gun-target line, especially with 155mms! The 155mm rounds were known for landing short of the target on a regular basis.

*LT Henry Thompson and SGT Carl Hudson on Marble Mountain
Combat Outpost 1, near CCN 1969
(Picture courtesy of LT Henry Thompson)*

A lot of NVA bodies were scattered around on the ground between the two COPs. COP 2 had two team members with gunshot wounds who would be evacuated the next morning. RT Michigan had three with not-serious shrapnel wounds. The rest of us were okay. We stayed alert the rest of the night, but there was no more activity—or so we thought!

## Day 9

When the sun came up there were no bodies to be seen. Under the cover of darkness, they had all been dragged or carried away, a common practice by the NVA. While observing the absence of bodies the TOC called for an update and to let me know that the CCN Commander wanted me to report to his office at 0800. I thought that maybe he was going to tell us we did a good job the night before, but I didn't really think so. We did a short AAR and I took Cantua, Hieng and Carl and headed down the mountain.

When I got in LTC Isler's office he confronted me about the drinking and partying going on at my COP. I assured him that was not the case. He said he heard me say "if we had another case of beer." I told him I said "a" case of beer and it was just banter while I was pinned down in my fighting position and not able to return fire. I said that I was sure he noticed that SSG Saunders and I were mixing a lot of "talk" in with the information we were exchanging. His final words were, "No partying on the mountain!" I said, "Yes, Sir," and Carl, Cantua, Hieng and I headed for the mess hall to get a real meal before climbing back up the mountain. I never did hear "good job."

No snipers or attack that night. It was nice to get some sleep.

## Day 10

Beautiful sunrise. Everyone was excited because we would be going back to the compound that afternoon after briefing the new team. We were told that we would receive a 1600 mission brief.

I did a quick AAR even though we were going back to CCN. I discussed being careful about what was said on the radio. Cantua inserted, "COL like NVA. Always listen." I told them to do a good police call (pick up trash) before we left and take it with us.

When we got back to CCN we ate in the mess hall, turned in Carl's equipment, and got him transportation back to his unit. It was great sharing some action adventures with him. It's not every day you get to have a "live fire" action adventure with your cousin.

## Lessons Learned

- Being in a static defensive fighting position is different (they know exactly where you are) than a team fighting and maneuvering.
- Sandbags got shredded very quickly. Not sure why we didn't use concrete.
- Snipers get your attention!
- Be careful what you say on the radio.
- Should have considered using helmets and flak jackets. No reason not to in a static position.
- We were trapped on a small peak with limited cover in fixed positions that the NVA could observe during the day.
- We could have lots of ammunition because we did not have to carry it.
- The M-79s played a critical role in our defense. We could "fire down" on the NVA and shoot longer distances than normal.
- It was very hot on COP 1 with limited man-made shade.
- Cousin Carl's visit was a great action adventure we would never forget.
- We had to learn how to shoot inside the stone caves.
- Team members get bored when confined to a small peak. We had to provide operations to break the boredom, e.g., clearing caves, trips to the village, etc.
- Eating the monks' dog did not make the monks happy.
- The view from COP 1 was fantastic during the day.

Our break/healing time was over. That afternoon we would get a new mission. What follows below are summaries of my last three missions as 1-0 of RT Michigan. They were great missions, and I thoroughly enjoyed my time in and out of combat with Eldon Bargewell. He would become one of my two special operations mentors for over 50 years.

# RT Michigan Mission 3: Search & Destroy
# Who Let the Dogs Out? SOG #7 Summary (7 FEB 69)

RT Michigan's mission was to search, find and destroy an NVA Regimental Unit (~2,000 men) operating near the Laos–North Vietnam border.

### Mission 3 Team Roster

| Name | Position |
|------|----------|
| LT Thompson | 1-0 |
| SGT Bargewell | 1-1 |
| Cantua | Interpreter |
| Hieng | M-79 |
| Camba | Pointman 1 |
| Pua | M-79 |
| Acat | Tail Gunner 1 |

Part of the mission prep was conducting a VR of the AO. To maximize time, I left Bargewell with the team to work on skill development while I flew the VR, which did not go well. The air was very rough, and the plane's right wing was hit with three rounds of NVA .51 caliber machine gun fire. The flaps were okay, but we were leaking fuel. We returned to base with only a few pictures of the AO, but I did see several small clearings that could be used for LZs. There were also some small cliffs that could be used for observation of the highway.

When I got back, Bargewell and I decided that Hieng and Pua would carry M-79 grenade launchers, and I would carry a sawed-off grenade launcher in addition to my CAR-15 and .22 pistol. The additional area fire weapons would give us more fire power in this terrain. Our close proximity to the North Vietnam border required us to have a flight of F-4s flying combat air patrol (CAP) to keep North Vietnamese MiGs away.

## Insertion

We inserted using two Kingbees. Cantua, Hieng, Camba and I were on the first aircraft, with Bargewell, Pua and Acat on the second. It was a smooth insertion and we moved out quietly after a security halt. As we started to move, I could smell decomp in the air. Soon Camba signaled that he smelled it too. We found a day-old, partially eaten deer. Cantua said, "Tigers." That got everyone's attention. This was a Yard team. They grew up in the jungle and were very familiar with what tigers could do to a human. Camba became even more vigilant.

The ridgeline was wide and rugged, with thick canopy and lots of undergrowth. The thick underbrush restricted airflow, increased the temperature and reduced visibility. Within two hours after our insertion, we heard bamboo clackers being used by trackers and a muffled dog bark. We were not expecting dogs—or tigers! A few minutes later Pua found tiger scat. His village had had a lot of problems with tigers. They were snatching people at night and running off into the jungle with them. The scat made him more afraid of being snatched and dragged off into the jungle by a tiger than walking up on an NVA. I noticed my search pattern had automatically added new factors: tiger "smell," and more sensitivity to the color orange.

Tigers can weigh 500–600 pounds and easily run 40 miles an hour. The fastest human can run 27.5 MPH (Usain Bolt ran this fast for a little under ten seconds in 2009). A tiger can take down and drag a 1,500-lb guar bull a long distance. One swipe of a tiger's paw can easily decapitate a human. They like to go for the neck for a quick kill. Avoid tigers!

We had been on the ground for an hour and were adjusting to thoughts of tigers when two North Vietnamese MiGs tried to approach our AO. Our F-4 Combat Air Patrol (CAP) destroyed one MiG and sent the other scrambling back to North Vietnam. The aerial combat engagement was too far away for our team to know what was happening. Covey transmitted an alphanumeric code to let me know there had been some MiG activity in the area, but all was clear.

## RON

We continued to move until about 30 minutes before EENT and found a good RON site. We did a fishhook maneuver to enter the RON. I put out toe poppers on the path just before we made our turn to go to the RON. Once in the site we put out our normal defensive Claymores. Around 2220 we heard a muffled dog bark and yelp about 100 meters from us. Cantua whispered, "Tiger eat dog. This number ten. Not good." I knew no one would sleep that night. We heard vehicular traffic on the road, but we were not in a position to see what was happening, and it was too dangerous to try to move closer to the road in the dark. It was very likely that the trackers knew our general location. It rained very hard for about 90 minutes during the night, hard enough to help conceal our path.

## Day 2

About 30 minutes after BMNT, we recovered the toe poppers and Claymores and moved to a cliff site I saw during the VR. The cliff gave us a good view of the valley and a couple of segments of the road. The air was very calm, allowing us to see smoke from cooking fires hanging in the jungle canopy. There appeared to be three areas of troop concentrations. We set up our defenses and began to observe the valley. Because we did not get much sleep the night before, we rotated sleeping during the day. We were going to have a long night ahead of us as we began putting air strikes on the NVA positions. By late afternoon we were confident that we knew the location of the leadership element of the regiment. Covey relayed all the targeting data to the launch site, which was given to the Air Force for targeting.

About an hour before dark, Covey returned with F-4s and A-1s. The amount of anti-aircraft and machine gun fire combined with secondary explosions confirmed that we had dialed in the targets. The strikes were too accurate to have been a lucky guess. The NVA knew there was a team nearby directing the strikes. The enemy patrol activity in the area around us picked up dramatically. It was now dark making it more difficult for them to move quietly, thus, easier for us to hear them. We were not moving which gave us an advantage. But we still

*A small-to-medium size tiger killed in the area.*

*RT Michigan String Extraction*
*(Picture courtesy of Rich Niles)*

had to deal with the dogs.

Dogs have extremely good hearing and smell. They don't always have to follow a scent on a trail. Under the right conditions dogs could pick up our scent from a distance of several miles (depending on the type of dog). Fortunately, a breeze was blowing toward the team relative to the dogs' locations reducing the distance they could smell us. (A tiger's sense of smell is much shorter than a dog's.) The dogs were still trying to pick up our scent on the ground and follow it to us. I had learned from previous encounters that dogs learn to detect the powdered CS (tear gas) at greater and greater distances as they encounter more places where we have left some behind to disrupt their sense of smell. Soon they learned to follow the CS deposits from a distance and go around where we put it on the ground. Dogs are smarter than they look. We stopped using CS and began leaving black pepper, which worked better.

Around 0330 we heard a tiger get a dog and its handler. The handler's scream was scary. As the NVA continued to get closer to finding us we got lucky. Covey brought in a C-130 Spectre gunship that could link to our Spectre transponder and shoot all around us without us having to mark our position with flares or strobe lights the NVA could see. Technology was continuing to enhance SOG RTs' mission abilities.

By 0400 we were in heavy contact and had to declare a Prairie Fire Emergency and bring in Close Air Support (CAS) to help us try to get to our extraction LZ. It soon became evident that we could not survive to get to the LZ. We adapted our plan to be extracted by strings. We had put on Swiss seats while we were in the RON just in case we could not get to the LZ. At first light we were extracted by strings while the whole area was pounded by napalm and Cluster Bomb Units (CBUs) from F-4s and rockets, miniguns and 40mm grenades from Cobras.

**Lessons Learned**

- Tigers are out there even if you can't hear them.
- Tigers will eat dogs and their handlers if they get a chance.
- Dogs have a better developed smell (and range) than tigers, and

they learn and adapt quickly. Carry a backup bottle of black pepper.

- The hand-held transponder for the Spectre worked great.
- Tiger scat raises everyone's situational awareness and fear to a level that can become a distraction to sensing the enemy's presence.
- Always have an alternate means of extraction available.

## RT Michigan Mission 4: Pipeline Destruction & Monkey Business. SOG #8 Summary (18 FEB 69)

RT Michigan was assigned the mission of finding a high-volume fuel pipeline coming out of North Vietnam and running to refuel points along the Ho Chi Minh highway and destroying a section of it.

### Mission 4 Team Roster

| Name | Position |
|------|----------|
| LT Thompson | 1-0 |
| SGT Bargewell | 1-1 |
| Cantua | Interpreter |
| Hieng | M-79 |
| Pua | Pointman |
| Chung | Tail Gunner |
| Aita | Pointman 2 |

The VR I flew was cut short because of the heavy AAA and damage sustained to the aircraft.

We made an early evening insertion, security halt, then moved quickly to a predetermined RON position. Two venomous snakes were discovered during our movement to the RON. We also heard trackers with clackers who had picked up our trail. All the conditions were right for this to be a long night. Our plan was to find the pipeline before going after the trackers. At approximately 2300 a ten-man NVA search team walked within eight feet of our perimeter.

There were several close calls with the NVA as we got closer to the pipeline. Around 1600 on Day 2 we found the pipeline and discovered that there were regular NVA security patrols of 3–4 NVA that passed by our area approximately every four hours. We moved 300 meters away from the pipeline to a rocky area near some cliffs for our RON. This area would provide a relatively safe place while we prepared our demolition charges and got some rest. Everything went great until 0130, then we heard movement between us and the cliffs. As they got closer the size of the group seemed to grow to squad size, then platoon and finally company-size (120–130). I called Moonbeam and requested support. Moonbeam found a Spectre gunship in range of our position and diverted it to us.

I used the new, experimental transponder I had been given to send out an electronic signal to mark our position so the NVA would not know where we were. Spectre flew several passes between us and the cliffs. We could hear the screams as over a hundred 20mm HE rounds hit the ground beside us and the side of the cliffs. I had Spectre hit two other spots in the AO to help confuse the NVA as to where we might be. You had to see the impact of those rounds to comprehend the firepower. In less than ten seconds, a Spectre gunship could put one 20mm HE round in every square yard of a football-field-sized area. There were a few moans and groans for a while, then silence. Spectre had done its job. We got a big surprise as we moved out at daylight. The jungle around us was littered with bodies and body parts—of big apes. There has been no definitive proof of "rock apes"—people-like creatures standing six feet tall, but these were really big apes. When asked for an estimated body count, I replied, "Forty."

When we arrived at the pipeline, I notified Covey that we were on target waiting on the security patrol. When the patrol arrived, Bargewell and I quickly terminated the NVA using our .22 pistols with integrated silencers. Our designated security team moved into place while the rest of us set the charges (20 pounds of C-4 with a WP grenade). We then activated the time fuse with 20 minutes' burning time and quickly moved 100 meters to a second spot on the pipeline, placed our second charge and ignited a five-minute time fuse.

We then began moving quickly toward the extraction LZ. I left toe poppers along our path as we moved. The two 20-pound C-4 charges made tremendous explosions letting the fuel run out on the ground. The WP grenades made sure the fuel ignited. It was an awesome fireworks display. We heard one set of toe poppers explode and knew the NVA were close to us. Then we ran into a group of 20 who seemed to be unhappy. Fortunately, by this time Covey had F-4s on station following our targeting directions to hit the pipeline in more places with a mixture of HEs and napalm. Their strikes produced secondary explosions at the refueling stations. A-1s provided close air support for RT Michigan, which was now a Prairie Fire Emergency. After about two hours of difficult fighting, we were extracted under heavy fire. The mission was a success, and we did not lose anyone.

**Lessons Learned**

- Rock apes travel in large groups and will attack RTs as they did us.
- The Spectre transponder works great and does not give your position away.
- The NVA patrol their pipelines.
- WP grenades and Napalm help ensure a great fire.
- The .22 pistols with integrated silencers worked great on small patrols.
- Rocky terrain provides cover and concealment but slows and channels movement.
- Rocky terrain creates an urge not to move. The NVA are always maneuvering.

## RT Michigan Mission 5: Bomb Damage Assessment & The Chinese Connection. SOG #9 Summary (25 FEB 1969)

RT Michigan's mission was to follow closely behind a B-52 strike in Laos and assess the bomb damage, collect intelligence from bodies and take a prisoner if possible. The indigenous team members were told we were going on a PW snatch; Bargewell and I were the only members of the team who knew about the B-52 strike.

### Mission 5 Team Roster

| Name | Position |
| --- | --- |
| LT Thompson | 1-0 |
| SGT Bargewell | 1-1 |
| Cantua | Interpreter |
| Hieng | M-79 |
| Camba | Pointman 1 |
| Pua | Pointman 3 |
| Rapun | Tail Gunner |

While I went on a VR of the area, Bargewell prepared the team for the mission by doing more PW capture training—especially how to secure them, put on a pre-made Swiss seat and a flak jacket and helmet. They worked with handcuffs, gags, head bags, morphine syrettes, duct tape, control ropes, etc. We really wanted to get a live one back to the launch site this time.

The VR did not go well. The flight was rough, it was cloudy and rainy with lots of AAA. The right wing took some damage causing us to only have approximately 15 minutes over the AO.

When it was time for our team to be inserted, our flight to the LZ had to be closely coordinated. All aircraft and RT Michigan had to remain over 3,000 meters from the target box (a one by two mile area) for at least 15 minutes after the last 500 pound bomb landed on target. With the exception of the smoke, rough air, fires all across the target area, and what looked like the aftermath of a Level 5 hurricane, we were able to get into our insertion LZ (approx. 500 meters from the target box) without contact and move quickly to a security halt. It took a little longer than normal to acclimate our senses.

As we neared the target box, trees were scattered all around and there were lots of bomb craters throughout the area. Over 300 bombs (75 tons of explosives and shrapnel) had been dropped in the target box. We made our way slowly around, over and under the fallen trees and around craters that were large enough to set a house in.

The smell of smoke and explosives was very strong. The air was difficult to breathe without choking. It was difficult to see because of the smoke, dust and ashes. We could still hear secondary explosions and an occasional tree falling. There were screams and shouting in the distance.

We took pictures of the damage, body parts and bodies. Everything was surreal as we cautiously moved toward the center of the target box. As we moved into our RON around 1830, just before last light, we heard what everyone agreed was a helicopter flying just above the canopy and landing on the other side of the ridge. I notified Covey. He said it was cloudy and low light and he did not see an aircraft in the area. He had no knowledge of a CIA mission taking place in the area. We put out our defenses and settled into our RON. During the night we continued to hear explosions, screams and a lot of vehicular noise. Bargewell and I were confident we would get a PW the next day.

**Day 2**

We made heavy contact with a company-size NVA force. As the NVA initially withdrew they left a concussed NVA soldier behind. We were all over him. He was quickly put in a flak jacket and helmet, gagged, head-bagged, handcuffed and lightly sedated with morphine. The NVA realized we were a small group and had captured one of their people. They regrouped and assaulted us. I called Covey, told him we had a PW, were in heavy contact, were declaring a Prairie Fire Emergency and moving toward the extraction LZ.

It seemed strange, but we could already hear the extraction helicopter approaching. I told Covey we were approximately 100 meters from the LZ but moving very slowly. He might want to have the helicopter circle around and come back. Covey said our helicopter was still 45 minutes out from the LZ. That did not make sense. It began to rain harder as we continued to fight our way toward the LZ. Then we saw a group of NVA running to the LZ in front of us with a tall soldier, dressed in a different type of uniform running with them. I could not get a good camera shot. I told Covey there was another team with us. The tall guy looked Chinese. A strange looking helicopter (not

216

US, not Vietnamese) popped out of the clouds down to the LZ, and a few seconds later, it was back up into the clouds with people on it. The pictures I took of the men running toward the LZ and the aircraft lifting off were blurred and cloudy when reviewed later. We weren't able to determine the nationality of the men or origin of the aircraft.

We remained in contact and used A-1s to pound our attackers for an hour before we were extracted. The team was tired and hungry and eager to get back to CCN. We boarded the Kingbee and bounced all over the sky in the bad weather all the way "home." Our prisoner bled out on the way back. Two AK-47 rounds went through the flak jacket and penetrated his lung. I don't think the flak jacket even slowed the bullets down. I had been considering wearing one, but it appeared it would have been a waste of my time. Flak jackets do not stop bullets, plus they were heavy, hot, and restricted our movement, which is why SOG teams did not wear them.

### AAR

- No one seemed to believe we saw a Chinese helicopter and advisor.
- The team really performed well. Great execution of IADs and movement during contact.
- Even if you see the damage a B-52 strike does, it's difficult to believe.
- The whole area was covered with bodies and body parts.
- Roads, bridges, houses, vehicles and the terrain were destroyed.
- Once again our prisoner was dead by the time we got back to the launch site.
- We did, however, recover a lot of high value documents from the bodies.

### Lessons Learned

- We were not the only ones out there.
- The enemy who survives a B-52 strike is really upset and will try to kill you.
- The team put out enough firepower during initial contact to

cause an NVA company to initially run from us. We scared them. They are human too.

- The only way you knew the B-52s were there was when the world began to explode. You could not see nor hear them.

It was a relief to get back to CCN. We had been promised a two-day R&R starting the next day. No new missions for two days, and we needed it. At this point I had completed 9 "across the fence" SOG missions as well as some in-country missions.

We were all looking forward to cleaning up, eating and starting recovery. I knew that within a couple of hours I would have a full stomach and be sleeping like a baby. Bargewell and I would do a quick AAR and lessons learned with the team right after breakfast the next morning and let them go for a couple of days.

When we landed, Bargewell and I cleaned up and met at the mess hall to eat and do our own quick AAR/LL. We finished eating around 1930 and went back to our rooms. I did a quick clean and reload of my CAR-15 and web gear and lay down across my bed. Then I heard a loud knock on my door followed by, "Lieutenant Thompson. Are you in there?"

"Yes. What do you want?"

When he told me, I said, "You've got to be kidding me!"

"No, Sir. 2000 hours. That's eight minutes from now. Careful what you say, Sir. He's on the other side of your plywood wall!"

"Crap! Just another day in SOG."

***To be continued...***

# Coming soon to Amazon…

The second book in this series. If you thought Book 1 was intense, wait until you read about the insane missions in Book 2.

# Acknowledgments

I found that writing a semi-autobiography about traumatic events of war that occurred in my life over 50 years ago to be the most difficult and emotional writing task I have ever undertaken. That probably contributed to putting off this project for most of my life. To accomplish this task required the support, participation and patience of my wife, my family, relatives, HPS team members, MACV-SOG survivors, many friends, experts, colleagues and people who wanted to see the end product, and especially my SOG friends and teammates who made the ultimate sacrifice during 1968-69 and all the air crews who saved me on a regular basis. This project, like MACV-SOG missions, was a team effort. I do not know how to thank everyone beyond mentioning some of you in this section—and to apologize to the many more contributors who did not get mentioned here.

## SOG Colleagues/Friends

MG (Ret.) Eldon Bargewell, MG (Ret.) Ken Bowra, John Stryker Meyer, MAJ (Ret.) Richard (Dick) Meadows, Bruce Lombard, COL (Ret.) Richard Todd, LTC (Ret.) David Carr, Lynne Black, Gentry Deck, CW4 (Ret.) Vernon Ward, Terry Cadenbach, Dan Thompson, Don Haase, COL (Ret.) Barry Pencek, Russ Mann, MAJ (Ret.) Nguyen Quy An, Mike Stahl, Ken Holmes and Bill Barkley.

## SOG History Keepers

Steve Sherman, Bonnie Cooper, Jason Alexander, Bud Gibson, Jason Collins, MAJ (Ret.) John L. Plaster, MG (Ret.) Ken Bowra and John Stryker Meyer.

## Manuscript Readers

Grenae Thompson, Michele Thompson Bruce, Stephen Thompson, Eric Brown, Debra Cannarella, Andy Cannarella, Rob Graham, Carl Hudson, MG (Ret.) Ken Bowra, John Stryker Meyer, Bruce Lombard, COL (Ret.) Richard Todd, LTC (Ret.) David Carr, Dan Thompson, Don Haase, COL (Ret.) Barry Pencek, Jason Collins, COL (Ret.) Mark London, Bruce Christensen, Holly H. McClellan and Faith Meyer.

## Graphics and Imaging Team

Rich Niles, Ian King, Merry Maxey, Sam McIntire, John Stryker Meyer, Vivian Edwards, *Pucker Factor Magazine*, Jason Collins, Rob Graham and Jacqueline Cook.

## Special Encouragement and Support

Grenae Thompson, Michele Thompson Bruce, Stephen Thompson, Jennifer Thompson-Brown, Eric Brown, CW4 (Ret.) Larry K. (Butch) Thompson, Mary Margaret McClellan, Jamie McClellan, Isabella Bruce, Kendall Brown, Shiloh Brown, Carl Hudson, Derrill Thompson, Debra Cannarella, Julie Gentry, Marcia Swoger, Curt Cisrow, Farrell Collins, Merry Maxey, Dana Smith, Ian King, Rose Niles, Susan Hunter, MAJ (Ret.) John Reichley, Dr. Harvey Gayer, Mike Hamor, COL (Ret.) Mark London, Randy McGhee, Richard Fitts, Jr., Mike McGee, COL (Ret.) Larry Hammack, Jocko Willink and Andy Strumpf.

## Final Editing

Grenae Thompson, Faith Meyer, Jacqueline Cook and John Stryker Meyer.

I want to reiterate my thanks to my two SOG/Special Operations mentors, colleagues and friends, MG Eldon Bargewell and MAJ Dick Meadows, both of whom are Special Ops legends who stayed awake in the cold of night protecting the freedom of our country as the rest of us slept. I am honored, humbled and proud to have had time in your presence. They say that not all of God's angels sing. Some are warriors. I'm sure you are among those. Rest in Peace, brave warriors. You will never be forgotten. *De Oppresso Liber.*

**MG Eldon A. Bargewell**
APR 29, 2019

**MAJ Richard J. Meadows**
29 JUL 1995

# In Honor of My SOG Teammates/ Friends Lost During 1968–1969

# Glossary

**1911A1** – The Army issue .45 caliber pistol.

**A-1 Skyraider** – Sometimes called "Spad" or "Sandy" was a single-seat, propeller-driven attack aircraft that was used between the late 1940s and early 1970s. The A-1 could carry a very heavy load and variety of ordnance, fly low and slow, and provide accurate close air support. These planes and pilots played a major role in supporting SOG operations.

**AA** – Anti-aircraft gun

**AAA** – Anti-aircraft artillery

**AAR (After Action Review)** – When teams returned from a mission they would be debriefed in detail on the different stages of the mission, including things that went well and those that didn't. A detailed report would be written about the operation that could be used by future teams going into this area or conducting this type of mission. The AAR helped the team learn from each mission and increase their skill set.

**ABCCC (Airborne Battlefield Command and Control Center)** – This was an EC-130E aircraft that provided a tactical airborne command post that orbited very high above a SOG team's Area of Operation. It monitored all radio communications and provided SOG teams 24/7 radio contact. The daytime call sign was Hillsboro and nighttime was Moonbeam.

**Across the Fence** – Across the South Vietnam border into another country, mostly Laos, Cambodia and North Vietnam.

**AGL (Above Ground Level)** – The actual altitude above the ground directly below the aircraft.

**AH-1** – Cobra attack helicopters which could carry mini-guns (firing 4,000 rounds a minute), a 40mm grenade launcher (firing up to 250 rounds per minute) and up to 48, 2.75-inch rockets with

17-pound high explosive warheads. They provided exceptionally effective close air support.

**AK-47** – The Avtomat Kalashnikova assault rifle (designed by Mikhail Kalashnikov in 1947) was the primary assault rifle used by the NVA. It fired a 7.62x39mm round at a cyclic rate of automatic fire of 600 rounds per minute. It also had a semi-automatic mode.

**AO (Area of Operation)** – The area in which a team would be operating in Laos, Cambodia, North Vietnam or the DMZ. Many had specific designations within the general area, e.g., Oscar 8.

**Arc Light** – A B-52 bombing mission that normally consisted of 3–6 planes flying in formation from an altitude of around 40,000 feet with each plane dropping up to 110, 500-pound bombs.

**Arm Squeeze** – A technique for silently waking up team members at night without making any noise by slowly squeezing the person's triceps. This was practiced before going on a mission.

**ARVN** – The Army of the Republic of South Vietnam. South Vietnamese soldiers. Our allies.

**AST-North** – Area Support Team-North. Responsible for collecting target data and supporting RTs going into northern targets.

**AST-South** – Area Support Team-South. Responsible for collecting target data and supporting RTs going into southern targets.

**Avgas** – Aviation fuel (gasoline) used in spark-ignited internal combustion aircraft engines (like the H-34 Kingbees).

**B-40** – A very effective reloadable shoulder-fired Rocket Propelled Grenade launcher (RPG-2) used by the NVA to engage tanks, helicopters and personnel. Sometimes carried by SOG teams.

**BDA (Bomb Damage Assessment)** – Assessing the damage caused by B-52 strikes (and sometimes other types of air strikes).

**Beeper** – A radio transmitter that sends a high pitch tone on the "Guard" frequency monitored by all friendly aircraft. All US SOG team members carried a URC-10 that had a beeper as part of the radio.

**Binh Tram** – A regimental-sized logistical unit responsible for specific sections of the Ho Chi Minh Trail. Much less skilled and aggressive than the Anti-SOG NVA soldiers.

**Blackbirds** – US Air Force C-130 and C-123 aircraft painted black. Used to transport SOG personnel and for other classified missions.

**BMNT (Beginning of Morning Nautical Twilight)** – The time in the morning when the sun is just below the horizon (about 12 degrees) but giving off enough light so you can see about 100 meters and move relatively quietly and accurately. The term "attacking at first light" comes from this time of day.

**Booby Trap** – A "homemade" device made using available explosives (artillery shells, grenades, etc.) and detonating devices (trip wires, phones, etc.) and usually hidden so you don't see it before it explodes.

**Born On the Path** – Some people seem to be born on a particular path (abilities, skill sets, etc.) that moves them toward a particular fate or accomplishment in life.

**Box Breathing** – A breathing pattern of inhaling through the nose for 4–8 seconds, pausing for 4–8 seconds, exhaling through the mouth for 4–8 seconds, pausing for 4–8 seconds and then starting the cycle again. Doing 5–6 reps of this cycle at a time causes the Vagus nerve to begin relaxing the heart and arteries, taking the mind out of the fight, flight or freeze response.

**Bright Light** – A code word for a heavily armed RT that is inserted across the border to recover downed pilots, missing RT members/ teams or bring back proof of death. These were very dangerous missions.

**Browning Hi-Power** – A 9mm, semi-automatic pistol with a 13-round magazine carried by some SOG members.

**BRU** – Montagnard tribesmen used on SOG teams.

**C-4** – A plastic explosive which uses RDX as its primary explosive agent. It can be shaped by hand. Requires a detonating device to make it explode. It will burn slowly if lit and is poisonous.

**CAP (Combat Air Patrol)** – A flight of F-4s flying high overhead looking for NVA MiGs that wanted to attack the RT. The F-4s destroy or chase them away.

**CAR-15** – A submachine gun with a collapsible stock. Starting in 1967, this was the preferred weapon carried by RT members.

**CAS (Close Air Support)** – The tactic of aircraft (e.g., gunships, F-4s, A-1s) providing support to friendlies on the ground when they are engaged with the enemy.

**CBU (Cluster Bomb Units)** – An air-dropped canister that breaks open while in the air and spills out approximately 250 bomblets (about the size of an orange, depending on the type) that rain down on enemy personnel or vehicles/tanks. There are several types and sizes of CBU that can be deployed.

**CCC (Command and Control Central )** – The SOG base in Kontum, for running missions into Southern Laos and Northern Cambodia. Formerly FOB-2.

**CCN (Command and Control North)** –The field headquarters in Da Nang, near Marble Mountain, for SOG missions into Laos, the DMZ and North Vietnam. Originally called FOB-4.

**CCR (Creedence Clearwater Revival)** – A popular American rock band.

**CCS (Command and Control South)** – The SOG base at Ban Me Thuot for running missions mostly into Cambodia and South Vietnam. Formerly FOB-5.

**Charlie** – A nickname given to the Viet Cong, local communists who fought in South Vietnam.

**Chief SOG** – The title of the MACV-SOG Commander, for example, COL Stephen E. Cavanaugh, AUG 68–AUG 69.

**Claymore Mine** – A directional anti-personnel mine. The inventor, Norman Macleod, saw it as a large medieval Scottish sword cutting a swath through the enemy. It contains approximately 700 steel balls propelled by 1.5 pounds of C-4. The steel balls travel at approximately 4,000 feet per second.

**Cleared Hot** – Giving the gunships/TAC air permission to fire on their targets.

**COP (Combat Outpost)** – In general these outposts are small bases used to provide early warning and defense of larger bases. Marble Mountain, located approximately 300 meters from CCN, had a COP located on each of the two peaks of the mountain to provide security and early warning for the compound. RTs rotated through these positions between missions.

**Covey** – An Air Force Forward Air Controller (FAC) that flew into the team's AO with a Covey rider (an experienced SOG team 1-0) on board. The FAC could talk to and control Air Force assets (A-1 Skyraiders & F-4 Phantom jets) and the Covey provided control of Army, Marine and ARVN assets and communicated directly with the SOG team. Covey was the team's lifeline, without which the team would probably not survive.

**Covey Rider** – The Covey rider was an experienced SOG team 1-0, such as Robert "Spider" Parks, drawing on his extensive ground experience to provide recommendations and calming words to teams—especially during a Prairie Fire Emergency.

**Cravat** – An olive drab, cotton, triangular bandage that could also be used for a tourniquet. SOG team members wore these "Rambo style" around the forehead. They had many uses in addition to bandages.

**CS** – A type of non-lethal "tear" gas (2-chlorobenzalmalononitirile) used by the military as a riot control agent and used by SOG teams to incapacitate the NVA and deter dogs tracking the team. Developed by Ben Corson and Roger Stoughton in 1928, the gas name is derived from their surnames (CS).

**Danger Close** – An artillery term meaning that you are calling the rounds to land within 600 meters of friendly forces. Also used to emphasize to gunships and TAC air that the target is very close to friendly forces.

**Det Cord** – Abbreviation for detonation cord. An explosive cord used for detonating other ordnance and clearing small trees.

**DMZ (Demilitarized Zone)** – The 17th parallel dividing North and South Vietnam. It was off limits to all military personnel, but SOG ran missions there any way. So did the NVA.

**Dominance Response Hierarchy** – This refers to the concept that the more times you perform an action the more likely you are to do it again, especially under stress. You are building mental and muscle memory through repetition. This helps you get better. Practice. Practice. Practice!

**DZ (Drop Zone)** – A landing area for parachutists.

**EENT (End of Evening Nautical Twilight)** – The time in the evening when the sun is just below (about 12 degrees) the horizon but giving off enough light so you can see about 100 meters and be able to move relatively quietly and accurately. The term "attacking at last light" comes from this time of day.

**F-4 Phantom** – A two-seat, twin-engine, all-weather, long-range supersonic jet interceptor and fighter-bomber (often called "fast movers"). The F-4s provided Combat Air Patrol missions when operating close to the North Vietnam border to ward off NVA MiGs and maintain air superiority. They also provided bomber support to teams in contact or to attack ground targets.

**FAC (Forward Air Controller)** – An Air Force Forward Air Controller that flew into the team's AO with a Covey rider (an experienced SOG team 1-0) on board. The FAC could talk to and control Air Force assets (A-1 Skyraiders & F-4 Phantom jets).

**Fishhook** – The technique of an RT making a wide, 180° fishhook-shaped turn in its direction of movement, and stopping for a security halt or RON. If the enemy is following the RT, they will walk past the team before realizing the RT changed direction.

Hearing the enemy going by alerts the RT that it is being followed.

**Flak Jacket** – A flak jacket was a form of body armor (ballistic vest) that members of the regular military units wore to provide protection against bullets and shrapnel. SOG teams did not wear them because they were too heavy, too hot, restricted movement and were not bulletproof.

**FMB (Final Mission Brief)** – The final mission briefing with all the asset representatives, operations and the team just prior to launch.

**FNG (Effing New Guy)** – The new guy. Dangerous. Does not have experience or knowledge of how to operate. Also gets teased a lot.

**FOB (Forward Operating Base)** – SOG operations bases located around South Vietnam from which RTs and Hatchet Forces operated.

**Guard Frequency** – An international distress and emergency frequency monitored by all aircraft in the area of operation. The URC-10 radio gave the Americans on RTs a way to contact Covey and other aircraft if the RT's main radio (PRC-25/77) quit working or a team member was separated from the RT.

**HALO (High Altitude, Low Opening)** – Freefall parachute jumps. These jumps could be from 30,000 feet or higher and open as low as 2,000 feet (falling 28,000 feet) with full combat gear (and oxygen) to avoid enemy detection.

**HE (High Explosive)** – a military term that describes rockets, bombs, grenades, etc., that explode with great force and usually sends many pieces of shrapnel out in all directions.

**HF (Hatchet Force)** – SOG platoon (approximately 40 indigenous commandos plus American leaders) and company sized forces (3–4 platoons plus Company leaders) used to conduct large scale offensive operations against the NVA.

**H & I Fire (Harassing and Interdicting Fire)** – Periodic firing of a few artillery rounds on random trails to harass the enemy and keep him guessing as to where and when the next rounds would land.

**High Standard HD** – A .22 caliber, pistol with an integrated silencer. Very quiet. Carried by SOG teams to take out dogs, trackers and guards.

**Human Combat Reaction** – A set of human behaviors/reactions I identified by observing the NVA and SOG team members during combat. For example, right handed people tend to shoot around the right side of a tree/rock (from their perspective) unless they had received a lot of training not to react that way. The NVA had not received that training. My teams used this information to increase their lethality significantly.

**IAD (Immediate Action Drill)** – A set of immediate reactions to specific situations, e.g., enemy contact, ambushes, man down, engaging multiple targets, assaulting, withdrawal, etc. We trained over and over on these responses and variations of them. They were life savers.

**IED (Improvised explosive device)** – A "homemade" device made using available explosives (artillery shells, grenades, etc.) and detonating devices (trip wires, phones, etc.) and usually hidden so you don't see it before it explodes.

**Invisibility** – I trained my teams on how to go beyond camouflage and be totally invisible to all the senses. What makes the enemy visible makes us visible.

**Isolation Area** – A restricted, classified and "isolated area" that is accessible only by the RT and mission support personnel in mission prep.

**Jody Call** – A song used to keep soldiers in cadence when marching or running. It is about the mythical "Jody" who is living a life of luxury in your hometown, dating your girlfriend or boyfriend while you are away from home. Not all are about Jody despite the name.

**JP-4** – Jet propellant version 4. A 50-50 blend of kerosene and gasoline designed for use in turbine engines like the UH-1 Huey and AH-1 Cobra helicopters.

**KA-BAR Knife** – A fixed-blade combat knife first adopted by the Marines and later used by Special Operators. It comes in two blade sizes: short (5 inches) and standard (7 inches).

**KIA** – Killed in action.

**Kingbee** – Call sign for the South Vietnamese Air Force 219th Special Operations Squadron H-34 pilots who supported SOG teams. They were known for their heroism.

**KZ (Kill Zone)** – That point in an ambush where maximum firepower is produced to quickly kill the enemy.

**LBE (Load Bearing Equipment)** – A shoulder harness attached to a wide belt around the waist used for carrying ammunition, grenades, water, etc. Could weigh up to 35 pounds. A handle on the top back of the harness facilitated dragging a wounded warrior.

**Lift Ships** – Consisted of CH-34 Kingbees flown by the 219th Squadron, South Vietnamese Air Force (VNAF) and UH-1C/D Army helicopters. Two sets of lift ships were involved in the insertions and extractions. One set of aircraft carried the team to the insertion Landing Zone (LZ) and from the extraction LZ. A second set of lift ships flew empty as "chase" aircraft prepared to pick up crew and team members of aircraft that went down during the mission.

**Little People** – A term of endearment used by SOG Americans when referring to their indigenous members.

**Long Range Patrol Rations (LRP)** – Dehydrated meals carried by many RT members on missions. They were reconstituted by soaking in water.

**LZ (Landing Zone)** – A clearing large enough that a helicopter can land to insert RTs or extract them.

**M or Mike** – Minutes. For example, "The cobras are 5 mikes out."

**M-26** – Old fragmentation grenade.

**M-33** – New "baseball" fragmentation grenade.

**M-60** – A 7.62mm machine gun occasionally carried for additional fire power.

**M-72** – A Light Antitank Weapon (LAW), single shot and disposable.

**M-79** – A 40mm grenade launcher. RTs normally carried at least one per team. Sometimes more. And sometimes one or more that had the stock and barrel sawed off making the M-79 a big fat pistol that kicked like a mule.

**Makiwara Board** – A mounted striking board, sometimes wrapped in rope, for martial artists to practice striking to toughen their knuckles and increase power.

**McGuire Rig** – A nylon rope of 120–150 feet with a large loop made out of a heavy padded strap attached to the end of it. A bag of sand is tied to the loop to give it enough momentum to penetrate the jungle canopy. The other end of the rope is attached to the floor of the helicopter. It is used when team members have to be extracted from the jungle where the helicopter cannot land. A small strap at the top of the loop fastens around your wrist to prevent you from falling out.

**MIA** – Missing in Action.

**MiG** – The MiG-21 was North Vietnam's best jet fighter aircraft and was similar in capability to the American F-4. It was manufactured in China.

**Mike Force (The Mobile Strike Force Command)** – A critical part of the Army Special Forces during Vietnam. It consisted of highly trained indigenous forces led by American Green Berets. They were considered a force multiplier.

**MM or Mike Mike** – Millimeters, for example, "a 40mm high explosive round."

**Montagnards** – Mountain tribesmen who were recruited to fight on SOG RTs and Hatchet Forces. Fearless fighters.

**Napalm** – A weaponized mixture of jellied gasoline that stuck to people like glue. Very difficult to extinguish or remove from skin. One of the most horrifying weapons in our inventory that burned bodies to a crisp. Similar to the gates of hell opening.

**NCO** – Non-commissioned officer.

**NKP (Nakhon Phanom Royal Thai Air Force Base)** – A launch site located in Thailand at Nakhon Phanom (NKP) approximately 75 miles from the North Vietnam border.

**Number 10** – English slang used by the Vietnamese. "Number 10" is very bad. "Number 1" is very good.

**Nungs** – Highly respected Chinese tribesmen recruited for SOG.

**NVA** – The North Vietnamese Army. Probably the 4th best Army in the world at the time. SOG RTs' primary opponent.

**One-One (1-1)** – Code for the American SOG RT assistant team leader.

**One-Two (1-2)** – Code for the American SOG RT radio operator.

**One-Zero (1-0)** – Code for the American SOG RT team leader. Position based on experience, not rank. Required vetting. The 1-0 had final say about who stayed on the team.

**Oscar 8** – The most deadly area of operation in Laos.

**PCI (Pre-Combat Inspection)** – A type of inspection I used with my teams just prior to being launched on a mission to make sure everyone had what he was supposed to have and it was secured properly and he knew his role during the operation.

**Pen Flare** – A small flare fired by a single shot "pen gun." Flares came in different colors and were used to signal an RT's location. Sometimes confused for enemy tracers, especially green and white flares.

**Post Mission Training** – I used Post-Mission Training to increase team member/team skill sets in areas we did not do well on during the last mission. I tried to instill the philosophy of every time you do something you need to do it better than last time.

**POW** – Prisoner of war.

**Prairie Fire Emergency** – An emergency alert that an RT was in contact with enemy forces and could not continue its mission and was fighting for its life. The RT then became the number one priority in Southeast Asia. Every asset (Army, Air Force, Marine and Navy) within range and with ordnance was diverted to assist the team.

**Project Eldest Son** – Various types of enemy ammunition were rigged to explode when fired. SOG teams inserted this ammunition in enemy ammunition caches or on enemy trails. This was a black psychological ops project.

**Pucker Factor** – Pucker factor was/is a slang term referring to the correlation between fear and the tightness of the sphincter muscle around your anal orifice. The higher the fear/pucker factor the tighter the sphincter.

**Quang Tri** – Launch site for FOB-1 and CCN teams going into Laos, the DMZ or North Vietnam.

**Real World** – The United States. Home.

**Rear Echelon Mother %&$ (REMF)** – A non-operator SOG support person who worked in the rear.

**Ringer's Solution** – A solution containing sodium chloride, potassium chloride, calcium chloride and sodium bicarbonate used to restore blood volume rapidly when given intravenously.

**RON (Remain Overnight)** – A location where the RT planned to spend the night.

**RP (Rendezvous Point)** – A prearranged meeting place. Gunships, F-4s and A-1s would often have assigned RPs near where an RT was being inserted or extracted while they waited to perform their part of the mission.

**RPD** – The Ruchnoy Pulemyot Degtyaryova 7.72x39mm, drum-fed, light machine gun with a high rate of fire. By late 1969, some SOG teams were making modifications to the barrel to reduce the RPD's weight and increase maneuverability in the jungle. A powerful weapon, but still heavy.

**RPG (Rocket propelled grenade)** – A shoulder-fired anti-tank weapon used by the VC and NVA. Sometimes referred to as a B-40.

**R & R (Rest and recuperation)** – Time provided to allow a team or team member to have some time to rest and recover.

**RT (Reconnaissance Team)** – Usually, 2–3 Americans and up to nine indigenous members.

**Rucksack** – A backpack used by SOG team members to carry extra ammunition, food, water, smoke grenades and special equipment. It was typically very heavy (60–80 pounds).

**Sandy** – Another name for an A-1 Skyraider.

**Sapper** – Well-trained North Vietnamese forces that penetrated US Forces' perimeters with explosives and created significant death and damage.

**Scarface** – Radio call sign assigned to Marine gunships assigned from the HMLA 367 Squadron to support SOG missions.

**Scat** – Animal poop.

**Schrodinger's Cat** – A quantum physics thought experiment created by Erwin Schrodinger in 1935. If you place a cat and something that could kill the cat in a box, you do not know if the cat is alive or dead until you open the box. The cat exists in all quantum states until you open the box. When you open the box all quantum states collapse into one—the one that you see. A cat that is alive or dead. You don't know what will happen on a mission until you open the box.

**Slicks** – UH-1 helicopters used to transport SOG teams.

**Sling Rope/Swiss Seat** – A 12-foot-long piece of nylon climbing rope used to make a Swiss seat for extraction on "strings" and extemporaneous uses.

**Situation Report (SITREP)** – Reports sent by radio from RTs explaining their situation during their mission.

**Snake Eaters** – A nickname for Special Forces.

**SOG** – Military Assistance Command Vietnam's Studies and Observations Group (MACV-SOG), a highly classified special operations unit that conducted unconventional warfare operations in Southeast Asia from 24 January1964 to 1 May 1972. They were the elite of the elite, the most BA men who walked the face of the earth during that period. They had the highest kill ratio as well as the highest casualty rate of any unit in the Vietnam war. They were the secret warriors that did not exist.

**Spad (SPAD)** – Another name for an A-1 Skyraider.

**Spectre** – A Lockheed C-130 Hercules converted to a gunship that housed two 20mm M61 Vulcan cannons, one 40mm L60 Bofors cannon (120 rpm) and a 105mm M102 howitzer (6–10 rpm).

**STABO Harness (STAbilized BOdy)** – A modified LBE harness with leg straps that can be quickly fastened if you need to be extracted by strings. You cannot fall out of the harness, and it provides a more stabilized flight when flying through the air under the helicopter.

**Sten Gun** – World War II Sten Mk IIS Submachine gun carried by some SOG teams until replaced by CAR-15 in 1967.

**Strap Hanger** – Someone who is assigned to an RT at the last minute to help fill in for a missing team member. Sometimes a person who volunteers to go with the team to help out.

**Strings** – Up to four nylon ropes 120–150 feet in length hung from a helicopter that the team members could attach to by various methods (Swiss seat, McGuire rig, snap link, STABO) and be extracted up through the jungle canopy from an area with no LZ.

**Strobe Light** – A small, powerful blinking light used to mark the team or a team member's location.

**Swedish K** – A 9mm submachine gun carried by some SOG teams until replaced by CAR-15 in 1967.

**Swiss Seat** – A simple improvised rappelling or extraction harness quickly made from a piece of 12-foot-long nylon rope that provides a "seat" that can be attached to a rope and used for rappelling or "string" extraction. Hanging in the seat for periods of longer than 20 minutes may cause the legs to "go to sleep" due to restricted blood circulation. See also McGuire Rig, STABO Harness.

**Syrette** – A small syringe with a metal tube containing morphine with a needle attached. Each American RT member carried several of these on missions.

**TAC Air (Tactical Air Support)** – It usually came as F-4 Phantom jets and/or A-1 Skyraiders.

**TBI (Traumatic Brain Injury)** – An injury to the brain caused by a traumatic blow to the head. Often caused in combat by concussion from explosions.

**TOC (Tactical Operations Center)** – A command post staffed with specially trained personnel who provide guidance and support for RTs during missions.

**Toe-Popper** – An M-14 plastic mine large enough to blow off an enemy's toes or foot if he stepped on it.

**Tracers** – Ammunition that has a pyrotechnic charge in the base of the projectile that burns very bright once the projectile leaves the barrel. The projectile is visible even in the daytime. It burns very hot and will cause the weapon's barrel to heat up more quickly than normal, especially with automatic fire.

**URC-10** – An ultra-high frequency emergency radio with a beeper. All SOG team Americans carried one. You could communicate to any aircraft within range on the Guard frequency.

**VC (Viet Cong)** – Vietnamese communists who operated in South Vietnam. Sometimes referred to as "Charlie."

**VR (Visual Reconnaissance)** – Flying over a target area to pick LZs for insertion and extraction, to view and photograph the terrain, and check for activity.

**VS-17 Panels** – Brightly colored (orange on one side, pink on the other), 24" x 70" panels used by SOG RTs for marking their position, LZs and other objects. RTs often cut the panels to make them smaller and easier to carry. I had the orange side sewn into the inside of our boonie hats. We would turn the orange side out when running for the helicopter under fire to prevent the door gunners from mistaking us for the enemy.

**WIA** – Wounded in action.

**WP (White Phosphorus)** – WP is one of the common forms of phosphorus used for creating dense white smoke, illumination and incendiary munitions. It is used in WP grenades, rocket warheads, artillery rounds and bombs, etc. WP causes severe burns when it comes in contact with the human body and is extremely caustic to the eyes and lungs.

**Zero-One (0-1)** – Indigenous leader on the RT. Zero-Two (0-2) – The indigenous RT interpreter. Zero-Nine (0-9) – SOG team M-79 member.

# About the Author

**HENRY L. (Dick) THOMPSON, Ph.D.**
*(aka Dynamite)*

**LIEUTENANT COLONEL**
US Army, Retired
President & CEO of High Performing Systems, Inc.

LTC (Ret.) Thompson enlisted into the Army in 1967 at Fort Jackson, SC, as an 11B Infantryman. After completing Basic and Advanced Infantry training, he attended Officer Candidate School at Fort Benning, GA, and was commissioned as a Second Lieutenant in the US Army Infantry in January 1968.

**MILITARY AND CIVILIAN EDUCATION:** LTC Thompson earned a Bachelor of Arts Degree in Sociology from Methodist University, Fayetteville, NC; Master of Science Degree and Doctoral degrees (Ph.D.) in Psychology from the University of Georgia, Athens, GA; and a Master of Science Degree in Continuous Military Operations from the US Army Command and General Staff College, Fort Leavenworth,

KS. He is also a graduate of the Infantry Officer Advanced Course, Fort Benning, GA, and the US Army Command and General Staff Officers Course, Fort Leavenworth, KS.

**ASSIGNMENT HIGHLIGHTS:** After commissioning, LTC Thompson's first assignment was as an Instructor, US Army Special Warfare School, 3rd Special Forces Group, Fort Bragg, NC, in February of 1968. In September of 1968 he was selected to be a team leader with MACV- SOG, 5th Special Forces Group, in the Republic of Vietnam. In January 1970, after finishing his combat tour, he was assigned as an instructor in the US Army Infantry School Ranger Department and stationed at Camp Frank D. Merrill, Dahlonega, GA. In May 1974, he assumed command of Company B (Ranger), 1st Battalion, 23rd Infantry, 2nd Infantry Division, Korea. In June 1975, he moved to XVIII Airborne Corps G3 (Training) as an Action Officer until taking command of Company A, REPTRAIN Battalion, Fort Bragg, NC. In February 1977, he returned to XVIII Airborne Corps G3 (Training) as an Emergency Readiness Deployment evaluator for Special Forces and Ranger units. In June 1979, he became an Assistant Professor of Military Science and Executive Officer at the University of Georgia Army ROTC Department. In June 1982, he became the Leadership Author/Instructor, US Army Center for Leadership and Ethics, US Army Command and General Staff College Leadership Department, Fort Leavenworth, KS. He served in several instructional and research roles until being assigned as the Professor of Military Science at the University of Georgia Army ROTC department in June 1986. He retired from the US Army in January of 1988 after 21 years of military service.

**AWARDS AND DECORATIONS:** LTC Thompson's military awards and decorations include 4 Bronze Star Medals, 2 with a "V" for heroism, 2 Meritorious Service Medals, 2 Air Medals for aerial combat, one with "V" for heroism, Vietnamese Cross of Gallantry for Heroism, 3 Army Commendation Medals, Army Achievement Medal, Presidential Unit Emblem, Meritorious Unit Emblem, Presidential Unit Citation for Extraordinary Heroism, Army Good Conduct Medal, National

Defense Service Medal, Vietnam Service Medal (5th award), Army Service Ribbon, Overseas Service Ribbon, Korean Defense Service Medal, Combat Infantryman's Badge, Master Parachutist's Badge, Military Free-Fall Parachutist's Badge, Vietnamese Parachutist's Badge, Pathfinder Badge, Ranger Tab and Special Forces Tab.

You can contact Dr. Thompson at: hpsys2@aol.com

# Other books by
# LTC (Ret.) Henry Thompson, Ph.D.

*The Communication Wheel®: A Resource Book*, 1995, 2000

*Jung's Function Attitudes Explained*, 1996

*Introduction to The Communication Wheel®*, 2000

*Introduction to FIRO® Element B® in Organizations*, 2006

*The Handbook for Developing Social and Emotional Intelligence (Co-Author)*, 2009

*The Stress Effect: Why Smart Leaders Make Dumb Decisions—And What to do About It*, 2010

# Veteran Support

During my time in SOG I had many opportunities to learn about stress, fear and the human reaction to combat. I incorporated what I had learned, into leading and training my teams and the units I led and trained during my military career. I adapted my learnings and experiences into my work with corporate organizations, especially high stress groups, during my corporate career. I compiled many of these insights into my book, *The Stress Effect* (Jossey-Bass, 2010).

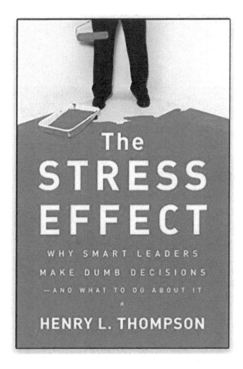

*Available everywhere books are sold.*

# Veteran Suicide Awareness

In 2019 I participated in a challenge designed to raise veteran suicide awareness. At that time, it was estimated that 22 veterans a day ended their life by suicide. The 22 pushups challenge (started originally by Honor, Courage Commitment, Inc.) was/is to do 22 pushups a day for 22 consecutive days.

When I began this challenge, my research indicated that the actual number of veteran suicides was closer to 50 a day and active-duty suicides was at least one a day. I increased my daily pushups to 60+ a day and decided not to stop the consecutive days at 22. I put my pushup activity on social media and did pushups during Veterans Day speeches and other presentations. At times I do 220 a day for 22 consecutive days.

*The Pushup Challenge*

I work with the Military (U.S. and allies), veterans groups, law enforcement, fire fighters, first responders and individuals using the ARSENAL™, a Stress Resilience questionnaire. The ARSENAL™ is an online questionnaire designed to help individuals identify their current Stress Resilience level by providing a scientifically validated summary of their current performance level in the seven best practice areas that most influence their ability to combat the negative effects of stress. The higher the Stress Resilience level, the longer individuals can manage high levels of stress, maintain optimal health and make effective decisions. As a result of completing the ARSENAL and properly applying the seven ARSENAL best practices, respondents can:

- Improve stress resilience
- Make better decisions
- Increase effective brain functioning
- Control emotions and stay calm
- Build new brain cells
- Improve physical functioning
- Increase longevity
- Decrease the negative effects of stress

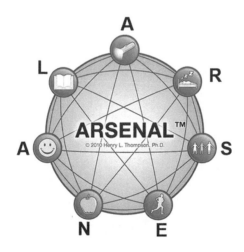

To complete the ARSENAL™ and receive feedback or to become certified to administer the ARSENAL™ Assessment Call 800-535-8445 or email info@hpsys.com.

If you or someone you know needs immediate help, text or call the **National Crisis Line at 988** (if you are a vet or military, enter a "1" when the line answers). They will provide immediate confidential crisis support.

Visit our Stress website at **www.thestresseffect.com** and/or our company website at **www.hpsys.com**.

High Performing Systems, Inc. P.O. Box 868 • Watkinsville, GA 30677 • 706.769.5836 • info@hpsys.com • www.hpsys.com

# Arma 3: S.O.G. Prairie Fire

Arma 3: S.O.G. Prairie Fire is a video game made for PC, which builds on a military simulation game (Arma 3) but creates the world of the Vietnam War, with jungle terrains as large as 150 square miles. As a military simulator sandbox, it has highly realistic weather, day- night cycles, terrain, aircraft, vehicles, personal movement, weapons and ballistics, radio communications and squad co-operation.

Its creator, Savage Game Design, worked closely on the game with MACV-SOG Recon Team Leaders John Stryker Meyer, Jim Shorten Jones and Ken Bowra, as well as aviators, like Don Hasse, who supported SOG operations in slicks, gunships and Cobras. Due to this cooperation, the enemy AI tactics and mission planning and parameters closely match the MACV-SOG experience, and the sounds take veterans back to the moment they step into the helicopter with their team, loaded for bear, heading out over the fence into Laos or Cambodia or North Vietnam. The game is even played regularly by a team comprising MACV-SOG veterans and their families and friends.

You can team up with friends and form a virtual Recon Team

and tackle the campaign's eight co-operative missions, which follow RT Columbia as it progresses through gradually tougher targets, culminating in Oscar 8, the baddest of the bad. The emphasis on teamwork and evading overwhelming enemies in the jungle makes this a real test of your friendships and stress resilience. The pressure grows during the campaign, until the final mission pushes your team way beyond its breaking point.

For those teams who make it through, General Bowra personally reads the SOG Recon motto on the flight home:

"For those that have fought for it, life has a special flavor, the protected will never know." **www.sogpf.com**

Made in United States
Troutdale, OR
09/16/2023